Philip Algar, B.Sc. (Econ.) F.I.J., has written five previous books. For many years, as a freelance editor and writer, he contributed regularly to UK and overseas publications on energy, economics and crisis management. He also wrote a regular and humorous column, on business topics, for a national newspaper and for a business magazine, but is now concentrating on writing books

Praise for *Goodbye Old Chap, a Life at sea in Peace and War*

Philip Algar tells a fascinating story full of period detail about the oil and shipping industries in which he skilfully relates the personal story of his father, Stanley Algar, to events in the wider world. The book provides a rare insight into the life of a merchant seaman and prisoner of war during one of the most critical periods in the history of the 20th century.

Dr Paul McDonald, Historian and Author

There are many facets to this book. There is the context of a long life full of change and innovation, painted in vivid terms. Goodbye Old Chap then confronts the dark side of the 20th Century, with its conflicts, inhumanity and hardships. The book brings many rewards to the reader.

Tony Redding, author of Flying for Freedom-Life and death in Bomber Command

This is a fascinating, well-written account of an extraordinary life. Relying heavily on personal diaries, wartime logs and other writings, Philip Algar has illuminated the life of his father by skilfully setting his exploits in the context of the bigger, historical picture.

Ray Dafter, author and former Financial Times journalist

GOODBYE OLD CHAP

PHILIP ALGAR

peakpublish

Peakpublish
An imprint of Peak Platform
Hassop Station
Bakewell
Derbyshire
DE45 1NW

First published by Peakpublish 2009

Printed in England

A CIP catalogue record for this book is available from
the
British Library

ISBN: 978-1-907219- 04-7
www.peakplatform.com

Dedication

This book is dedicated to the memory of my brave and generous father and to those wartime members of the Merchant Navy who gave so much but received such little recognition for their courageous and essential contribution to the war effort.

Acknowledgements

Hundreds of sources have been used in the research for this book. It is impossible to list them but I thank them all. I also acknowledge the contributions of those who contributed to parts of my father's war log but who are no longer with us.

INDEX

GOODBYE OLD CHAP

Foreword

On 27th June 1992, in a pleasant suburban flat still illuminated by late evening sunshine, an elderly man stretched to turn on his television set to see the news. As he did so, he suffered a massive heart attack and stumbled. Falling, he shattered a cut-glass vase, a wedding present from 60 years before, and hit his head on the stone fireplace, slumping, lifeless, to the floor. He remained, ignored and alone, until the next morning when a neighbour called.

Stanley Algar's death, one of some 1,400 in the United Kingdom on that day, was no mere statistic. He was my father. His fascinating life, from 1899 to 1992, spanned nearly an entire century. During this time, he witnessed and confronted the hard life endured by millions, caused partly by employers' bullying and arrogance in the early part of the 20th century and the horrors of the First World War. At that time, as a marine apprentice, in his early teens, his vessels were bombed, mined and torpedoed and he had to jump for his life as his ship sank after a collision. Between the wars, he served for three-year long periods in the Far East before being allowed leave and, like millions of others, suffered unemployment and financial problems during the depression.

In the Second World War, the vessel which he captained was the first tanker to be attacked from the air. Later, he was captured by the Germans in the South Atlantic and spent four long and increasingly hungry years in a prisoner-of-war camp before being liberated by the Welsh Guards, days before the end of the conflict.

Despite lacking a good formal education, and being brought up in a modest household, largely ignored by his callous and sometimes cruel mother and timid father, he read extensively and gained an admirable command of English literature.

He enjoyed writing and contributed many articles to specialist publications about his life at sea and the countries that he visited from 1916. Given his background, it was much to his credit that he became the third most senior master in the worldwide Shell fleet, denied the rank of commodore only by enforced retirement.

This book is based, in part, on these published articles and on his remaining and meticulously-written diaries. When 88, he wrote his life story for his family. This, augmented by the diaries and a war log, hidden from the Germans during his long period of captivity, provide a fascinating and inspiring look at a self-educated and brave man of the 20th century, his experiences, aspirations and hardships, in the context of a world that has now vanished. His success, in raising a family of three boys with Maidie, his devoted wife, and giving them a start in life that he had been denied, is scarcely mentioned in his writing but this must be his lasting legacy.

His surviving diaries, intriguing social histories in themselves, reflect his own life and times and reveal much of the man and his fierce desire to experience the happiness, success and freedom denied him in the early days and later eliminated by incarceration. Married relatively late, when nearly 33, in 1932, his new life was abruptly interrupted by the war but he frequently claimed to have been very lucky as countless respected colleagues paid the ultimate price. He had to wait for two years before seeing his first son and the delay in making the acquaintance of his second son was nearly five years.

This book leans heavily on his own words but is augmented by information from numerous other sources relating to the context in which his life was lived. Of course, it is not intended to be an objective effort to chronicle even a tiny proportion of all the developments in a tumultuous and complex century. Nor is it supposed to be a detailed account of

the lives of all prisoners of war in Germany in the Second
World War.

More simply, it is an attempt to recount the tale of an
ordinary yet extraordinary individual whose life was
influenced by some of the key events in a century of major
change that altered the world for ever.

Note: Prices have not been changed into today's currency:
One "old" pound was made up of 240 pence or 20 shillings
and there were 12 pence to the shilling. Figures in brackets
after a number of pounds have been quoted indicate,
approximately, how many pounds would have been required in
2007 to achieve the same value. The source for these
calculations is:
www.measuringworth.com

CHAPTER 1

Early days

Stanley Algar was born at home in 3 Murray Street, West Hartlepool on 8th September 1899. He was to live through nearly 92 years of the next turbulent century, to see the dreadful social conditions in the early 1900's and to experience the inhumanity that characterised two world wars.

When Stanley entered this world, Adolf Hitler was ten years old and Joseph Stalin was 20. Queen Victoria was on the throne, but she was to die two years later, at the age of 81. The Boer war, which lasted until 1902, was about to begin. The day after Stanley's birth, *The Times*, as well as reporting on the situation in the Transvaal, noted that a naval stoker was to face trial for placing a 21 pound stone on a railway track. 1899 saw the arrival of the aspirin and an electric vacuum cleaner was invented within a year of Stanley's arrival. The birth of the Labour Party was still five months away, although the Independent Labour Party had been set up in 1893, and women lacked the vote.

Even by 1905, there were only 5,000 cars on British roads and when Stanley rode in one, possibly for the first time, it merited a note in his 1912 diary. In 1896 the speed limit was four miles an hour but this was increased to 20 mph in 1904. By 1914 there were 140,000 cars on British roads and the

1

annual death toll was about 1,500. In the early years of the 21st century, the corresponding figures were about 26.2 million and 3,200. Although the first American car had been sold in 1898, the creation of the Ford Motor Company was still four years away. The first motor buses made their London debut only in 1903 and the Paris Metro system was opened in 1900. The New York network started operating in 1904. The first powered flight in a heavier-than-air machine was in the future: the Wright brothers, who had previously repaired and sold cycles, made their historic flight in December 1903. The first flight over open sea was even further away: Louis Bleriot claimed the world-first in 1909 when he crossed the English Channel and won £1,000 (£75,000) from the *Daily Mail*.

Only 210,000 domestic telephones existed in the UK in 1900 although the first telephone exchange had opened in 1879. As literacy levels improved, postcards became very popular: hundreds of millions were sent in 1904. New technology encouraged the development of newspapers and the *Daily Mail,* which had first appeared in 1896, was followed by *The Daily Express*, priced at a half of an old penny in 1900, by which time the *Mail*'s circulation had reached one million. The *Daily Mirror* came on the scene seven years later.

The disparity between the very rich and the rest of the population in 1914 was marked: four per cent of the population owned 90 per cent of the wealth. Working hours for the non-privileged classes were long and unpleasant. At the turn of the century, millions in Europe, and in the United States, lived in slums, dogged by bad health, poor living conditions, little real education, high levels of infant mortality (163 per thousand in 1899 in the UK) and confronted by low life expectancy. Between 1905 and 1909, nearly half of all working-class women had chronically bad health. Indeed, by 1905, so many Europeans were disenchanted with their lives that around 2,000 a week were leaving for a new life in the United States.

Despite all this, at the beginning of the new century, there was a hope that a new era of relative prosperity was imminent, partly because of the new developing technology. Such hopes were to be dashed by the war and the reluctance of the leisured classes to surrender their advantages. By 1911, Britain had suffered a series of major strikes, involving seamen, dockers, miners and railway workers and Germany and Italy had also experienced significant labour disputes. Russia was to undergo continuing turmoil and the First World War erupted in 1914.

The sea was to dominate Stanley's life: his father, notwithstanding a lack of connections with anything marine, was named Francis Drake Algar. Young Stanley, when he was six years old, lived in the hotel, "not very high class, more a pub", that his father managed, just outside the dock gates at Middlesbrough, the population of which was then some 90,000. "From our upstairs window, I could see the ships in the dock, the officers in their uniforms, pacing up and down the decks, and hear the ships' sirens before they sailed. It thrilled me then, as it did in all my years at sea. Occasionally, I would glance timidly into the saloon bar where the ships' officers gathered. As a young boy, dressed in a sailor's suit, I would be invited in and I listened eagerly to their tales of the sea before being hustled out by my father."

Francis Drake Algar was born in 1861 in Wingate in Yorkshire and was married twice. His first spouse, Mary Eliza, born in 1862, married him in 1888 but died in 1897. Eliza Thompson, born in 1871, became Francis Drake Algar's second wife in 1899, a few months before Stanley was born. She survived until 1943. The family expanded: Arthur arrived in 1905 and Sylvia was born in the following year. Additionally, Francis Drake's first marriage had resulted in Joseph, born in 1889, Frank in 1892 and Eva two years later. In Germany, on 22nd August 1902, a young German boy, Theodor Detmers, was born in Witten in the Ruhr: he was to have a significant impact on Stanley's later life.

Before becoming a hotel manager, Francis Drake Algar was a master grocer. Stanley liked his father but thought that he was a weak but good man who was loathe to call in customers' debts which led, inevitably, to financial difficulties. He retired in his early sixties and died in poverty in Middlesbrough, aged 86, in 1946. However, in 1912, family finances may not have been too serious: in October Stanley took a camera for repair. The Eastman company had produced the first celluloid film roll for Kodak cameras in 1899 and box cameras, sometimes made of cardboard, were available from 1888. By 1901 they were priced at 5/- or less and some models were designed specifically for children. In November 1912, aged 13, he attended a fireworks display, probably a communal event, but, significantly, it was one of the few occasions in which his parents may have played a part.

In April 1944, Stanley, then a prisoner of war in Germany, was distressed to learn that the allowance he asked to be sent to his father had to be cut as the family bank balance was shrinking. "Poor old father, he has had a poor life and, at 84, has had to ask Sylvia [his daughter] to take him in. His old age pension and £2 a month from us means he has 24/3 a week to live on!" Stanley's attitude to his mother was totally different. Seemingly ignored in his childhood, although that was common in large families and hard-working marriages, he was later seen just as a source of income and, despite sustained hostility, he never wavered in giving financial support whenever possible, even when the pressures on his own finances were severe, as when he was setting up his own home. His mother fought to prevent his marriage in 1932 and made little attempt to disguise her preference for Arthur, to whom she frequently diverted some of the money that Stanley sent home to Middlesbrough.

Stanley noted in his diary for 5th April 1944, ironically Maidie's birthday, "received news via Red Cross of the death of my mother. When the padre said that he had bad news for me, my heart thumped. 'Who is it?' Cruel as it may sound, I was relieved that the bad news was not related to Maidie or the boys. The news of her death makes me sad, yet, now that she has gone, I can't think differently about her. I still remember many unkind actions and the deliberate attempt to destroy my

4

only chance of happiness, with Maidie. I hope she has gone to a better place." It had taken about 10 months for the news to reach Stanley. A few days later, he recalled the neglect and occasional cruelty from his mother whilst his father remained indifferent. For example, nobody visited him, when, aged 15, he joined his first ship in Middlesbrough. "Nobody was sufficiently interested to see my ship, my accommodation or the food I would get." He sent money home, out of the miserly pittance he was granted for his clothes, whilst other boys received money from home. Towards the end of his own life, Stanley became very embittered towards his mother.

A diary entry for 13th May 1944, when incarcerated in a prisoner-of-war camp in Germany, reveals something about his early life. "Another few months will see me reach 45. What have I had out of life? Literally a few months of happiness. As a boy, the only real happiness I had was when I was away from home at camp with the Boy Scouts."

1912 and the Boy Scout movement

In 1912, the local club room, the gym, library, Sunday School and the swimming pool, costing up to three pence per week, were important to the young Algar. Home and family are hardly mentioned. It was the Boy Scout movement which took him to places he would not otherwise have visited, some by train, and which filled his spare time by providing him with useful skills and, importantly, offered him an extended family of friends. It also contributed significantly to the development of his character. Indeed, the discipline instilled in the scout movement doubtless influenced many men who were to serve in the First World War.

The Boy Scout movement was established in 1908. Lord Robert Baden-Powell, the founder, had become a national hero for defending Mafeking during the Boer war and on his return, aged 50, he wrote *Aids to Scouting* followed by *Scouting for Boys* in 1908. In 1910, an office for the fast-developing scout movement was set up in London and the movement then claimed 100,000 members. Some of the originator's comments, in his last letter to the movement before he died in 1938, may have been recalled by Stanley when subjected to the horrors of a prisoner-of-war camp. "I believe that God put us in this jolly world to be happy and to enjoy life. Happiness does not come from being rich nor merely by success in your career nor by self-indulgence....Be content with what you've got and make the best of it. Look on the bright side of things instead of the gloomy one. Try and leave this world a little better than when you found it." Stanley undoubtedly achieved this.

Some of Baden-Powell's outrageously simplistic and unscientific comments were ridiculed when his classic book, *Scouting for Boys,* was reprinted many decades later by Oxford University Press. They reflect Baden-Powell's experience in the Boer war but it is not apparent how relevant such remarks were to young boys in Middlesbrough. BP claimed that by observing how people dress and behave, it might be possible to detect that they were "up to no good" thus avoiding a crime. All boys should know how to obey orders and to shoot, otherwise, if war broke out, they would be no more good than an old woman and would be killed like squealing rabbits. BP favoured bees which respect their queen and killed the unemployed. Snakes were not good pets as they might frighten the servants. Scouts should know what to do to save a man who has tried to commit suicide and boys should not loaf around with their hands in their pockets. Even American cowboys cleaned their teeth, thrice daily, and smoking made a boy look like an ass.

The young Stanley, now living at 110 Grange Road, West Middlesbrough, joined the 1st Middlesbrough Peewit troop, also of Grange Road, on 16th January 1910 so became one of the first recruits. He acquired his second class badge on 21st August 1911 and the first class badge on 17th June the following year. He was promoted to patrol leader in 1912 and taught younger boys knots and other skills.

Stanley Algar's copy of *The Boy Scout Note Book and Diary 1912*, bound in khaki cloth and costing six old pence, was preferred to one priced one shilling although the latter was bound in leather and was accompanied by a pencil. His diary contains not only interesting insights into his own life but into the emerging movement. We learn, for example, that a scout is to be trusted, is loyal and that his duty is to be useful and to help others. "A scout smiles and whistles under all difficulties…when you just miss a train or someone treads on your favourite corn, not that a scout ought to have corns, or under any annoying circumstances, you should smile at once and then whistle a tune and then you will be all right." Whistling must have been a regular feature of daily life as there was so much about which to be angry.

A scout had to be thrifty, which, in 1912, would not have been too difficult for the 12 year old Stanley. During the year, his diary only records one gift of money, a postal order for 1/- from a Miss Hood, although he does buy *The Scout* every week, so he had some spending money. "A scout saves every penny he can, and puts it into the bank, so that he may have money to keep himself when out of work and thus not make himself a burden to others or that he may have money to give away to others when they need it." Contemporary readers may be surprised at the assumption that scouts had bank accounts. This comment, like so many other utterances, reflects BP's privileged status and a profoundly breath-taking ignorance of how others lived. Indeed, this failure to understand the less privileged raises the inevitable question of why his movement was so popular. Was it because it offered friendship, access to different subjects not covered in any more-formal education, such as it was, and was affordable at a time when there was little competing for young boys' attention?

Absolute loyalty to the King, his officers, his country and to his employers was required. In 1915, did the young Algar, when seeking an apprenticeship, at a time of war, and all its attendant risks, feel loyalty to the employers? They were to pay him £40 over four years, in wartime, for the privilege of providing them with cheap labour and being taught little, despite the requirements laid down in the indentures. Loyalty then was only in one direction, as millions of workers discovered during the century.

The scout was also required to "do at least one good turn to [sic] somebody every day". In 1912, Stanley listed, *inter alia*, taking dinner [lunch] or tea to his brother, believed to be working in the docks, and to his father and looking after the house when everyone was out, sometimes until 11.00 pm. He also washed up crockery, ran regular errands for his parents, cleared away snow, helped at whist drives, collected "cinders at the cinder yard", often very early in the morning, and cleaned bugles and bayonets. He even walked into a river, wearing his socks and shoes, to retrieve an errant hat, the ownership of which is not mentioned, nor the reaction of the hitherto-hatted person.

Scouts should have been able to "mend and even make clothes and boots". Stanley could not mend his boots which were repaired four times during 1912, confining their owner to his home while the footwear was at the cobblers. Allegedly, every scout, even if he were small and weak, could become strong if he did the required exercises for ten minutes a day. To encourage such activity, there was a section in the diary devoted to "my physical development" but this remained blank for young Stanley who was less than 4 feet ten inches and had a collar size of fifteen and a half and a hat size of six and seven eighths.

Advice was also offered on swimming, at which Stanley was to excel, and how to become a competent signaler, which proved helpful in his career, especially in the Second World War, as did his skill with knots and splices. Perhaps of less relevance to most scouts in 1912 was a guide to foreign currencies. The US dollar was then valued at 4 shillings and a penny halfpenny, yielding an exchange rate of \$4.95 to the pound sterling. Stanley may have studied these rates when he visited America, for the first time, in 1915.

A few advertisements appeared in the diary. A patent kit cart, made by Braggins of Banbury, was offered at £6-10-0 free on rail. William Pope of St. Mary Axe in London, which would later become familiar to Stanley, when it was the location for the London head office for Shell, his long-term employers, was publicising Army bell tents and marquees. A new scout patrol tent was just 17/6 but second-hand ones were available at only 12/6. B.S.A of Birmingham were offering rifles "which are absolutely accurate, no matter at what price they are retailed". One shown in the advertisement, available to boy scouts for just 30/- was "by far the best value ever offered in rifles".

Stanley's year

Scarcely a day passed in Stanley's 1912 diary without a reference to some aspect of scouting. As he remarked in his diary, 32 years later, the only time that he knew real happiness in the early days was when he was away at a scout camp. He notes with pride that, on 5th January, he attended the junior scouts' (cadets) party, won the signaling competition and came second in "ambulance", (first aid) and in shooting. A few days later, he was at the local fire station learning fire drill. On 13th January, he went to Eston, some four miles away, near Middlesbrough, with the scouts, and, now hopefully skilled in fire drill, was permitted to have a fire, followed by some scouting games before returning home at 6.00 pm. A few days later, he was practicing signaling but only went home at 9.00. This was his usual time but, during the year, even during term time, he occasionally went to bed at 11.00 pm or even later. There is no indication that his parents objected to this. Did they know or care?

Trips out with the scouts were eagerly anticipated. On Saturday 9th March he accompanied the scouts to the local Primrose Valley and one week later he returned to Eston. Occasionally, he paid unspecified sums into the camp fund and went on several camping "holidays", including one with the Territorials in about 1913. He also participated in many church parades with the scouts and, on one occasion, was a member of the guard of honour for the Archbishop of York.

Day trips to nearby Barnaby Moor were popular for scout games and tuition but, in April, Stanley was disappointed that he could not accompany his friends to the Moor because his boots needed repairing. Another scouting destination was Guisborough, some nine miles away, and one visit was memorable as the tent fell down. The scouts also chopped down a tree, presumably to burn, as the night was sufficiently cold for it to snow, even although it was early April. Unusually, his mother visited him at this camp.

Other forays under canvas were dominated by bad weather. "It rained all day and water flowed through the tent like a stream. I moved to a bell tent and went home that night for more food but returned to camp the following day on the 3.00 train." Eston was another camping venue in August. Possibly because of bad weather, Stanley slept in the Walkers' farm loft and had his photograph taken at dinner. Proudly, he records that he climbed the hills, although, on one occasion, he was "helped by the Walkers' car", had tea at a farm and ran nearly four miles back. He also watched an artist painting Barnard Castle, which was about 33 miles from Middlesbrough, and this and other trips suggests that he used the train frequently. Another destination for the scouts was Middleton, some 40 miles away, where Stanley took part in a church parade. He also attended a rally at Ronaldskirk, about 40 miles from home, and walked around the village. In September young Algar went to a Thornaby Scouts display and saw a presentation of colours before giving an exhibition of signaling and walking home the six miles.

Apart from teaching young Stanley some skills, scouting trips introduced him to nature. During the year, obviously impressed by the new world he was experiencing, he saw a dog chasing a rabbit, not an everyday occurrence near the docks, and, on a visit to a farm, he found a nest and then a blackbird's egg and also watched butter being made in a small churn. Other discoveries deemed sufficiently important to be mentioned in his diary included finding a moorhen's egg, skinning and cooking a rabbit and seeing a dead fox, being given some birds' eggs and discovering a skylark's egg and a thrush's nest with two eggs. The scouts also found mushrooms and apples and watched deer on Lord Barnard's estate. Stanley spoke to Lord Barnard but the nature and duration of the conversation were not revealed.

Later in the year, he enjoyed a walk along the sands at Marske-By-The-Sea, just 11 miles from home, with the Sunday School and saw Princess Louise open a bazaar which he had helped to publicise. Two stark reminders of the age occurred when Stanley was sufficiently interested to follow a fire engine and, in July, saw an aeroplane which had flown from Thornaby, six miles from Middlesbrough, over the town hall.

A social life?

There are few mentions in the 1912 diary of either parent. That might reflect the times as both parents were fully occupied and it was an age when, in some families, children were neither seen nor heard but, clearly, Stanley was never his mother's favourite. In the entire year, there is not a single reference to his father and there are very few entries relating to his family. He went out with his mother in April and again in September when the two went to Stockton, four miles away. In the summer, his mother and sister visited him at the scout camp. The sister returned to the camp two weeks later and Stanley made her tea. "Uncle Walter" visited home in September and may have stayed for nearly a month. There is also a fleeting reference to an Aunt Jane who visited briefly but uncle and aunt may have been courtesy titles.

School receives few mentions in the diary, apart from references to homework. Having read about the *Titanic* disaster on 21st April, he had to write a "composition" about it two days later. The new, luxury 46,000 ton liner, owned by the White Star Line, hit an iceberg off Newfoundland and sank at 02.20 am on 15th April 1912. It was on its maiden voyage from Southampton to New York and 1,500 passengers and crew lost their lives, partly because there were insufficient lifeboats, although, given the presence of icebergs, it is doubtful if many more of the 2,224 people on board might have been saved. 11,000 workers had constructed the vessel which was widely believed to be unsinkable.

There is little information about Stanley's school but he acknowledged in later life that it was "one degree better than a council school" and that his father always did his best for him, as, indeed, Stanley was to do for his three sons. Schooling was compulsory to the age of 12 but Stanley went to the secondary level and in the period between 1910 and 1929, only a fifth of all pupils continued to this level. The fees were two pence a week which doubled when Stanley went to the senior school. Many decades later, he remarked that "if there were one thing for which I am thankful, it is that I have been able to send my [three] boys to Highgate School. Whatever happens, at least we have given them a good start".

Sunday School at St. Michaels and choir practice also absorbed much spare time. During the year, he passed a medical examination, carried out by the school doctor, and only twice does Stanley mention his health. In June, he had a headache and was bilious, necessitating an early night, and he burned his foot in November, after standing on a poker. Away from school, he begins courses in shorthand, but the reason for this is not explained. He made further attempts to master shorthand during his long stay in the prisoner-of-war camp.

Clearly, the young Algar was obliged to develop his own social life. There are very few references to other people accompanying Stanley to anywhere but names and addresses of ten fellow scouts are listed in the diary and it may be assumed that they were involved in both scouting and social activities. During the year, apart from trips with scouts or the school, Stanley notes that he saw a whaler in the docks and he also went to a police carnival and in September travelled to Wingate, 16 miles away, in a donkey gig.

Sport figured prominently, either through the school or the scouts. 1912 began brightly for Stanley as he saw Middlesbrough beat Wingate Albion 7-0 and later in the year he watched Middlesbrough playing Sunderland Rovers in a cup tie. Middlesbrough football club had been founded in 1876 by some cricketers, keen to keep fit during the winter. The club finished third in the 1913-14 season in the second division of the Football League. Stanley enjoyed football and took part in the 4-2 defeat of the bible class at the hands of the scouts and helped to defeat East End Cadets 8-2. In early February, during a period of cold and snowy weather, Stanley went skating, possibly in the local park. 1912 was in the middle of what some analysts later described as a modest ice age. He also enjoyed cricket and table tennis and records that, late in the year, after a billiards table arrived in the club rooms, he played with some of the adults. Card games are also mentioned and this seems to have been a popular pastime at the rooms.

There are also references to shooting, presumably with the Boy Scouts, and he watched and participated in boxing. This, and swimming, were to be life-long interests. On 10th September, erroneously noting that it was his birthday (which was on the 8th), prompting thoughts that his parents made a mistake, he finished second in a school race at the local swimming baths. Four days later, possibly inspired by having bought a "new swimming costume", he managed seven lengths of the pool and he was soon selected as reserve for the swimming team. He completed two lengths in 51 seconds and soon managed 20 lengths. On 29th October he competed in the school swimming championships.

In 1912 there was relatively little for a young, and largely impecunious, boy to buy. Stanley methodically records what, to him, were significant acquisitions. In July he was given a new suit and boots and this was followed by his purchase of a walking stick. An advertisement for a man's suit in 1911 indicated that the price was about 35/- so Stanley's suit, if it were new, would not have been cheap. The following month, he bought a scout's knife and fork and in September, he received new shorts and slippers. October was significant for the arrival of a new overcoat and cap and in December, a new pair of boots was welcomed. The diary entry for 21st December announced the purchase of a scout's diary for 1/- Presumably, this was the leather edition, complete with pencil. On Christmas Eve he bought a water pistol and the following day received a box of paints. On the last day of the old year, he acquired a "flash lamp and an extra battery".

Almost every day, "read book at home," was a standard diary entry and this habit of reading was to persist for many decades until his eyes failed to co-operate. Usually, the books came from the local library but some originated in the scouts' library. Volumes chosen included traditional schoolboy stories as well as books about history, travel and the sea. Stanley also read every issue of *The Scout*, out every Thursday, price one penny. "Every boy should read it. Full of good articles and other matter of interest to boys" read the advertisement.

He enjoyed films and the diary records 13 trips to "Kelly's Pictures" in the year, including nine visits in the first quarter. He also patronised "Smart's Pictures" and went to the Bedford with a fellow scout. Whilst all these venues showed films, they may not have been cinemas in the modern sense. Some may have been shops or halls and even houses were converted to show the new films before small and local audiences. Mitchell and Kenyon were successful film producers who specialised in making shorts about the local area and then showing them to a thrilled audience just a few hours later. However, the first English cinema had opened in 1907 and by 1912, there were some 4,000. Stanley also went to the Empire, possibly a theatre, at least three times in the year and even went with his mother on one occasion. He also visited Scarborough, about 50 miles away, to attend a concert and patronised the Hippodrome. The absence of any information to the contrary suggests that many of his 46 listed visits to films or the theatre were by himself and that many were the late show which meant that he returned home after 11.00 pm.

CHAPTER 2

Apprenticeship and war

Before Stanley went to sea, he became a Sea Scout and also attended some camps with the Territorials in 1913.

On 4th August 1914, Britain declared war on Germany after the latter had invaded Belgium. Germany was able to call on 8.5 million armed men, backed by 40 battleships, 12 cruisers and 33 U boats. Great Britain had some 711,000 men under arms and operated 64 battleships and 121 cruisers. President Woodrow Wilson, on the same day, announced that the United States would neither participate in the war nor take sides. However, this decision was reversed in April 1917, about 20 months before the end of the war, when Congress voted in favour of intervention by 373 to 50. By early June, 50,000 members of the US forces were arriving in Europe every month.

At the outbreak of the conflict, Stanley, then nearly 15, was at school. Before the war ended the schoolboy had become a man. He was to be apprenticed in July 1915 but, before then, events showed how local citizens might be affected by the conflict. Stanley had been born in Murray Street, West Hartlepool but, by 1901, two years later, the national census records the family's address as Inkerman Street in Stockton. By 1906, the family had moved to Grange Road in

Middlesbrough, where Francis Drake became the manager of a local hotel, near the dock gates. The distance from Middlesbrough to West Hartlepool, attacked on 16th December 1914 by three German warships, is about ten miles so the young Stanley may well have heard the gunfire. Nearby Scarborough was also attacked.

The hostile vessels approached the English coast early in the morning, doubtless attracted by the concentration of the shipyards and engine works. The warships, based at the German centre on Heligoland, reportedly flew a "British" flag, before substituting the German flag. The attack on West Hartlepool commenced at 8.10 am and 40 minutes later, 127 people had been killed and more than 400 injured by the 1,500 shells fired at the town. Panic ensued when it was realised that this was an enemy attack, possibly the prelude to an invasion, and not a harmless practice by the Royal Navy. Thousands fled, not knowing what to do. One consequence of the enemy action was that the gasworks were unable to operate for some months, thus denying the local people much-need heat and light in winter. In total, some 200 people were killed by the German navy and about 600 houses were damaged.

In 1916 and again in 1918, Hartlepool was attacked by Zeppelins on three separate occasions. These airships, with a metal frame, were fuelled by hydrogen, with engines outside the frame and steered by a motor-driven propeller. They could cruise at about 85 miles an hour, carrying up to two tons of bombs. Shops and houses were damaged during the raids and eight people were killed at Middleton Beach, which Stanley had visited with the scouts in 1912. One of the airships was shot down over the sea and the bodies of the crew were washed ashore.

Stanley's desire to go to sea was not diminished by war. In July 1915, aged nearly 16, he tried to become an apprentice. There is no indication that any alternative work was considered or that he had even been on a vessel. He must have heard about the German warships which had shelled Hartlepool the previous December but did Stanley know that, in January 1915, the German battle cruiser *Blucher* had sunk off the Dogger Bank and that nearly 800 sailors had been drowned? Was he aware that the Germans, after warning that they would attack any merchant ship carrying armaments, had torpedoed a Cunard liner, the *Lusitania*, en route from New York to Liverpool on 7th May 1915? Over 1,200 passengers perished when the vessel sank, in 18 minutes, off the coast of Ireland. The calamity was converted into a propaganda exercise by the British who claimed that innocent citizens had been slaughtered. However, recent efforts by divers have suggested that the liner was, indeed, carrying munitions. Reportedly, some four million rounds of .303 bullets have been found in the vessel's hold. The loss of 128 US citizens may have played a part in eventually changing American sentiment on isolationism.

Stanley must have been aware of some of these events but there is no evidence that it influenced his desire to go to sea. Later, when he was first engaged by a shipping company, he acknowledges the dangers he could face and his resolution to pursue a sea-going career was confirmed after his potentially disastrous incident in 1916 when his vessel sank after a collision. Later, when still a teenager, his ship was mined in Swansea Bay in 1916 and torpedoed in the English Channel in March 1918. When he began his career, the conflict was less than a year old and people and politicians alike, enthusiastic for the war, were optimistic, believing that it might even be over by Christmas. Perhaps the young Algar concurred with this view?

At that time, there were several ways to commence a career at sea. The best, and most expensive, was to serve two or three years as a cadet on a training ship, such as the *H.M.S Worcester,* followed by three years with a reputable shipping company. This was the marine equivalent of the "old school tie" and eased entry into the best shipping companies and into the Royal Naval Reserve. Another system was to join a reputable company which would require a guarantee that the individual would complete his apprenticeship satisfactorily. Such fortunate individuals were provided with good accommodation, allowed to dine with the captain and officers and were trained competently.

The method that Stanley's father selected, for financial reasons, was for his son to be apprenticed to a company which paid for the privilege of taking on cheap labour. Stanley was to be granted £40 over four years, plus £1 in lieu of washing facilities and a bonus of £5 on successful completion of the apprenticeship. Another approach was to start as a deck boy and to become an able-bodied (AB) seaman after three years but this scheme did not impress the best shipping groups. After four years, or three for those who had been on the training vessels, it was possible to take the examination for the 2nd mate's certificate.

Stanley's mother took him to the local offices of the Shipping Federation. "I was 15 years old and my height, only 4'10," immediately created an adverse impression. The atmosphere was heavy with pessimism. The official shook his head sadly and muttered that I was so small that no London company would accept me. The alternative was to find a local firm and the one selected, one of the worst companies, occupied an office opposite the Federation. Understandably depressed, I think I lost an inch or two, just crossing the road, and my arrival in the ship owner's office prompted the official, smiling pityingly, to observe that I was so small and would not be much good to them for a long time."

"Then, suddenly, after a long pause, he said that they would take me. The war was on, which meant that I could be blown up by a mine or torpedo or drowned but he was prepared to engage me. I was to be paid £7 for the first year, then £8, £10 and £15 in each of the succeeding years. 'The master agrees to provide said apprentice with sufficient meat, drink, lodgings, medicine and medical assistance and 20/- will be given in lieu of washing'.

"A few days later, I went to the offices with my father and signed the indentures, an impressive parchment document, littered with red seals. I had a brief moment of pride as my

18

father signed as Francis Drake Algar. The indentures confirmed that I was to be housed and fed, taught the duties of a seaman, would obey all lawful commands and that I would not frequent ale houses, taverns or houses of ill repute. I did not know what they were but my new shipmates kindly enlightened me."

Aged 15, the tiny and apprehensive newcomer to the nation's war effort joined his first ship at Middlesbrough. It was a dirty coal-fired oil tanker, built around 1890, and Stanley's initial voyage was to the Humber to load a full cargo of fuel oil for the Royal Navy at Scapa Flow, in the Orkney Islands, north of Scotland. His colleagues comprised a capable but unpleasant master, frequently drunk, an elderly and amiable chief officer, a second mate of 70, blind in one eye and with a face that suggested that it had once been subjected to a massive blow, and some apprentices and sailors with experience of sailing ships who were contemptuous of those who had not.

The apprentices were accommodated in a good-sized room with five bunks, each with three drawers underneath. A rough table and two benches constituted the remaining furniture and the entrance to the room was used to hang working clothes. It was also the area where the buckets used for washing and toilet facilities were kept. The only bath was used exclusively by the captain. Sometimes, the firemen allowed the apprentices to bath in the stokehold, where the temperature was more acceptable, although coal dust was a problem. Food, in terms of both quality and quantity, was a permanent problem. For example, one tin of condensed milk had to last for three weeks. Very poor deserts appeared thrice weekly. The fruitless and remarkably heavy Christmas pudding in 1917 was dropped overboard by the apprentices who believed that the spot ought to be marked by a wreck buoy lest passing ships be damaged. Poor quality curry and rice was frequently served at breakfast. Meanwhile, in the UK, there was a food shortage and rationing was imposed.

The last meal of the day was at 5.00 pm and breakfast was at 8.00 am so apprentices on watch during the night became hungry. The working day extended from 6.00 am to 5.00 pm and the day seemed endless to the new apprentice, recently out of school. The uninspiring work was dominated by chipping rust off the decks, washing paintwork, cleaning filthy fuel oil tanks and overhauling gear. On Stanley's first night at sea, having told the chief mate that he had acquired signalling experience as a scout, he was called upon to read signals from a navy ship. He records, with no little pleasure, that, in his first few hours, he had proved the Shipping Federation official wrong when he said that the diminutive boy would not be of any use for some years.

On entering the Flow, young Stanley was most impressed. "It seemed that the whole of the British fleet was there. I had read at school, and had heard so often of the invincibility of the British navy and, now, to my boyish eyes, was the proof as we steamed between the lines of ships which included *Resolution, Revenge, Royal Oak, Marlborough* and, most impressive of all, the *Iron Duke*, flagship of Admiral Jellicoe…We anchored amongst merchant ships, colliers and supply vessels and immediately began fuelling destroyers but we had to go alongside the larger cruisers. The largest ships, usually coal burners, were not our customers."

A decision to switch from coal to oil as the main fuel for the Royal Navy had been taken by Winston Churchill, then First Lord of the Admiralty, and the government in 1912. Some other vessels had been converted as early as 1904. Oil-fired vessels were faster, had a bigger range and could be loaded more swiftly and required fewer personnel who would otherwise have been occupied in shovelling coal. Oil provided 50 per cent more steam than coal per ton and occupied significantly less space than that taken by the rival fuel. However, at the beginning of the First World War, less than five per cent of the global fleet of merchant vessels used oil.

When his own vessel needed coal, Stanley, some firemen and other apprentices were required to carry out a dirty, frightening, unhealthy and dangerous operation. Coal burners required huge effort from humans who had to put coal into sacks, the sacks into nets, swing the nets from the collier into their own bunker hold and empty them, then trim the supply so that it was level. All this had to be accomplished with the aid of only a small lamp as the remaining daylight was snuffed out by the incoming coal.

Stanley spent some time in the region because his vessel took oil from larger tankers and then supplied it to the naval ships. Summer in the Orkneys was pleasant and on Sunday mornings, the apprentices went fishing but Stanley, because of his lack of stature, was excused rowing and, instead, had to clean the fish. This did not appeal and he soon "resigned". After a few weeks, the ship's stores were depleted and the steward was despatched, once a week, to Kirkwall, the small town on Orkney, to buy the necessary provisions. He took advantage of this by drinking excessively so Stanley, presumably because he was young and doubtless naïve, was ordered to collect the necessary provisions. He went ashore in a fishing boat and then travelled by a horse-drawn carriage to the clean little town. Eventually, such was the volume of purchases he made for the vessel and its crew, the shops gave Stanley commission of £7 (£300) over the period. "I lost control and bought an Ingersoll watch for 5/- and a chain which also cost 5/-."

In 1916, another tanker, the *Hermione*, came alongside to supply Stanley's carrier with fuel oil from Trinidad. "As daylight faded, the wind increased to gale force and the sea became very heavy. The mooring wires and ropes linking the two vessels began to snap and the stern of our tanker sheared into the *Hermione* and her propeller cut right through our hull into the engine room." Efforts to plug the hole by covering it with tarpaulin proved fruitless and attempts to pump oil out to bring the ship's stern out of the water to bring the hole above the water line also failed. The oil left the pipe in a solid jet and, as a nearby vessel turned on its searchlight, it showed a grey warship gradually becoming brown with the oil. "It must have been a weird sight: the wind was howling in the darkness, the huge waves were rolling away to leeward and the stricken vessel was pitching and slowly sinking by the stern."

Wisely, Stanley packed his seabag in anticipation of disaster and the lights went out when the ship lost all power, leaving the apprentice to stagger to the deck. A tug, the *Alliance,* came alongside but initially inspired little confidence as it rose above and then fell below the height of the stricken tanker as it was engulfed in the trough of a wave. "I was standing, undecided what to do, when McPherson, the chief mate, saw me, grabbed my shoulder and took me to the bulwarks. I stood on the angle bar, he gripped my ankles, to prevent me from slipping and my hands were tight around the rigging of the foremast. 'When I say jump, let go the rigging and jump as far as you can.' I suppose I realised the danger but I was too excited and tense and there was no time to be afraid. I watched the tug rising and falling and, at the right moment, I heard the shout of 'jump'. I did and fell across the bulwarks of the rising tug where eager hands pulled me aboard. I was cold, wet and shaken, but safe, thanks to McPherson. Sadly, he never returned to sea and died a few months later."

Everyone was saved and was taken to a comfortable old wooden warship, the *Imperious,* where they stayed for a few days. Stanley only had what he stood up in, a blue sweater, a pair of working jeans, and boots. He was given a pair of Royal Marine trousers, cut to fit, and a naval overcoat and returned home in this outfit, prompting his mother, unusually showing some interest in her son's career, to ask if he still wanted to go to sea. His response was unambiguous. "The idea of leaving it had never entered my head." That firm reply explains why he had not been deterred from realising his ambition when he became an apprentice in 1915, notwithstanding the war.

To the United States

Stanley's next vessel was a coaster, the *Teesdale,* which carried only a few hundred tons and had a crew of eight. It was a democratically-run ship where "everyone was someone". Iron segments for the new London underground system were loaded at Thornaby on Tees for discharge at Erith in Kent but this did not appeal to Stanley who then joined a decrepit oil tanker, the *Hotham Newton,* which was to sail from Middlesbrough for the United States. The departure was characterised by weeping wives on the quayside and drunken crew on the vessel so the apprentices had to steer the ship and keep watch until someone more senior was sufficiently sober to take over.

In the United States, in 1916, the young Stanley must have been astonished at what he found. Because Henry Ford had standardised car production and created an assembly line, thus reducing unit costs, many Americans were able to own cars. By 1910, there were 200 car manufacturers in the United States, producing some 200,000 cars annually and in 1913, the price of the Ford T model had fallen to $500 ($11,000). The only colour in which it was available was black and it was produced until 1927.

The New York subway system had been operating for about a decade and the skyscraper buildings, which had first appeared in the late 1860's, dominated the urban landscape. Public transport systems were expanding and there was a general sense of optimism in the New World, influenced, doubtless, by the fact that it was not involved in the grim war being fought in distant Europe. By 1913, US gross national product per capita was not only 25 per cent higher than in the United Kingdom, but was equal, in total, to the combined GNP of the UK, Germany and France.

Something that exercised the young apprentice, still under the age of 17, was the war risk bonus. It was £3-0-0 per month for senior men and £1-10-00 per month for all other ranks. Stanley felt that his life was as valuable as that of more senior men but wisely decided against challenging this injustice at that time. Now, in his second year, he was earning £10 per annum. He left the *Holtham Newton*, one voyage before it succumbed to old age and sank, and joined a larger and more modern ship, the master of which was the same unpleasant man that had captained the vessel that sank in Scapa Flow.

23

The chief mate, also later known as chief officer, decided that the young Algar could be trusted to keep watch, from the bridge, across the Atlantic. This meant a total of four hours on and four hours off over the week, resulting in a working week of 84 hours and maximum periods of sleep of less than four hours. The primitive open bridge offered little protection from the weather for those at the wheel. "I remember those voyages across the North Atlantic in winter and the intense cold, being called at midnight or 4.00 am, the mountainous seas smashing on board, the ship shuddering and shaking with the impact, and the sickening, never-ending rolling and pitching. Very often, I was soaked on my way to the bridge and then I would wedge myself in a corner of the bridge, holding on to a convenient rail...The minutes passed reluctantly, I stood peering into the compass, dimly lit, trying to make the ship's head keep to the course, feeling the cold slowly rising from my numb feet, the rain and spray finding and exploiting a vulnerable point around my neck, and, despite all this discomfort, struggling to keep awake. Sometimes, shivering and wet, I wondered why I had chosen this career, but it was all I ever wanted."

Stanley remained on this vessel for two years. Regular voyages were from the UK to the United States which was then the world's leading oil producer, providing two thirds of global crude oil supplies, and then to France with aviation gasoline for the Royal Flying Corps or the Royal Navy Air Service. These units combined in April 1918 to become the Royal Air Force. One of the most unpopular tasks was tank cleaning which had to be undertaken as the previous cargo, fuel oil, would have contaminated the aviation spirit.

Shore leave and cash advances were at the discretion of the master who was unhelpful when the vessel visited New York. The refusal to assist financially was because a crew member, who might have only worked for the two week trip across the Atlantic, might then desert. American rates of pay were virtually double those paid to UK nationals. Such was the perceived potential of the promised land that as early as 1905, some 100,000 immigrants had sailed from Europe each year, driven by desperation, the need for work and freedom.

The master allowed the apprentices one dollar each and, because that would have been absorbed in transport to New York, the young men contented themselves with a trip to Bayonne, close to the docks. Their first destination was an ice-cream parlour where Stanley consumed two banana splits, each consisting of three blobs of ice cream and a cherry, of such quality that the dish became the standard by which other similar fare was judged for many decades. Shunning ale houses and also houses of ill repute, the apprentices visited a picture palace for which the entry charge was just ten cents. The music came from an automatic piano. A bar of chocolate, costing ten cents, helped to induce a degree of euphoria as did a meal of bacon and egg, followed by a slice of fruit pie and a cup of coffee, priced at 25 cents. After this conspicuous consumption, the young men still had a few cents left from their original dollar.

On one voyage, part of the cargo was discharged at Le Havre and the vessel then proceeded up the Seine to Rouen. "It was summer and the river was lovely. The colourful small towns and villages that lined the river bank and the friendly people, waving to us, the woods, peaceful fields and farms and even the occasional chateau, all seemed so far away from the misery of war." A crew change followed at Swansea but some of the replacement personnel were disturbed to learn that they had signed on to a tanker, and worse still, it would be carrying aviation gasoline to Dunkirk. "Even the most unimaginative could grasp what might happen if a torpedo hit us."

Some of these voyages were marred by serious fighting. Firemen who had signed on in New York, unable to secure a job on an American vessel, were lazy, feigned sickness and often resolved their differences with a knife. The crew, living in the forecastle, the front part of the vessel under the deck, had to endure conditions scarcely fit for human beings. The men had little space and lack of natural light was not offset by the few and low wattage bulbs.

Christmas Day 1916

In 1916, Stanley made a few trips to and from America and, usually, an escort was only provided near the UK coast, so the vessel was exposed to the risk of an attack by enemy submarines. On Christmas Day, the 17 year old Stanley was on watch, looking out for floating mines.

"About 9.00 am, when only a short distance from Swansea, our destination, I was told to finish the look-out and go aft to hoist the ensign on the poop. As I was doing this, there was a terrific explosion forrard and the ship shook and shuddered as it hit a floating mine. There was a cloud of smoke over the fo'c'asle head and cork fenders were sailing up into the air. The captain ordered me to take the wheel to replace the Spanish sailor who was then trying to launch the lifeboat. Panicking, they did not see that the boats were still secured to the deck. A sailor from Newfoundland realised what the problem was and the boat was lowered over the side until I noticed that another mine was floating directly under where the lifeboat would have taken to the water. I was not feeling too happy at the wheel but the captain told me to 'keep her head steady' so I assumed that there was no danger." One of the firemen, a coloured American, promised that he would complain to President Wilson about the mining of the ship. Perhaps he did because the Americans entered the war soon afterwards!"

The mine had created a huge hole in the bow but the ship was able to continue to Swansea for repairs. At this time, the apprentices, who were the only personnel to live on the ship, were not allowed to cook onboard. They were given an allowance of 10/6 per week for food which Stanley described as absurd and it was a reflection of the times and the relationship between employer and employee, that no protest was made. Breaking into the ship's stores proved futile because there was little there: there was a strong suspicion that the captain had appropriated the contents. Such pilfering by senior personnel was rampant for many decades and persisted well into the 20th century. Some removed fridges, for example, with apparent impunity. Fortunately, in 1917, friendly apprentice engineers in the docks allowed their colleagues to visit their youth club where tea and cakes were cheap. Kind Welsh people invited the apprentices into their homes for tea and waitresses in local cafes forgot to include every item on their bills.

Despite the requirements imposed on the company by the apprentices' indentures, there had been no tuition on navigation or seamanship and the young men, frustrated, angry and impotent, sought coaching from a retired officer who charged two shillings per person for two hours. Soon, it was apparent that he was not good enough. "I think he must have been a navigating officer for Noah. We retreated to our own books and resources." Repairs to the vessel took three months and it proved a happy time, despite the war and lack of cash. Depressingly for all concerned, the repaired vessel was to carry aviation gasoline. The first trip after the repairs had been made was memorable because Stanley encountered an alcoholic 40 year old bosun and tried, unsuccessfully, to curb his consumption by looking after the older man's money and only allowing him cash when necessary.

Food and war

The lack of food had haunted Stanley and his apprentice colleagues in their early days at sea and provoked them into many ruses designed to ward off hunger. The problem was to recur when Captain Algar was detained by the Germans in the Second World War. Meanwhile, in 1916, the availability of food in the UK was severely curtailed: butchers were offering customers squirrel and woodpeckers. In 1917, as the war raged, the amount of food that could be taken from the UK for a voyage to the United States was restricted and the volume was determined in relation to the length of the journey. On one trip, persistently bad weather reduced the speed of the vessel, adding several days to the journey time. Eventually, the only food left was biscuits taken from the lifeboat, some tins of marmalade and some rock-hard unappetising cheese. When younger, Stanley disliked both marmalade and cheese but realised that this was no time for fads. "As soon as we anchored in New York, the ship chandler's launch was alongside with provisions and the cook hastily prepared the quickest meal. Delicious white bread, not the standard grey available in England, real butter, fried sausages and coffee with milk and sugar may not have been a gourmet's choice, but it always remained high on my list of memorable feasts."

If he had the time to browse American magazines, the young Stanley would have found some fascinating advertisements. One manufacturer claimed that its product would banish the tobacco habit. "Mail now for free brochure." Another offered "the only smart model in the small car class for $695, including five wire wheels". The Milburn light electric car was available for $1,685 but the Studebaker was $300 more expensive. In a different league, *The Boy Mechanic,* volume two, suggested 1,000 interesting things to make and do, including how to make a Ferris wheel. The book cost $1.50. There were many advertisements for phonographs and records, "which can be played on both sides" and "Mr. Edison's wonderful new phonograph" could be sent for $1 for a free trial. If subsequently bought, the balance of $36 could be paid in easy payments of $3.50 per month. An advertisement for a Kodak camera assured potential buyers that, "wherever the purr of your motor takes you, wherever the call of the road leads you, there you will find pictures, untaken pictures, that invite you".

In 1918, which was to be the last year of the war, Stanley was still making the same potentially dangerous voyage between the US and France. Another German offensive meant that the battle line was approaching Dunkirk and the occasional shell was landing near the town. When in Dunkirk docks, Stanley saw about 100 Chinese labourers marching, commanded by a sergeant of the Royal Army Service Corps. A shell exploded nearby and within seconds, the Chinese had vanished. The possibility of a shell hitting the ship prompted the order that the crew should leave the docks, late one afternoon, and return the following morning. There was a threat that the vessel might be attacked overnight by submarines, aircraft or motor boats. The evening passed without mishap but the mood was gloomy.

On the next voyage, the vessel discharged at Le Havre en route to Swansea. As the tanker approached the English coast, a destroyer provided cover which made Stanley "rather proud" and he felt safer than on previous occasions because their usual escort was a trawler with a 12 pounder gun. A close watch was kept on the shore side, with the destroyer outside, presumably because any attack would come from seaward, not from inshore and in shallow water where a submarine would be more vulnerable.

At 8.30 one morning, everyone, apart from the watch keepers, was at breakfast. "Suddenly, a terrific explosion on the starboard side made the ship stagger and shake. We had been torpedoed by a submarine between us and the shore, the cheeky swine." A few feet further forward or an attack a few minutes earlier would have caused severe loss of life. There was a hole the size of a bus on the ship's side and the deck's plates were curled up like pieces of tin. The destroyer wheeled around and dropped a few depth charges but failed to locate the submarine, before leaving the tanker with the message "better luck next . Stanley's vessel went to Devonport and joined a queue of other ships awaiting repair. When in drydock, the apprentices watched the water drain out of the damaged tank and then looked for souvenirs. Stanley found the brass blade of a small propeller and the shoulder of the torpedo but had to hand over his find, allegedly for onward despatch to the Admiralty. Notwithstanding the temporary repairs, water entered and left the hole in the ship's side but, after a slow journey, the vessel reached North Shields for permanent repairs.

Stanley was given a week's leave and, as he lived in Middlesbrough, some 38 miles away, the apprentices decided, after all their torrid and frightening war experiences, that the young Algar should represent them with the locally-based shipowners. His challenge was to argue for an increase in their war risk allowance. At that time, the youngsters were still paid £1-10-0 monthly and officers and senior ratings collected twice as much. The owners were then receiving £10 per ton for freight which meant some £60,000 every six or seven weeks. The meeting did not go well. The contemptible owners failed to thank the apprentices for their work or even to say that they were pleased that the young men were safe and well. Instead, the official barked out "what do you want?" "My carefully prepared speech deserted me and I stammered out that we apprentices thought that we should be given an increase in war bonus to £3." The official said that he would ask a director but Stanley believed that he merely left the room, counted to ten and returned with a total rejection. "I was very dejected and became angry when I remembered all that we had been through, all we had done, all that we had risked, for a ridiculous pittance. What miserly behaviour." Such managerial behaviour was to influence Stanley's politics for many years.

Algar and his young friends found an alternative way of augmenting their minute earnings, by six pence per day, whilst they were at sea. The navy provided gunnery courses to apprentices and attendance at a course in Portsmouth offered a welcome release from the noise, the grime and, of course, the problems of trying to eat on a pitiful allowance. Accommodation was provided on an obsolete cruiser, the *Black Prince,* and every morning, a launch took the participants to the gunnery school at Whale Island. The instructors were petty officers who gave their lectures and gun drill in a dull monotone "as if the tongue was performing an exercise without any direction from the brain". Sometimes, the students, maliciously, would halt the torrents of words with a question. "The instructor would slowly grind to a halt, answer the enquiry and then start all over again because his rhythm had been disturbed."

Back at home, Stanley received a letter from a friend. He had been accepted as a fourth officer by Elder Dempster, despite lacking a second officer's certificate. One potential problem was that Stanley, who wanted to join the company, had completed only three of his four-years of apprenticeship but his employers waived their rights. "Perhaps they were glad to see the back of me: after all, I had had the temerity to ask for more money, which, in those days, was almost the action of a Bolshevik." In his last year as an apprentice, having risked losing his life through enemy action, and having been on a vessel carrying essential aviation gasoline for the allies, he had earned just £1-5-0 in wages and £1-10-0 in war risk bonus per month.

CHAPTER 3

The end of apprenticeship
and the war

Three weeks later, no appointment had been offered by Elder Dempster so Stanley, unable to wait any longer, was appointed as an Able Bodied Seaman, AB, and lamp trimmer on the *Edna*, a coal-carrying vessel from Middlesbrough to Rouen. Returning to Hull, he received a letter from Elder Dempster appointing him as fourth officer but the problem then was being signed off from the collier. The captain agreed, providing that Stanley found his own replacement. A few beers and 10/- achieved this and Stanley reported to Liverpool to join the 5,000 ton *SS Palma* on 20th September 1918. The end of the war was but two months away. "All I recall from my apprenticeship is hardship, poverty, exploitation, constant danger and a total lack of consideration by the shipowner, and, with few exceptions, by the captains and officers under whom I served. Admittedly, it was a wartime period, but, somewhere, there should have been some kindness and just an occasional glimpse of a happy carefree youth."

The *Palma* was a 5,000 dwt cargo vessel running from the UK to West Africa and the tropics. This excited young Stanley as his previous voyages overseas had been confined to the United States. More significantly, the new officer thought that money worries were at an end. Time would prove him, woefully and repeatedly, wrong. Misgivings about working on a cargo vessel vanished because the officers and others helped each other. Everyone lived ashore until the vessel was ready for sea and the new uncertificated fourth officer was only required to watch the holds being loaded with cases, bales of cotton, machinery, barrel staves, bags of salt and rice, cast iron cooking pots and beer, spirits and cigarettes.

Stanley's remuneration of £19 a month, £4 more than he had received in his last year as an apprentice, induced a sense of affluence even after giving his mother an allowance. His morale was further boosted as he had his own room and a degree of privacy never previously experienced. He could dine in the saloon and the menu included a sweet every day. The first destination was Dakar, a quiet and orderly port where the French influence was apparent by the *joie de vivre* and colour. Here, as on the north coast of Africa, even the smallest town had a central square ablaze with flowers and shrubs, shade-giving palm trees, pleasant boulevards, cultivated gardens, cafes, and hotels with bright sunblinds, coloured umbrellas over seats and tables and people drinking and talking. It all seemed so civilised.

After Dakar the *Palma* called in at Bathurst and Conakry, further south, before reaching the main destination, Freetown in Sierra Leone. The 19 year old fourth officer was in charge of a gang of 30 natives who were assisting in the unloading of myriad cargoes. Typically, these men stayed for the duration of the trip along the coast and could be on board for some six weeks, loading and unloading. They were incredibly naïve in that they wore strips of coloured celluloid on their wrists on which was painted a paper watch face.

When discharging was completed, passengers, men, women and children, were taken on board. Awnings were spread over the deck space and in a move that was reminiscent of package-holiday tourists many years later, the passengers established their claim to a particular area on the deck by spreading a blanket over the favoured spot. They were noisy, colourful cheerful groups who caused little trouble. The next destination was Monrovia, the capital of Liberia. "We anchored well outside the surf and so-called surf boats came out to us, to be towed back, laden, towards the shore by a steam launch. The tow rope was released just before reaching the surf and then the men propelled their boats through the breaking waves and on to the beach where a gang waited to pounce on the cargo and drag it clear." Supervising the loading and discharging was a demanding and time-consuming task. Occasionally, the officers would work to midnight, and then heave up the anchor. The ship steamed all night and arrived at the next port at daybreak and discharging was resumed. The picture was rather different to that with which the young apprentice had become familiar.

"The ship rolling in the swell, the sun beating fiercely from a cloudless sky, the breaking surf, the dazzling sands and the low-lying land with a background of trees, the red-roofed huts further inland and the noise and colour of the surf boats and their crews were unforgettable." The life was exciting and interesting even if it entailed hard work. The vessel continued along the coast, calling at many ports, including Accra, Lome and then Lagos. The first evening ashore in Lagos proved disappointing. It was dark, there were no lights, the roads were nondescript, and the buildings seemed small and ugly. Stanley and friends eventually found a "hotel", run by a Brazilian. "I had a glass of warm lemonade and a running fight ensued with various insects which seemed determined to share my drink."

The next destination was Port Harcourt to the east of Lagos. "We approached land early one morning and, as the waves followed us in, there was a sudden bump as the ship struck the bottom, the masts vibrated with shock and the vessel stopped. The next few waves increased the depth of the water over what I discovered was a sand bar, the ship refloated and we surged forward into deeper water. Although the officers laughed at my concern, the ship's bottom was inspected for damage every time we drydocked in Liverpool."

Although the master had said that he did not want anyone to go ashore, a plot by an engineer involved taking a canoe and Stanley succumbed to temptation. The canoe was so crowded that it was only a few inches above the crocodile-infested waters. Once ashore, the young men were invited to the chief's house, which resembled a museum of clocks. The following day, Stanley went ashore, legitimately this time, and was amazed to see that nearly all the women were naked above the waist. "Most of the young girls and women were graceful and some were lovely. They all walked with a dignity, possibly the result of carrying things on their heads." Not everything was good: the old women were "hideous".

One of the main sources of entertainment for the natives, who were working on the vessel, was catching the rats, one of which was so large that it was given a collar and lead and marched around the deck. Stanley hated and feared rats which infested the ship. The West coast of Africa was known as "the white man's grave" and fever was very prevalent, especially just outside the ports. Stanley, who had had some mild bouts of fever during this period, was alarmed to learn that one engineer had died of Blackwater fever, one of the most dangerous forms of malaria.

The immediate plan was to load for home and the prospect was enhanced by the announcement on 11th November 1918 that an armistice, with effect from 11.00 am, was operating on the Western Front. There is much uncertainty on the statistics but it seems that the United Kingdom, out of its population of 46.40 million, had no less than 5.70 million serving in the forces. Over 700,000 were killed or missing and more than 1.6 million were wounded. A further 170,000 were taken prisoner. This meant that, out of the 5.70 million in the forces, nearly 45 per cent were killed, missing, wounded or captured. In addition, another 1,386 civilians lost their lives.

France, with a total population of 39.60 million, saw 5.7 million members of its forces killed, wounded or missing and 446,300 became prisoners of war. A further 40,000 civilians died. Doubtless, the scale of this loss, exceeded only by

35

Germany and Russia, as well as the devastation to their country, played a part in the country's early capitulation in the Second World War. The number of Germans killed, wounded or missing, excluding the toll of civilians, has been quoted at more than 7.7 million, or 11.5 per cent of the total population. Another 700,000 civilians died.

Russia recorded a total of 6.75 million members of its forces as killed, wounded or missing and 3.9 million were captured. Two million civilians lost their lives. The US, which only entered the war in April 1917, lost some 280,000 killed, wounded and missing. By the end of the war, however, over two million Americans were in France.

In aggregate, although the real total figures will never be known, some analysts claim that at least 13 million people lost their lives and 21 million were injured. The last man to be killed was a Canadian who was shot at 10.58 am., just two minutes before the Armistice took effect. The impact of the war on the British Merchant Navy was significant: the gross tonnage lost was 7.8 million tons and nearly half of this occurred in the penultimate year of the war.

What was not realised was that the peace conditions imposed on Germany would contribute significantly to initiating another bloody and sustained war just 21 years later. On the morning after the armistice, US President Woodrow Wilson wrote "Everything for which America fought has been accomplished. It will now be our fortunate duty to assist by example, by sober, friendly counsel and by material aid, in the establishment of just democracy throughout the world." The mood was euphoric but the rejoicing was to be undermined by another major problem that was to claim even more lives than the Great War.

In March 1918, in a military camp in Kansas, an outbreak of Spanish influenza occurred: it spread rapidly around the world and reached Europe via the American forces engaged in the last year of the war. Some analysts contend that the disease originated in birds and began in China. In the last quarter of

1918, some six million people around the world died. In two years, it killed between 15 and 70 million people and even the lowest estimate was probably above that for the total of lives lost in the First World War. Originally, it was thought that the number of deaths was at the lower end of this range but more recent studies favour the higher figure. In the UK, up to a quarter of a million people died from the virus and streets were sprayed with chemicals to prevent the spread of this appalling disease. Some estimates suggest that a fifth of the world's population was affected and, in the US, where up to 700,000 died, the average life span plummeted by ten years.

Stanley's vessel was in Opobo when the news of the end of the war came but, although obviously relieved, he scarcely mentions it in his written recollections. His return trip from Las Palmas, in the Canary Islands, to Liverpool was completed on 13th January 1919. Plans to sell his 18" long crocodile, bought in West Africa for a large sum, were thwarted. It was sold for only 2/6. Stanley had lacked many opportunities to spend, so after sending money home to his mother, he had saved the not inconsiderable sum of £20 (£650). After a few more trips, he headed for home, Middlesbrough, on 29th December 1919.

Just five days before, as if to remind the world that universal peace was unlikely, civil war had broken out in Russia and the victory of the Red Army in 1921 put an end to the anti-communist movement. However, the greatest threat to lasting peace had occurred in June 1919 when the Treaty of Versailles between the allies and Germany was signed. The European powers were too greedy and divided in their demands and German resentment, not least on the extent of reparations payments, proved to be helpful to Adolf Hitler and the spread of Nazism and another global conflict. In 1921 Hitler was to become leader of The National Socialist German Workers' Party. In Britain, labour relations were poor and violent strikes in favour of a shorter working week heralded a period of severe problems which culminated in the General Strike in 1926. Civil war broke out in Ireland in January 1919 and by the end of the year, a new Home Rule Bill was introduced which proposed Parliaments in Dublin and Belfast.

CHAPTER 4

Studying, promotion and a problem

Two weeks later, in early 1920, Stanley left Middlesbrough, after a short holiday, to go to a nautical school at Liverpool, believing that this would offer fewer counter attractions. In those days, pay stopped on leaving a vessel and no wages were paid whilst individuals studied but he thought that he had saved enough to pay school fees, travelling expenses and board and lodging in Liverpool. To avoid having to accept a position as an able-bodied seaman or even a bosun, it was essential to acquire a second mate's certificate and Stanley was in a hurry to become qualified. Lacking the time and money to spare for a social life, the self-motivated Stanley studied hard and confined his extra-curricular activities to occasional visits to the cinema.

Before being allowed to begin an examination on first aid, candidates had to produce a certificate stating that they had attended relevant lectures given by a doctor. His experience in first aid with the scouts proved helpful and the necessary certificate was soon obtained. However, after minimal training from the doctor, Stanley, wisely, unconvinced that he could deal with any medical emergency at sea, studied *The Shipmaster's Medical Guide*. Over the years, as chief officer and captain, he had to treat many cases and the guide proved valuable.

Stanley passed the examination for second mate at the first attempt. He did not want to return to West African trade but was keen to spend another year at sea, as second or third mate, as this was obligatory before sitting the exam for first mate. Another 12-18 months had to be served as 2nd or chief mate before individuals were allowed to sit the exam for the master's certificate. All this meant that some seven years had to elapse between starting at sea and obtaining a master's ticket. The main objective, therefore, was to return to sea as soon as possible, to serve the necessary sea time. The first opportunity came from a Newcastle tramp-owning company which appointed Stanley as third mate for a cargo boat, the *Derindje*, then at Newport in Wales. He joined on 30th March 1920.

He knew that tramp vessels were strictly utilitarian but he was in for a shock. Nothing that increased the initial cost of the ship and which could reduce profits was incorporated into the vessel. Towels and soap were not provided. Personnel had to work at least 84 hours a week because of under-manning. The captain, fat and over 60, had wanted his nephew to be appointed and he seemed to blame the innocent Algar for taking his place. After travelling overnight, the cold greeting from the captain, and the fact that there was no bed for Stanley augured ill. The young officer had to go ashore to buy a "donkey's breakfast" which was a cover of cheap material, filled with straw. This "bed" could not be delivered as it was a Saturday morning, so Stanley had to carry it to the ship himself. On the first morning, he was rebuked for failing to do something that the night watchman should have done and this incident was followed by similar occurrences which suggested that the other officers were trying to ingratiate themselves with the brutish captain.

The tramp sailed for Buenos Aires, to load maize but, despite the unpleasantness, Stanley decided against resignation as unemployment in the Merchant Service was increasing and national economies were deteriorating. On the homeward voyage to Hull, after being provoked with many unfair demands, one specific incident prompted him to change his mind. When on watch in the English Channel, Stanley was ordered to clean the chartroom. He obeyed but a deck boy saw him shaking the mats and grinned. Stanley returned to the chartroom and flung the mats down, only to be told to clean the floor. This order was not well received and he retorted that there were "stewards and deck boys to do that, I am a certificated officer on this ship and I refuse to do it." Fearful of receiving a bad discharge, Stanley tried to explain to the captain but he would not listen.

"I left the vessel at Hull on 2nd July 1920 and my discharge book was stamped 'very good' for conduct and ability and there was a comment that, 'I always found him sober,' which implied that I avoided being seen when drunk. I realised later that he had little choice but I was concerned at the time." Throughout his entire career, his continuous certificate of discharge never deviated from the highest ratings.

Financial pressures, not least from his family, who, "to some extent depended on me", prompted many letters to potential employers. Eventually, after an interview in London, The Royal Mail offered him temporary employment, as third officer on a German vessel which had been surrendered as part of the reparations agreement. Stanley travelled to Leith to see the handover of the vessel to the British. "A curt naval commander, representing the UK government, made the Germans open their cases as they left, depriving them of anything that belonged to the ship." The accommodation was comfortable, if not luxurious, and the crew were friendly, except the captain, who seldom spoke to his third officer.

Stanley was to spend four months on the *Polaria* and the first voyage commenced in September 1920 when the ship sailed to Newport in the United States to carry coal to Buenos Aires. New technology enabled the cargo of 6,000 tons to be loaded in six hours but the discharging method was rather different. The coal was moved into railway wagons or horse-drawn carts. The Buenos Aires docks were notorious and it was unsafe for sailors to walk alone at night. One thief, stealing just one piece of coal, was shot in the leg by a policeman and the dockers immediately went on strike. The following day, as the vessel moved further along the wharf, a body floated to the surface. Local shop windows were full of knives and revolvers. One trick favoured by the locals was to drop a wallet so that a foreign passer-by would find it. A fireman from the ship saw this, chased the man and dutifully returned his wallet. The owner then inspected the item and found it empty. By a happy coincidence, a nearby policeman stopped the fireman and made him empty his pockets. Having just been paid, unsurprisingly, he had money on him but was forced to give it to the wallet owner.

After loading grain at San Nicholas, up river, the ship discharged at Hamburg and then returned to the Tyne, arriving on 30th January 1921, to be laid up. The captain and chief officer agreed to support Stanley's application for permanent employment but, notwithstanding the increasingly harsh economic context, typified by a three-month-long strike by the coal miners, he did not want to join the Royal Mail. His ambition was to become a master before middle age and he did not think that this could be achieved with this group.

The political climate, too, was bad and the immediate employment outlook was bleak. Stanley's father had a mediocre job with poor pay and his young brother was an apprentice engineer earning a few shillings a week, so Stanley's financial contribution was important. He had earned just too much to qualify for the unemployment pay and was also denied benefit because he was not a manual worker. He had earned very little during the war, when he had risked his life when carrying aviation fuel, and now, less than two years later, "like so many, I was out of work, with absolutely no income…What had happened to the politicians' slogan of a 'country fit for heroes to live in?'"

Some captains had to sail as able-bodied sailors and Stanley's many letters to potential employers failed to elicit any response. "I called at the offices of all local shipowners

42

and was received with scant courtesy by junior clerks and office boys. More and more ships were being laid up. Immediately after the war, many new tramp companies had been set up by newcomers, attracted by the large profits made during the war. They had paid too high a price for the ships, possibly reflecting their inexperience, and the optimism that war profits would continue. They did not and the freight rates were falling dramatically so that it became impossible to run the expensive ships at a profit. One South Wales ship owner sold some of his ships at an inflated price to a newly-formed company and bought them back at the half the price within two years." Stanley admitted to being, "broke financially and I did not want to be bankrupt in spirit too".

After five months out of work, Stanley, very reluctantly, was forced to apply to the company with whom he had served his three years apprenticeship. On 6th June 1921, he was appointed third mate on the *Paul Paix,* at Middlesbrough. Unfortunately, the master was a man whom he neither liked nor respected but at least he could record more sea time and earn some money. This time, he had his own room but the atmosphere on board was unpleasant and overtime payments were cancelled.

This coal-burning vessel, carrying oil, was running from Port Arthur, in Texas, to either the UK or France and every time that coal bunkers were taken on board, the whole ship was covered with a thick clinging coal dust. When loading oil at Port Arthur, with the deck of his own vessel piled high with ashes and galley refuse, Stanley gazed at a Shell tanker, the *Mytilus,* about four years old, lying quite close. "It was an oil burner so there were no ashes on deck. I looked in envy and admiration. It was a picture: all the brass work was gleaming in the sun, the paintwork was fantastically clean, the woodwork on the bridge sparkled with good quality varnish, there was no rust to be seen, not even over the side of the hull, and the wooden bridge deck and poops were as clean as a hound's tooth. The crew were Chinese and the British officers were in clean uniforms, not in shabby old lounge suits, as on our ship. I looked at our vessel, with the ashes from the stokehold and the galley refuse stoked up on deck, and was filled with disgust."

After two voyages to the Gulf of Mexico, Stanley had sufficient sea time to apply for permission to sit his next examination but he opted to undertake one more voyage, to bolster finances. After a grim nine months on this vessel, his happiest memory was in a Hull theatre where he saw Jose Collins in *Maid of the Mountains*. Leaving the ship at Middlesbrough in February 1922, he decided to live at home and study at West Hartlepool which would be cheaper than at Liverpool. After one month at the school, Stanley passed the examination for first mate and assumed, that, armed with a superior ticket, finding a job would be easier. He was wrong. His next appointment, hardly compatible with his new qualifications, was in July, after a total of five more months of unemployment.

Unemployment again and then to Singapore with Shell

Once again, he wrote over 100 letters to shipowners, few of whom replied. He also applied on board vessels and, one day, feeling very depressed, climbed the gangway of a filthy ship discharging manganese ore, seeking a job as a second or even third mate. "Christ, you must be hard up" was the response of an apprentice who had asked him what he wanted. He frequented Missions to Seamen places where he played billiards and exchanged stories about ships and seamen. A letter to The Merchant Services Guild to see if they could offer any advice or prospects of employment prompted a note of regret and a gift of £3 (£100). "I accepted the money gratefully, but somehow I felt vaguely ashamed, forgetting that I had subscribed to that fund in happier times."

Having been out of work for so long and aware that his family faced financial problems, Stanley, and a friend, secured work as quartermasters on an Anchor-Brocklebank vessel, the *Mahratta,* a coaster, then in the Middlesbrough docks, in July 1922, at £10 per month. It proved to be an easy assignment as the Indians did most of the work. The third officer had a

44

second mate's ticket and Stanley, the quartermaster, was qualified as a first mate but he was glad to be on a good ship and earning money.

On returning to London, he went to Fenchurch Street to visit the Anglo Saxon Petroleum Company. He was on their waiting list and had even completed an application form five months earlier. Initially, he was impressed and pleased to be treated as a human being and then, astonishingly, with minimal discussion, he was offered the position of third officer on one of the group's ships when he reached Singapore. This meant three years out East and he hesitated before accepting. "I had nobody at home to worry about, no girl friend, so later I was puzzled by why I had hesitated." It would be three years continuous employment, in contrast to the grim experience of the previous two years, and he would be able to save and to secure his master's certificate.

Stanley was home for one week and his letter of engagement, dated 20th July 1922, confirmed his appointment as a permanent third officer at a salary of £20 per month, his highest rate thus far. Repeatedly, he scanned the letter, scarcely able to comprehend its contents. His monthly income was twice what he had earned in his previous and unworthy post and about twice what his onshore friends were earning in Middlesbrough. "I borrowed £20 from a friend, gave my mother half, bought myself a new suit for £5 and joined the P&O ship, the S.S. *Kalyan,* as a passenger for Singapore with £5 in my pocket and a smile on my face."

There were 12 fellow seamen on the ship en route to joining Shell vessels. Stanley, nearly 23, was the youngest. Within a few years, only three of the original 12 were still in Shell, some of them having succumbed to excessive drinking. In those days, sailors were not keen to serve on tankers, perceiving them as dirty, dangerous and smelly. Stanley, recalling his time on a tanker built in about 1885, could understand this attitude. Consequently, as an inducement, senior and junior officers received, respectively, 10 and 7½ per cent above the usual rates of pay. The voyage to Singapore

45

took four weeks and Stanley enjoyed every day. He was impressed not just by his room but also the real curry made by the Indian cooks. Enjoying good food, accommodation and company, allied with the knowledge of firm employment, hopefully for at least three years, was an agreeable contrast to recent experience.

"As soon as we moored in Port Said, the Egyptians swarmed on board. There were fortune tellers, magicians, stamp dealers, barbers, carpet merchants, dealers selling scarabs, amber beads, pornographic material or small boxes made from olive wood from Jerusalem. The gullible were offered pieces of wood from the cross on which Jesus was crucified." Young men and boys in the water implored passengers to throw money into the harbour for them to retrieve and some even swam under the ship, emerging on the other side, although Stanley wondered if they were the same individuals who had dived in initially.

He was unimpressed by the Suez Canal which he described as a large ditch excavated in the desert but acknowledged that, when it was built in about 1869, there was little machinery to assist in its construction. The trip through the canal was uninspiring, "with a dull monotonous view of sand on both sides, as far as the eye can see, broken by the occasional signalling and control stations, attractive buildings   set in colourful gardens. In some places, the banks were so high that ships approaching round a slight bend showed only their masts, funnels and high superstructures and appeared to be floating in the desert."

Deck sports were organised and dances took place in the evenings. Stanley, who dressed up as Charlie Chaplin for a fancy dress ball, was particularly popular with the children and he provoked additional mirth when, just five foot four, he danced with a formidably statuesque lady dressed as Britannia. He was awarded first prize, a tobacco pouch, but he did not then, nor ever, smoke. When the vessel called in at Colombo, he and some friends hired a taxi and drove to Mount Lavinia, through the Cinnamon Gardens. The perfumed air was almost intoxicating. At the Mount Lavinia hotel, situated on a point overlooking the sea, the party stopped for a curry. "I had a sudden feeling of well-being and I chuckled to myself when I thought of my position less than one month before." Coincidentally, his last vessel, the *Mahratta* was in the harbour and Stanley went on board for half an hour. The *Kalyan* then called at Penang and then Port Swettenham for a few hours before sailing on for Singapore which was a very busy port crowded with ships en route to China, Japan or Java and many small ships engaged in the coastal trade. Chinese junks could be seen threading their way between the small wooden flat-bottomed fishing boats, the inevitable sampans.

The new recruits were escorted to a Shell ship, on 24th August, the *Myrshell*, at anchor, just off one of the many islands near Singapore. This was used as floating accommodation when the company's rest house or hotel was full. It had been a three-masted sailing ship but then, demasted, it was used as a storage hulk and hotel. The accommodation was comfortable, the cooks and stewards were friendly and life on board was easy but Stanley, who had done very little real work for nearly eight months, wanted to be occupied again. On 4th September 1922, he was appointed third mate, at £20 per month, of the *Adna*, a converted cargo boat of 7,500 tons. He was to spend one year on this vessel, during which time it visited Borneo, Hong Kong, Singapore and Japan. Occasionally, it crossed the Pacific, after discharging in Japan, to load at San Francisco. By now Stanley felt part of a large and secure group as many other Shell vessels were in the region.

On one visit to Takatoya, in Japan, in 1923, Stanley and the fifth engineer attracted attention when shopping ashore because they were foreign. The shop had straw mats on the floors and an elderly Japanese lady knelt before her potential customers. Stanley bought a small leather attaché case for seven yen, then worth about 14/- and his friend purchased a violin at a ridiculously low price. They wandered around the village and were surprised that some shops favoured narrow vertical strips of wood rather than windows. "Later we realised that we were in the Yoshewara district which was the brothel area. Apparently, when darkness fell, the prostitutes exhibited themselves in the rooms, hoping that clients would enter and indicate their choice."

When the vessel docked in Hong Kong for repairs, for about a month, Stanley discovered that everything was cheap, especially clothing, and tailors, shoemakers and trusty "sew sew women" flocked on board. They repaired clothes and were very competent. Tailors, if they could not persuade potential clients to buy a new suit, offered to turn an old one inside out. The main shopping street in Hong Kong was fascinating, with shops selling ivory, jade, pictures, vases, silks and many other items beyond the pay of a third officer, such as a red vase, about 9" high and priced at £40.

There were many robberies on ships in dock and Stanley took his turn in mounting a 12 hour watch but it was the harbour that attracted most attention. "I watched the tiny sampans drifting across the harbour like water beetles. They are very small craft in which families are born, live and die, seemingly making a very precarious subsistence living by ferrying people from ship to shore. The junks, some large, seemed slow and clumsy vessels, and had an eye painted on each bow. There was constant noise and bustle as the boats and ships scuttled around but imminent and seemingly inevitable collisions were miraculously avoided. One section of the harbour was dominated by ships sailing between Hong Kong, Canton and Macao. It seemed that a ship was leaving or arriving all the time. In those days, the Far East was often the last resort of men who had failed at home and some were employed by local Chinese companies."

It appeared to Stanley that there were only two classes in Hong Kong, the rich and the poor. The latter wore black tunics and trousers of cheap cotton, whilst the rich were dressed in luxurious patterned silk. Stanley also visited Paddy's Market where, allegedly, you could lose a watch at one end and then buy it back at the other end. He lost and bought nothing.

After the sojourn in dock, the vessel sailed for Tarakon on the east coast of Borneo to load for Yokohama, where the cargo was to be discharged into barges. A representative from the Missions to Seamen invited anyone interested to join a party he was taking to Kamakura, a religious centre. After about one hour on the train, passing through some very attractive countryside, the group reached Kamakura, which was the focal point for many pilgrims visiting the temples. The grounds were beautiful and well-kept but many of the trees and shrubs were unfamiliar. "We crossed a low bridge and I saw a huge goldfish. Soon we approached a long avenue lined with tall trees, leading to the square where the god awaited us. On each side of the road were posts on which the names of subscribers to the temple funds were listed.

"After climbing a few steps we stood before the god Diabutsua. It resembled a statue of Buddha, a human male figure, squatting, cross-legged, with his hands on his lap, and an expression on his face of complete serenity and compassion. Before him was a stone platform before which stood a few Japanese women, slowly bowing and praying. It was a calm and solemn picture and the only discordant note came from tourists taking photographs. The statue was of bronze, about 40 feet high and we were surprised to find a door at the rear of the statue and we entered, climbing inside, high into the statue."

On one of his early visits to Japan, Stanley was impressed by the kindness and politeness of the civilians but rails against those in uniform who were surly and impolite. Later, he notes that visiting Japan became increasingly unpleasant as the authorities seemed determined to "harass the Chinese crew and they were not very friendly to us, either".

There were problems, too, in the world away from the ship. An earthquake in September 1923 killed more than 100,000 people and rendered some two million homeless in Tokyo. Yokohama was also reduced to ruins. French troops moved into the Rhineland, against the wishes of the British and Americans, as the Germans were in default on their war reparation payments which had been pitched at unrealistic levels. This action induced civil unrest in Germany and hastened the decline of the Deutschemark. Hyperinflation set in and banknotes were used as wallpaper, as they were less valuable, and burned as fuel. Diners had to pay for their meals in advance and workers were paid twice a day. Within a day, a loaf of bread bought in the evening cost as much as a house in the morning. At its peak, inflation was running at 2,500 per cent per month. In 1923, the mark was valued at $US 2.38 but by the summer an American acquired 4,000 million marks for $7. Hyperinflation ended later with a revaluation of the mark, which was backed by land, railway networks and factories.

German unemployment was at least two million, or more than a third of the work force. Seeking to capitalise on the increasingly desperate economic situation, Hitler attempted and failed to mount a successful military coup in November 1923 and was jailed for five years but released after 12 months. The UK was not immune to the economic and political violence that characterised much of the decade. In the early 1920's, the country was in a recession. Unemployment figures for that time are misleading as many jobless did not seek work but up to 2 million were officially unemployed. In 1920 a million UK coal miners had taken strike action to secure a pay increase of about 8 per cent, equal to 2/- per week, on top of their rate of their weekly rate of 24/3.

The average annual income for industrial workers in 1920 was £150 whilst agriculture workers could expect to receive £120. The standard working week was 48 hours. The following year, when the government refused to sustain the wartime ownership of the coal mines, opting to return them to private ownership, the miners withdrew their labour for three months before capitulating. Their defeat, and the depressing economic climate, led to management imposing lower wages on many thousands in other industries. There was also major disruption in France and in the United States.

The spectre of unemployment was a constant feature of much of the Twenties and workers reluctantly accepted less money and worked longer hours in preference to having nothing. The post-war boom had ended as markets became saturated and a decline in trade, caused partly by protection, meant that ships were being laid up. There had been civil war in Ireland in 1920: the first election in the newly-created Irish Free State was held in 1923 and the communist victory in Russia was to cost millions of lives. The remorseless march towards communism and Nazism, feeding off the economic misery of the decade and fuelled by political frustration, gathered sinister and seemingly inevitable momentum.

Promotion

In July 1923, when the *Adna* reached Hong Kong, Stanley learned that his salary was to be cut by a quarter to £15 per month. First and second officers were to be paid £37 and £23 a month respectively. He did not feel that the situation demanded this reduction but acknowledged that the depression at home must have reached the East. The next appointment was on the *Sultan Van Koetei* which he joined on 24th September 1923 as second officer, at the standard rate of pay. He was on this 2,400 ton ship for two years, although he reverted to the position of third officer on 14th February 1924, but "returned" as second officer just ten days later.

The ship, named after a sultan of an area in Borneo where Shell acquired some of its oil, was to sail around Sumatra, Malaysia, Borneo, Java, The Celebes and all the islands east to New Guinea and to the north of the Philippines. The accommodation was below the main deck and, on leaving their rooms, the officers could look through a window into the engine room which was helpful if the vessel were trading in the Arctic but hardly suitable for the fine weather in the tropics. It was even too hot for cockroaches: silverfish, repulsive small insects with a half inch tail and a voracious appetite for silk, were the main enemy.

After periods of actual and feared unemployment and the grim prospect of having to accept work below his qualifications, on poor ships, these two years, spent exclusively in the East Indies area, were ideal and the source of many happy memories. The *Sultan Van Koetei*, being a small ship of less than 2,000 tons, could enter ports denied to larger vessels and this broadened the experience and pleasure. The weather was always warm and the nights cool, whilst the sea was as calm as a sheet of glass. Food, too, was good but the need to keep watch regularly meant that the maximum period allowed for sleep was 3½ hours. The heat during the day caused sleeping to be difficult so a bucket of water was kept on deck for splashing on the faces of those charged with keeping watch during the night. The first voyage was from Singapore to Bangkok in Thailand where Stanley was surprised to see bananas growing wild on the banks and "topless" girls infinitely more attractive than those he had seen in The last word is then Africa.

Balik Papan was the next destination and from then onwards it became the main loading port. The company operated a club for its employees there and the facilities included a swimming pool, a billiards table and somewhere to enjoy a cool drink and to read. A third officer was an accomplished pianist and to listen to him, playing Chopin, whilst looking through the palm trees to the silver sands and the blue sea, all in harmony, was memorable. The view in the other direction was dominated by large oil storage tanks.

Many voyages were in and around the islands to the North East of Borneo and through the Sulu Sea, 36 hours sailing time from Balik Papan, which had been infested by pirates in the early days of sail. Manila was then an attractive walled city, built by the Spaniards, but the town was largely American with its naval base in the bay. "We always managed to have two days in port there and one claim made by the locals was that it boasted the largest dance hall in the world, at Santa Ana. Two bands provided the music and patrons bought a ticket for each dance with a hostess who cashed in her tickets at the end of the evening." The favourite song was "Yes, we have no bananas". A few soft drinks, an enormous club sandwich and dance tickets were cheap. "We could have a great evening for just ten bob." The mangoes, nearly eight inches long and about two to three inches in diameter, were so juicy it was wise to eat them in private but those from India tasted of kerosene.

The authorities on Cebu Island did not allow a dance hall in the town so it was based in a village called Opon, across the strait from Cebu, which, happily for the crew, was also the location of the local oil refinery. The "dance hall" was a bungalow with a polished floor. The music was provided by four sleepy locals armed with their guitars and their repertoire, inevitably, included the banana song and, perhaps for the benefit of the visiting Europeans, "It's a long way to Tipperary". Ten dance tickets cost about two shillings and, including tips, the drinks and dances cost each individual about ten shillings for the evening. The girls used coconut oil liberally and its unmistakable aroma, when detected in later years, always reminded Stanley of Cebu. He liked one girl in particular and danced with her more than with any of the others. She told him that, if he left the ship and lived in Cebu, she would marry him. He was "not unduly flattered", although, doubtless with typical under-statement, he confessed that she was "rather attractive". The island was also memorable for the size of its cockroaches which "had nothing to do all day, except lounge around in the sun, eating copra and growing very big and very fat. Walking ashore at night, and unavoidably treading on them, produced a sound like footsteps on frozen snow."

In 1924, the vessel was ordered to Bula, on the north east coast of Ceram Island, some 50 miles west of New Guinea, where Shell had a small oil field. The European population there numbered but ten and only a very few ships, from Australia and from China, visited. Stanley took his camera to a nearby fishing village where the inhabitants were real Papuans with almost Negroid features. The children followed him and hurriedly hid behind a hut whenever he turned round. Eventually, they were persuaded to be photographed but Stanley was eyed suspiciously by the village elders. Sourabaya was a large town with many large European-style shops.

One voyage, to Madras, was memorable because of the heat and bad weather which caused the vessel to roll heavily. Although very busy, Stanley managed to do some studying and looked forward to leave, after three continuous years of service, during which time he had just one night ashore, in the rest house when awaiting to change ships. Meanwhile, in May 1925, he had been promoted to permanent second officer. He came home as a supernumerary on the *Achatina*, arriving in Hull in November 1925, after studying hard during the trip for his master's "ticket" whilst remaining on full pay as a second officer. This was very helpful as Shell's Eastern rates were about half as much again as the level paid for ships' crews operating out of the UK.

In 1925 in Italy, Benito Mussolini, now dictator, outlawed all left-wing political parties and took action against newspapers which criticised his draconian methods. Their freedom vanished. The ban on the Nazi party was removed in Bavaria whilst General Paul von Hindenburg, who was to prove feeble in resisting Hitler, was elected president. French troops withdrew from the Rhineland and the border between Northern Ireland and the Irish Free State was agreed. In the Soviet Union, a purge on Christians resulted in thousands being sent to labour camps. In the United Kingdom, in 1924, Ramsay MacDonald had become the first Labour Prime Minister.

Back to school and success

Stanley registered at a nautical school in West Hartlepool and sought to secure his "certificate of competency as master of a foreign-going steamship". After just one month, and not the three months favoured by his friends, he sat and passed the examination. Some colleagues advised him to leave tankers but employment prospects with Shell seemed good so he stayed. "There were easier ships at sea than tankers but the future seemed reasonably promising and stable." Later, those friends who had opted for employment on tramps admitted that they were wrong.

Once again, financial problems loomed. Wages for the two months of leave were due but would not be paid, even in part, until Stanley joined another of the group's ships, in early April 1926 in the Far East. This meant that he had not been paid for a total of nearly five months. His school fees and the cost of travelling to Hartlepool, as well as the allowance he gave his mother, created some financial difficulties.

To take him to his next appointment, in Singapore, Shell booked him on the P&O's *Macedonia*. Travelling to London, for just 24 hours, he secured an advance against his leave pay which would be given to him on arrival in Singapore. "However, a very significant incident occurred during my 24 hours in London. I stayed the night with some kind people whose relatives I knew in Middlesbrough. When I arrived at their house, after obtaining the various documents necessary for the voyage from the London office, the door was opened by the daughter of the house, whom I had never seen before. She was just under 16 and for the rest of the evening my eyes were drawn irresistibly towards her. The next morning, she, her mother, who, I learned later, had appeared on London's West End stage with the legendary Sarah Bernhardt, and I left the house together. The daughter went her own way at an underground station and I stood and watched her out of sight but she never glanced back. Singapore and the East had lost much of their attraction. There seemed something infinitely desirable for me to hope for and three years out East seemed an eternity. As for her callousness in not turning round after she left me, I often reproached her over the many subsequent decades of our marriage."

Stanley had taken rather longer than he had anticipated to obtain his master's ticket, because of periods of unemployment, but felt that he could now relax as he was in a good company where he could confidently expect to spend the remainder of his sea-going career. The Shell fleet was expanding and the possibility of quick promotion seemed good. He posted a letter to his London friends from Port Said, thanking them for their hospitality, and wondered if he might receive a letter from the daughter. Having reached Singapore on 26th March 1926, Stanley stayed in the company's two-storey rest house. A large veranda on the front gave a commanding view of all vessels entering and leaving the docks. Nearby was a hotel previously a sultan's palace and the rest house had been his harem's home. On the bank just below it, a small graveyard, enclosed within a low wall, contained several graves assumed to be those of the sultan's widows.

Whilst in the rest house, wages were paid at the end of the month, but advances could be secured, albeit that they were provided reluctantly. Stanley's next appointment, on 1st April 1926, was as second officer on the *Khodoung* at Palembang. The tanker, previously owned by Burmah Oil, was designed for the tropics and based at Balik Papan. He was delighted to receive a friendly letter from the young girl he had met in London and his hopes and ambitions were roused. When back at sea, freed from the necessity of studying, he wrote long letters, describing the places he visited and the unusual sights which he thought would interest her.

Life in the UK in 1926 was grim. The General Strike in May lasted nine days and brought key industries, including transportation and the iron and steel sectors, to a halt. Newspapers failed to appear and the docks were idle. The government, fearing an uprising, deployed armoured cars, with guns ready to fire, in central London and many soldiers were recalled from overseas. Fortunately, there was little violence and the relationships between the police and the strikers was sufficiently cordial to permit them to play each other in football matches. The strike commanded wide support although some 300,000 volunteers, mainly from the middle class, backed by some students, attracted class-related opprobrium as they drove buses and seemed to be enjoying themselves doing unusual work. The strike had been provoked by the harsh treatment, once again, of the coal miners. After rejecting wage cuts of up to 25 per cent, they were locked out by angry management but forced to return, on the mine-owners' terms, in November. Their slogan had been "not a penny off the pay, not a minute on the day". All this took place against a background of disappearing markets, declining productivity and too many miners and pits.

Elsewhere, power changed hands or freedom was curtailed in Portugal, Poland and Greece and in Russia Joseph Stalin was busy plotting to oust Trotsky in his struggle to impose his own vicious brand of socialism on the country.

The Far East

The captain and chief officer of the *Khodoung,* both affable men, were aged about 28 and Stanley was 26. Unusually, the captain, the chief officer and Stanley held master's certificates but the third officer had an extra master's ticket. At the beginning of the First World War, he held a first officer's ticket but was rejected by the navy so he enlisted in the army. When he was fighting in the trenches, the bureaucrats discovered their error and he was withdrawn from France to join the navy. He was killed in the Second World War when the vessel he was commanding was torpedoed.

The chief engineer, a Yorkshireman, was keen on cricket and improvised a form of the game to be played on the deck. The balls were constructed from old rope and were made fast to the end of a line to be hauled back on board from any successful shots for six. Bowlers were denied a run up and batsmen could not move forward because of a lack of space. Sometimes, the crew, who enjoyed the game, found a dusty space ashore, near the wharf.

One port of call was Djakarta and Stanley took his camera ashore to photograph the temple, the local children and a quiet village street. "The nights were memorable: the ship lay motionless at anchor, the sea was like a sheet of black glass, there was neither moon nor stars and all was black. The land was vaguely visible as a darker mass against the sky. The vessel was too far from land to allow noise from the frogs and the incessant chatter of countless insects to disturb the all-pervading silence. Everything seemed in a union of harmony and total peace. Later in the night, a fire was lit in the village and the human figures were outlined as they added more wood to the conflagration before playing native music that floated gently across the bay. I sat motionless, absorbing it all, the music, the night, the sea and the land."

Later, the vessel was destined to visit Ambon, in what became Indonesia. "We headed south down the Macassar Strait, rounded the southern tip of Celebes Island, and moved east into the Banda Sea. Ambon was then the headquarters of the Dutch East Indian Army and no British vessel had visited this small port since 1913 as it was effectively the preserve of a Dutch company. However, the first accent I heard was that of a Lancastrian. He visited Ambon every three years, selling cotton. It was a small port with a tiny wooden wharf and our oil was pumped, slowly, into a wooden tank. Away from the small town, there were some large huts, enclosed by wire fencing and occupied by figures covered from head to foot in folds of faded pink cotton. Sadly, they were lepers.

"We left Ambon in the evening and arrived off Banda at eight in the following morning. Initially, we missed the entrance because it was so narrow and, when we did find it, we proceeded very cautiously because the channel, although deep, was enclosed to port by the low-lying island of Banda and to starboard by the peak of an extinct volcano that rose abruptly from the sea and towered several hundred feet towards the sky. The island gradually opened up to show its beauty and to reveal the town and the red roofs and white walls of the houses. The tropical vegetation, bougainvillea, hibiscus and many different types of orchid produced a blaze of flamboyant riotous flames of colour. Equally impressive was the spice-laden perfume wafted by the offshore breeze. It was truly beguiling and that impression of beauty remained with me for ever. The sea was clearer than any I had ever seen and I could follow the anchor chain down to the bed of the sea. The coral was delicate pink or white and of various sizes and shapes. Many pieces were as dainty and fragile as filigree. The fish, of many and splendid colours, some striped like rugby players' jerseys, weaved in and out of them in their beautiful marine garden. The fine sand was white."

As soon as the *Khodoung* anchored, a launch arrived with some local officials, one of whom was excited because it was the first time that a British ship had visited the Dutch-dominated island. Two officials boarded the vessel. One was a Dutch harbour-cum postmaster who was also head of the customs and the other was an Indonesian chief of police, who was about to be married. The crew were invited to the wedding but missed the ceremony so joined the party on its way from the mosque to the house, where the festivities were to take place.

"The party was led by an Indonesian brass band, consisting of some independent, rugged individualists who insisted on blowing their instruments lustily in their own time, totally disregarding others in the group. Eventually, it became clear that their main tune, predictably, related to the confirmation of the absence of bananas. This was followed by another musical epic that bore some slight reference to 'It's a long way to Tipperary'. The happy couple followed, he in his policeman's uniform, she in white. In turn, they were followed by the village elite with the women wearing smart dresses. The men presented an odd picture. They wore old dinner suits, some of which had started to turn green, whilst others were too big or too small. The man inside the greenest suit, who also favoured a huge butterfly collar of unknown vintage, seemed to be the comedian of the party as he caused a constant ripple of laughter. Finally, others from the village joined the procession, dressed in their native clothes. The young people brought up the rear with most of the females wearing European-style dresses."

The local people gathered in a large well-built house with an imposing terrace, large pillars and a surprising profusion of marble. Banda once held a world monopoly of the spice-growing industry and the merchants became rich so that their ships, having discharged their cargoes of spice in Italy, returned with marble. Later Brazil entered the market and the merchants moved away, leaving the natives to occupy the miniature palaces at a minimal rent.

Food and drink were plentiful. The drinks offered were fresh lime squash or Coca Cola but no alcohol was served as these people were strict Moslems. The food was the Javanese rijsttafel, the most delicate and delicious of oriental cuisines. As the tropical night closed in, the guests gravitated towards groups attracted by western music from one room and oriental music from another. Suitably emboldened, Stanley addressed one girl in his best Malay and she responded in impeccable English, learned at school in Java. She had never been to England. On the following day, he walked through the town and saw many handsome but old and decaying houses and some boasted gardens that were spectacularly colourful and offered a rich perfume. Everyone was friendly and smiling. Two forts overlooked the narrow channel. One was built in 1617 and gun barrels lay on the parapet. Stanley noted that in such beautiful surroundings, he would find it difficult to fight anyone.

After loading at Balik Papan, the next destination was Makassar and the ship anchored some 50 yards from the shore. The crew took their football ashore and played the natives and, later, being hot and dusty, some of them opted to swim back to the tanker. Only later did they discover that the waters were infested with sharks. After a few more months around the islands, the vessel dry-docked at Surabaya, so the crew were able to have some time off. One Sunday morning, at 8.00 am, Stanley and some colleagues were taken in a dockyard company car into the mountains for the day. As they climbed, it became agreeably cooler and every square yard seemed to be cultivated. Lunch was taken in a country hotel and this was followed by a swim in a pool fed by a mountain stream.

The next port of call was Shanghai. It was February so the weather there would be cold. Worse still, the tanker was designed for work in the tropics, so lacked heating in the accommodation areas and electric heaters were totally inadequate. This was Stanley's first visit to Shanghai and he was impressed by the river, dotted with ships of every nationality, size and shape, which mingled with Chinese junks.

Returning later to Bula Bay, on the edge of the primitive jungle, the installation manager there suggested that the captain and some of his colleagues might like to hunt for wild boar, pigs and deer. He would lend them rifles and provide a native guide. Having been a dedicated scout, the idea appealed to Stanley who thought he knew "a thing or two about stalking game". Suitably dressed, the party met the guide and his dogs in the village at around 3.30 am but the local man contended that this late start meant that the group would reach the watering places after daylight. The dogs seemed as anxious as the guide to set out. "They circled round, beating their brains out with their tails or tripping themselves up over their lolling tongues." Soon, walking at a brisk pace, the party left the village behind and entered the jungle. The trees and long grass were dripping with dew and the men rapidly became wet up to the waist. After half an hour, trying to keep up with the guide, pushing through bushes, climbing over fallen trees, in and across gullies and up and down hills, perspiration completed the work started by the dew and all were completely wet through.

Stanley contended that the rifle he was carrying was assuming the dimensions and weight of a heavy machine gun and, despite transferring it from one shoulder to the other, he was feeling sore. The daylight was beginning to filter through the trees and the lighter it became, so did the pace quicken, but a breathless Stanley was consoled by the picture of the game he would shoot. After two demanding hours, the group arrived at the dry bed of the river that still contained some pools of water. Sore, wet and exhausted, Stanley was thrilled to see the footmarks of the game that had been down recently to drink. The guide, less impressed, said that they were late. "He suggested that I should hide behind a fallen tree whilst he and the captain went up river. I had just a faint suspicion that he had found some of us rather slow and this was his first chance to jettison me. The idea of sitting down, however, appealed and I waited for a pig or a deer to approach me, keen to be shot. Apart from my rifle, I also had the ship's revolver and my pocket knife, as well as my camera, so I was thoroughly prepared. I could shoot the animal with my gun, stab it if necessary and take its photo.

"Soon, when the cloud of steam from my feet was gradually dispersing and the prospect of my feet bursting into flames was fading, I heard a shout from the guide and he gestured me to follow him into the long grass. Picking up my paraphernalia, I hurried after him thinking that now was the time when my Boy Scout training would pay dividends. I crept cautiously through the grass and slowly raised my head to see, to my joy, a magnificent deer, about 200 yards away. I decided against shooting it at this range and moved forward, carefully and hopefully silently, before looking up again. The deer was now only 50 yards away. I raised my rifle and, just as I was increasing the pressure on the trigger, the captain shouted. I had nearly reduced the dog population of Bula Baai by one. Fortunately, the guide was unaware of my efforts as otherwise my stock would have slumped even further.

"Later I heard a shot. The guide had killed an enormous and distinctly unfriendly-looking wild pig. I thought that it was just as well that I had not encountered this animal as I suspect that my rifle would not have been very steady. I had my photo taken with my rifle in hand and my foot on the pig, surely suggesting...Justice was served in that the photograph was a failure and it was difficult to make out who was who. Natives then appeared, seemingly from nowhere, and cut up the pig into smaller pieces to facilitate carrying it. Later, rather unsportingly, I shot a bird sitting minding its own business, partly because I had seemingly carried this rifle since I was a boy and had a strong desire to use it. My colleagues on the ship opted for roast pig but I tackled bird stew. It tasted like stewed sandal and I soon asked for some roast pig."

Subsequently, Stanley was signed off at Surabaya, Java on 31st October 1927 and sailed on a Dutch passenger ship to Tarakan, Borneo, to join the *Bithina* as acting chief officer at a monthly rate of £37. The vessel, a coal burner, was one of two museum pieces, built in about 1895, which Shell had acquired after the 1914-1918 war. The new acting chief officer was not "unduly enthusiastic" about the elderly vessel, which carried some 5,000 tons. One of the two masts had gone and the funnel was tall and thin, presenting a weary and dejected appearance. The floor of the rooms midships was also the top of the cargo tanks and on one occasion, the second officer forgot that the tank tops were suspect and over-filled the tanks with fuel oil which covered the deck in ankle deep oil.

The ship also carried cargo and the itinerary was interesting as it called at several ports, staying but a few hours in each. Stanley felt that he was more familiar with the coast and ports of Borneo than of the UK. The resthouse at Tarakan, just a bungalow, was in the middle of an oil field and was surrounded by rigs. The only other resident at the time in the rest house was a Dutchman who collected snakes which looked particularly sinister and unhappy at meeting Stanley.

The first voyage was to Hong Kong, which Stanley had not visited since he was third officer. The slow pace of discharge and ballasting, which usually meant 48 hours in port, allowed him to visit the shops which were loaded with expensive jade, ivory and silk. The next destination was Fremantle in Western Australia and Stanley felt it odd to walk down a crowded street and to see only white people. Indeed, he had spent so much time in the Far East that he was surprised to see white men doing menial work.

One evening, back in Tarakan, as loading was completed too late to allow the vessel to sail that evening, Stanley accepted an invitation to go ashore with the chief and second engineers for a drink. He only had one glass of cheap and unpleasant wine but his comrades were thirstier and became progressively less capable so Stanley tried to help them back to the vessel. Fortunately, he noticed a small wagon on the railway line which led to the wharf and the ship. His friends were then loaded on to the obliging wagon which he pushed back to the ship. Ironically, Stanley discovered later that it had been their intention to get him drunk. He said goodbye to the *Bithina* on 2nd April 1928.

Outside the world of shipping, global events had not improved. In 1927 and 1928, allied military controls over Germany had ended and between 1929 and 1932 industrial production there fell by 40 per cent. In China, there were strong demonstrations against foreigners. There was violent unrest and a general strike in Austria, where the majority was keen to deny success to left wing movements and in Mexico the government's strong anti-clerical stand provoked violent opposition from the millions of Catholics in the country. Turkey became a one-party state. Joseph Stalin secured undisputed control of the Soviet Union when Leon Trotsky was expelled from the party and, on another continent, a war commenced between Paraguay and Bolivia. In 1928, a dam burst in Los Angeles, killing 400 people, and China and Japan were involved in a furious and deadly struggle. In the United States, the first television sets were made available for sale, priced $75. There had been a slump between 1919 and 1922, followed by a boom and now some analysts feared substantial problems in the near future.

Stanley's next appointment, back on the *Sultan Van Koetei,* as second officer, took effect from 20th April 1928 when he joined the vessel at Balik Papan. After six months, on the usual Borneo, Philippines and Java run, he returned to Singapore to join the 8,500 ton *Pleiodon* in November 1928 as acting chief officer. The vessel was built in Hong Kong just after the First World War and was the best vessel thus far for Stanley. The new run included two trips to Sydney and Adelaide. "After leaving Singapore, we steamed east, along the Java Sea and across the Torres Strait where we picked up a pilot to take us down the Barrier Reef. It was like being on an expensive cruise, passing between lovely tropical islands with their rich vegetation and white gleaming sands, seeing reefs and shoals, and coral banks and every day there was warm sunshine, calm seas and exquisite nights when the stars seemed to glow like green Chinese lanterns and the air was soft and cool."

On returning to Singapore the vessel was ordered home to the UK and Stanley was excited at the prospect of finding out if he had a future with the young lady with whom he had sustained "an assiduous and increasingly enthusiastic" correspondence. He must have been hopeful because she had sent him photographs of her and friends on holiday in Broadstairs in 1927 and to Seaton and Lyme Regis in 1928. "I had tried to keep my hopes and ambitions in control, well, comparatively soon I would find if I really had any hopes and ambitions to hang on to." The ship seemed to crawl to the UK and the nearer England became, so did his impatience and excitement increase. He was due for three months leave, which was for three years service in the Far East, and he would be paid at the beginning of this period. Additionally, he had managed to save whilst away in the Far East. "I wanted to relax and be happy and forget the miserable times of unemployment and lack of cash."

Leave in 1929 and back to sea

After one week in Middlesbrough, the hopeful suitor took the train to London, on 1st May 1929. The day was fine and "SHE was there to meet me at Kings Cross. She was very attractive when I first met her, three years before, but now she was beautiful." For the next few months Stanley enjoyed himself more than he had ever done before. In June, he bought a second-hand Morris and the garage owner took him out into the country and, after less than an hour's instruction, released him on a defenceless world, an unskilled driver with a lethal machine. (Driving tests were only introduced in 1934.) Initially the car controlled him but he took command before any accidents could occur and was sufficiently bold to drive to London where one of the couple's favourite haunts was Kew Gardens.

Maidie, who was keen on amateur dramatics and hockey, worked at Lloyds Insurance in the City and the two frequently lunched together and then, until 5.00 pm, whilst awaiting his friend's release from her office, Stanley would wander around London, visiting museums, art galleries, and, occasionally, going to a matinee. "I was really happy and for the first time for years, I had enough cash to enjoy myself. I felt that I was making progress and convincing her what a fine fellow I was but, as the months were drifting by, so did my departure draw nearer and I began to dread it."

Stanley was soon accepted, not just by Maidie but by her relatives and friends. This must have been most satisfying to him because his own family and home life had been so unpleasant. Stanley and Maidie spent time at Bognor, on the Sussex coast, and other photographs show them with John, his future brother-in-law, and Maidie's mother, Ethel, who was known as Bloss. His relationship with his brother Arthur was to turn sour but all seemed well in August 1929 as a photograph of him and his motor bike, which Stanley had probably and unknowingly bought, showed. Stanley and Maidie had a holiday together at the East Cliff House Hotel at Bournemouth.

For Stanley 1929 was probably the best of his life thus far: for millions of people, especially in the United States, it was the worst year of their lives. After some years of deceptive and relative prosperity, the US experienced the Wall Street crash in October and the decline was followed four days later in London. Values eventually plummeted by 89 per cent over a three year period. Many of those involved committed suicide whilst others lost all their pensions. On the first day of the crash, some speculators killed themselves, causing the New York Stock Exchange to close the spectators' gallery. One leading company admitted that there had been a "little distress selling" and that, "things were susceptible to betterment". Thirteen million shares changed hands, three times the previous record. The slide continued until 1932 and those who had bought at peak prices only saw their values restored in 1954. The economic recovery really only began after the Japanese attack on Pearl Harbour in 1941.

Predictably, politicians maintained that the underlying economy was sound but the economic and political consequences were awful. The losses helped to cause the Great Depression, governments to abandon the gold standard and to assist the development of the Nazi party in Germany where many banks failed. The causes of the calamity were complex, but, in the main, resulted from market saturation in foodstuffs and commodities which lowered prices and deterred some countries from importing and consuming other goods as protection was favoured. The harsh conditions imposed on Germany after the end of the First World War was another powerful factor. Acute speculation, increased borrowing stringency and defects in the banking system, aided by unstable businesses, further weakened demand and US unemployment rose to more than eight million by 1931.

In the United Kingdom, more than three million were jobless and much later, in 1936, the unemployed marched from Jarrow to London to demand food and better treatment. The Prime Minister, Stanley Baldwin, refused to see them. German unemployment peaked at around six million. The deteriorating economic conditions proved to be breeding grounds for communism and fascism, which, before long, were to claim millions more lives. It was re-armament that, effectively, ended the long economic nightmare, even if a more tragic political horror was soon to explode over Europe. On the political front in Europe, in 1929, King Alexander renamed the Kingdom of Serbs, Croats and Slovenes as Yugoslavia and took dictatorial powers, thus ending years of near civil war. Hitler attracted huge audiences in Nuremburg and at other venues in Germany.

After five very happy months on leave, despite the fact that only two were on pay, Stanley was appointed acting chief officer of the 10,000 ton *Elax,* one of the best vessels in the fleet, on the 19th September 1929 at Tilbury Docks. His monthly pay was to be £23-2-0. He had requested a home ship and, having spent so much time out East, his request was granted as the *Elax* was then in dry dock on the Tyne for ten days so he incurred a big telephone bill ringing his teenage friend. The tanker was employed mainly on the run from the UK to Curacao or the US. However, a Standard Oil tanker, the *Tacoma,* had broken down in Malta and the *Elax* was despatched to load its cargo and take it to Karachi and then to proceed to Singapore where it loaded for Auckland in New Zealand.

Thence it was back to Borneo, Balik Papan and then orders were received to load for the UK, after just three months away. Hopes of seeing his girl friend and, perhaps, putting the relationship on a more permanent basis, were immediately dashed as he was to be moved from the *Elax* back to the *Bithina* which he re-joined at Balik Papan at the end of January 1930. The frustration was partly offset by the thought that some encouraging savings could be made as his monthly pay would rise from £23, the coastal rate, to £37.

The initial voyage was to Hong Kong and thence to Borneo where the *Bithina* ran into a typhoon. Warnings had been broadcast from Manila regularly but their position denied the possibility of evasive action. "We had to heave to and try to maintain our position. The sky darkened, the violent rain squalls and the rising sea threatened and it became darker still as the wind became cyclonic force. Speed was reduced until we had just enough to steer the ship and keep her head up into the wind. We spent 36 hours hove to, which is a long time to watch the same lighthouse from a labouring and tossing ship, with huge waves crashing on board and the wind howling in the rigging like a crowd of banshees. I remembered, too, that the ship was old but, after two days, we were able to head south again to find the sun and calm waters. I doffed my hat to the old ship."

The next time that the *Bithina* visited Singapore was to be broken up for scrap. Sailors become attached to their vessels and Stanley felt sad. "During the night, some ballast had leaked from her tanks, she had a list to port and was down by the head and her funnel sagged one way and her remaining mast in the other. She looked old and tired and I had a fanciful wish that she should not end her days in a Japanese yard but off the lovely Banda. Aground on the reef, the sun bleaching her upper works, the rain and salt slowly eroding her steel sides until the sea gained access to her tanks turning them into a garden of tropical sea plants and coral and a playground for gaily decorated fish and a slow disintegration in the sun and spice-laden air."

The next appointment was as chief officer, from 2nd September 1930, on the 8,000 ton, UK built, *Saxicava*. The vessel was a "home ship" so, after voyages to Durban, East London, Abadan and Italy, it was reasonable to think that a trip to the UK might be imminent. In fact, Stanley did not return to the Far East for six years and trading was mainly in the Mediterranean. He enjoyed visiting Venice and Trieste although the goods in the shops were expensive. Above all, there were opportunities for Maidie to visit the ship.

The run often meant that the ship had about eight days steaming around the coasts of southern Arabia. There were no lighthouses for over one thousand miles until the vessel rounded Ras al Hadd. "Whenever we were near enough to see the coast, it appeared to be a dull, desolate place, with an eternity of sand and limitless desert. Very occasionally, there would be a clump of palm trees around which would be clustered a few huts. In the Gulf of Oman we could see the town of Muscat, one of the hottest places on earth. Parallel to the coast line, on the Iranian side, there was a fascinating rock which looks like a huge wave that was just about to break. The Abadan river bank on the Persian side was covered with date palms which supported many villages."

Alexandria in Egypt was not very interesting and Stanley did not seek out the lurid night life about which he had read. Another regular voyage was to the Black Sea to load at Constanta in Rumania. The town boasted numerous cafes and bars, some of which had dance floors and music and many potential dance partners. Dancing, however, was but a means to an end for the girls and after a few dances and drinks, and a firm rejection of their suggestions, they were usually satisfied with the equivalent of a few shillings. Stanley believed that Rumania was corrupt but, during the summer, it was interesting on Sunday afternoons to go into the town square and watch the people. There was a naval base in Constanta and soldiers were also stationed nearby and the square looked like a set from a musical comedy set in Ruritania.

One trip was to Naples. "We approached just as dawn was breaking. There was no moon, and at first all we could see were the stars and the lights of the town against an opaque background. As the light increased, the conical outline of Vesuvius with a wisp of smoke emerging from its peak became clearer and soon the whole image of the volcano was reflected on the sea. It was a strange picture, two volcanoes, separated by the low lying lights of the town. Walking along the streets of Pompeii, seeing deep ruts in the stones carved by the chariots many centuries before was exciting as was looking at the stone jars used by the wine makers and the unmistakable signs carved in the walls pointing the way to the houses of pleasure."

During 1931, there were several voyages from Constanta in Rumania to Shellhaven on the Thames. Whenever in port, Stanley looked anxiously for mail from Maidie, now his fiancée, and another regular worry was whether the next orders would route the ship back to the UK. He was fortunate and his intended wife was able to visit him often and learn what ships and shipping meant in the context of a marriage. However, as late as mid January, in 1932, the year in which he hoped to marry, he still had doubts on whether the couple could cope financially but he decided that it would be possible. They would marry during his long leave. During the first five months of the year in which he intended to marry, he earned £113-2-0.

In the early Thirties, the troubled world experienced new problems. The previous economic recovery had proved fallible when the Wall Street crash and subsequent Great Depression disrupted the lives of millions of people. Conflict was a regular visitor to many countries and the war between China and Japan was an unpleasant indication of the depths of depravity to which a modern state could sink. In Germany, the Nazis had become the biggest party in the Reichstag and by the beginning of 1933, Adolf Hitler was Chancellor of the German Reich, where the jobless total was around five million. Stalin was unleashing his brutal reign of terror in the Soviet Union and poverty and social unrest was evident in many countries. In the US, more than 4.5 million were unemployed by the end of 1930 and in the UK, where unemployment reached 2.75 million in 1931, a national government, headed by Ramsay MacDonald, took office. Oswald Mosley formed the British Union of Fascists in 1932.

CHAPTER 5

A busy weekend and a wedding

On Thursday, 21st January 1932, the *Saxicava* left Southampton for Plymouth and, after waiting for tides, was alongside the wharf the following day at 4.00 pm. The ship could not leave until the Monday morning, so Stanley, who had obtained the master's permission to go to London, "to see about buying a house", was on the 6.30 pm train. He was too tired and excited to sleep, read or to do anything but think about the future. He arrived at his fiancée's home at 07.00 am on the Saturday morning. That afternoon, Maidie and her mother, Ethel Watson, who lived in The Chine, in Muswell Hill, North London, but who had been born in Limehouse, in east London, her long-term friend Stan Slade and an excited Stanley, visited an estate agent's office. Then the quartet inspected several houses, and Maidie and her future husband selected 63 The Avenue, some two miles from his future mother-in-law's home and about eight miles from Charing Cross. Despite the expansion of the underground system in the 1920's and 1930's, the house was nearly two miles from either of the two nearest underground stations, Highgate and Bounds Green.

Stanley gave an IOU to the agent for £112-2-0 as a deposit, and asked him to apply for a mortgage which was to be in his name and that of his future wife. Later he put down £150 for the deposit and in 1934, paid another £200 when a policy matured. By the end of 1938, the outstanding balance owed was £416. He completed the purchase of the house in 1945, when he was 46. Stanley described it, costing £1,120 (£56,000) as "ideal". Similar properties were priced at more than £700,000 when prices peaked in 2007/8.

It was a terraced large house, built around 1900, with four bedrooms, a separate dining room and large lounge, bathroom, which was a luxury as the majority of homes even in the Thirties lacked an indoor water supply, toilet, kitchen and scullery and modest front and back gardens. There was no garage although in 1932, that was not a consideration. The house was connected to the electricity supply system: in 1930 only a quarter of houses had access and the proportion was still only a half in 1939.

It was a few hundred yards from Alexandra Park and its steam railway station, which had been opened to coincide with the completion of the £500,000 Alexandra Palace in 1873, offered a regular service to Finsbury Park with subsequent connections to the City and the West End of London. Ally Pally had had a chequered history. Within two weeks of its opening, it had been burned down by a worker who upset a coal brazier which immediately ignited the dry wood. During the First World War, the Park, which had been created in 1863, was used as an internment camp for up to 3,000 Germans and others. Later, the Palace was the location for television studios and a transmitting tower from which the first ever regular television programmes in the UK became available to a few hundred local viewers in November 1936, ten years after John Logie Baird had first demonstrated television. War brought an immediate end to the fledgling service.

That evening, in January 1932, the business completed by 8.30 pm, tired, and struggling to keep awake, but very happy after a long day, Stanley was alone with his future wife. Sunday started auspiciously with Maidie bringing him tea in bed. The day ended with Maidie accompanying her future husband to Paddington station in the evening. "A few months and we're united." By 5.00 am on the Monday morning, he was back on the vessel, tired, hungry and happy. The *Saxicava* sailed at 3.00 pm, delayed by the tide, and anchored off Falmouth some five hours later and the operation to free the tanks of gas commenced. They were wet, cold and gaseous but "how warm and happy I feel inside."

In February 1932, the *Saxicava* visited Batumi, on the east coast of Russia. This was Stanley's first visit to the communist Soviet Union, where Stalin, within the next two years, was believed to have imprisoned up to ten million of his fellow citizens in concentration camps. The weather was atrocious and, as no berth was available, there was a delay of a week. The wind was frequently at gale force and was accompanied by blizzards. Nobody was allowed ashore and nobody was allowed to board. The ship was searched by soldiers on its arrival and the captain was taken under guard to the agent's office before being escorted immediately back to the vessel. No installation officials were allowed near the vessel and the *Saxicava* crew pulled the oil pipes on to the deck and connected them to the ship's pipes. A Russian soldier stood guard near the gangway but the military still searched the vessel for stowaways. During a heavy swell, the vessel broke adrift at 12.30 am and was subsequently anchored and went alongside at 4.00 pm.

Later, having just gone thorough the Bosporus, Stanley laments that there was no letter from Maidie. In a poignant phrase that was to be repeated so often in the next decade, he notes that, "I would have given anything for just one letter" but he was soon to meet her again, at Thameshaven, before the vessel headed for Reykjavik in Iceland, some four days sailing time away. The town had cement and corrugated iron buildings and only the main roads were paved. The countryside was as bleak, bare and as desolate as Stanley had ever seen. There were no trees or vegetation and, by the sides of the road, at frequent intervals, there were cairns of stones to delineate the roads during the winter months when they would otherwise be hidden in the snow drifts. There were many hot springs which the people had utilised by building greenhouses around them.

"It was strange in an otherwise bleak landscape, bereft of any vegetation, to see sudden gusts of steam and hot sulphurous water shooting up into the air, some to a height of at least 20 feet".

The vessel sailed on 23rd March 1932 for Curacao, and immediately encountered very heavy seas which caused the ship to roll and pitch in the turbulent waters and the wind was howling and shrieking. Stanley felt unwell but after four unpleasant days the course was changed to avoid the bad weather and icebergs. By the end of the month, he wrote, "tired of it all, the bad weather and everything, just existing for the few months ahead of me when I will really start to live". More bad weather was still to come and the ship was "jumping about" to such an extent that it was difficult to find any rest anywhere. "Physically and mentally tired and beginning to get nervy, just living on the thoughts of our long, happy peaceful days together." Just how much he was investing in the relationship was indicated by his comment that, "if I don't find them, (long, happy peaceful days) what's left?"

April 1932 opened more brightly for Stanley. The wedding, previously provisionally planned for September, now scheduled for 9th July, was but weeks away and the weather had improved. On 5th April, Maidie's 22nd birthday, he mused on the future but he still felt unwell which was attributed to the gas on the tanker. The days were moving too slowly. On 1st May, his spirits were lifted when, on reaching Rotterdam, he received eight long letters from his fiancée and, on the following day, he sent off his mortgage papers noting that, "now it should be ours". He was "tired but deeply, so deeply, happy".

Two days later, the mood had changed. Another letter from Maidie was received just before the vessel sailed. She was disappointed that he was not coming to England but, initially, going to Belgium. Stanley was "plunged back into morbid depths and all the doubts that used to torment me before". Matters improved when the ship reached Augusta in Italy on 15th May and he received two more letters from his fiancée, of

16 and 26 pages. The voyage continued to Piraeus and then to Constanza, where orders were received to set sail for the UK.

The atmosphere on his vessel was depressing Stanley. The master had recently hit a bosun and a riot by the sailors, who had refused to work, because of the master's regular bawling, shouting and swearing over the previous 18 months, was only narrowly averted. Stanley was "sick of it all" and applied for leave, as he wanted to be married and was only three months short of the necessary three years service to qualify for leave.

He sent his future wife a cheque for £100 to buy furniture and she acquired suites for the dining room and bedroom, kitchen utensils, carpets and linen etc. for £95. Shell subsequently said that Stanley's leave pay would only be given when he had completed the full three years service. (If an employee came home from the Far East on a passenger vessel, the month at sea counted against leave!) This meant that the intending bridegroom had to join another vessel and work for three months before he received his money. He had hoped that a proportion of what was nearly due to him in full would be paid. Fortunately, he had saved hard so it was not the problem it would have been in earlier years. Because of the grim economic climate, the shipping sector was depressed but Stanley was too busy and happy to have any misgivings about the immediate future. May ended on an unhappy note. Passing through the Bosporus, he received two more letters from Maidie in which she complained of the quiet life outside the office and business. "This perturbs me. What will she feel like when I'm gone? I'm just a little worried. I feel restless and unsettled."

In early June, Stanley was tired and listless. "I'm reading all my old letters and looking at photographs. How great life is going to be after all the empty monotonous years". En route to Thameshaven, he received a depressing message from Maidie that he was to be relieved "on condition". "All I want is to be home with her. Another three days of suspense!" Maidie met him at Thameshaven and he lost no time in signing off on 8th June and learned that he was to have leave. On 10th June, he could "hardly realise that I'm clear of the ship at last". The happy couple saw a talkie, widely regarded as the first such film, at the Plaza. *The Jazz Singer*, had been released in 1927 but by 1929, the bulk of Hollywood's output was talkies. They then had tea at a Lyons Corner House. "Noise, buses, tubes, London, once again, and it's glorious." The following day was devoted to shopping and then the two listened in the evening to the wireless. "Just such a time as I have hungered for the last few years." On the 12th June, they went to morning service and heard the banns called.

Between the 13th and 17th of June, Stanley's visit to his home town of Middlesbrough plunged him into gloom. He was met at 3.20 pm by his mother and his sister, Silvia. The following day, Stanley went to Wingate and met friends but a conversation with his mother made him feel desolate. This was followed early the next morning with another session in which she appeared to challenge his right to happiness. He left on the 10.00 pm bus from Middlesbrough and reached 63 The Avenue the following morning at 9.30 am. A visit to the Marlborough cinema was followed by an evening at home, in the Chine, listening to the wireless. Preparations were now proceeding apace and more shopping in Oxford Street was financed in part by selling some national savings certificates. Midweek, the couple and his prospective mother-in-law went to the Astoria at Finsbury Park to see Jack Hylton and his band.

Any euphoria was then wiped out by the arrival of his mother, whom he met at Highgate Hill. The "usual" conversation, presumably acrimonious and unpleasant, took place but generously, Stanley completed payment on her house. This was extraordinary, given his mother's persistently hostile attitude and the fact that, within a few days, he was to be married and exposed to the costs of setting up and running his own home. On 25th June, his mother visited number 63 and then had lunch with Maidie and Stanley before he took her to a film. On the Sunday, 26th June, his mother had tea at her son's new home and the following day, they attended a matinee at the London Pavilion and then had tea at a Corner

House. Later, he accompanied her to the Watsons in The Chine where she caused "an unforgettable and sickening scene, such was her appreciation for all the past years". This rumpus occurred a few days after he had completed payment, for her, on her house which was a most eloquent comment on the woman.

On Tuesday, 28th June, she returned to Middlesbrough and Bloss and her friend, Stan Slade, Maidie and her future husband went in Stan's car to Wheathampstead. Stanley managed to shake off the pernicious influence of his mother's visit and noted that England beat India, in their first full Test Match at Lords, and the only Test they played that season, by 158 runs. Stanley would not have been pleased that Herbert Sutcliffe, of Yorkshire, failed in both innings but maybe he, not Sutcliffe, had other matters on his mind.

On the first day of the significant month, July, the presents started to "pour in" The couple went to see "a talkie, *Faithful Heart*. The first payment of the mortgage was made, and, as Stanley noted, "only 203 more", which implied that the mortgage was for 17 years, which would have made Stanley about 50 if the mortgage were allowed to run until its natural completion. The wedding ring was bought on the 4th and, on the day before the wedding, the 8th, he met his mother again, at Kings Cross station. Arthur, his brother, arrived in London on his motor bike. Stan Slade gave the couple a costly and magnificent canteen of cutlery and Stanley, who admitted to an onset of nerves, went to Pittmans, presumably a restaurant or bar in London, for his last night of bachelorhood.

Saturday 9th July, was "a beautiful day and everything passed off marvellously. She looked wonderful and I had to keep looking at her, even during the ceremony. There were 30 people at the reception, held in the lounge of 63, all happy, sociable and jolly. Stan made a splendid speech and I made a little one. Everything was just perfect and it was all that I could have wished for." The marriage certificate shows that Stanley and Maidie were living at 63 when the marriage took place. St Andrews Church, which was built in Alexandra Park

Road in 1903, was within walking distance of the couple's new home.

The honeymoon was at the Richmond Lodge Hotel in Torquay and the newly married couple reached their destination, "tired but oh, so happy" at 10.00 pm. The weather on the first full day of marriage was beautiful and the couple looked around Torquay, which was "great, with beautiful gardens, coves, beaches and countryside". That day and the next, the weather was fine and the couple luxuriated in their happiness, sun bathing and swimming. On the 13th July, they saw *Private Lives* at the Pavilion. They returned to Oddicombe Beach, their favourite, doubtless shunning the steep walk down through the cliff and opting instead for the cliff railway, still functioning today, some 90 years after its introduction. They enjoyed the countryside and the woods as well as Meadfoot beach.

A visit to *HMS Stuart,* in the bay, and a musical evening in the hotel lounge accounted for 17th July and the following day was spent shopping and then a visit to "truly wonderful" Kents Caverns. They walked through the woods from Ansteys Cove to Meadfoot beach and Daddy Hole Plain, supremely happy and visited Torre Abbey, founded in 1138. Torquay had developed in Victorian times as holidays became more popular. The railway line to Paignton, on the far side of Torquay, had been opened in 1859, thus allowing more to enjoy the delights of the area which was regarded as the Queen of the English Riviera. Napoleon had compared the region to Italy, when, in 1815, he awaited deportation and exile to St. Helena, whilst on the *Bellerophon.* The Channel fleet had anchored in Torbay in the Napoleonic wars and Admiral Nelson was given the freedom of nearby Exeter, the county town of Devon, in 1801.

The couple left Torquay on 23rd July at 10.00 am and arrived home at 4.00 pm. Bloss, Stanley's new mother-in-law, had prepared a meal and arranged some flowers as part of the welcome home. A few days of bad weather followed but on 29th July, the couple bought a wireless but either could not afford nor find a suitable table on which the large radio could sit, until the end of August. The British Broadcasting Company, later Corporation, celebrated its 10th birthday that year. Its first broadcasts had been in November 1922, when it offered concerts and news from 6.00 to 10.00 pm. The annual license fee was 10/-. By the end of 1939, listening had become very popular and there were some 8.9 million sets in the UK.

At the end of July, the couple had tea at the Oxford Street Corner House and walked though Hyde Park along the Serpentine and then home to listen to their new wireless. The summer of 1932 was the hottest for many years and the happily-married couple relaxed and enjoyed their new life together. They often visited the Hornsey and Finchley swimming pools: on 19th August the temperature rose to 99 degrees in the shade, which was the highest for 21 years.

The contrast with Stanley's life up to that point must have made him wonder how he had stumbled into such an agreeable world. With a car-owning friend, they went to St. Albans, Oxford, Windsor and other towns and villages on the Thames and, between August and October, they spent many happy days around London. Closer to home, they walked in Highgate and Queens Wood, in north London. This was a 70 acre site that had been given to the City of London in 1886 by the Ecclesiastical Commission, partly to prevent speculative building. They also spent time at St. Paul's, Hampstead Heath, Kenwood, The Tower of London, Hyde Park, Westminster Hall and Abbey and the Victoria Embankment. There were numerous visits to cinemas, theatres and concerts and shows. In the 1930's about 40 per cent of the population went to the cinema once a week and a quarter went twice or more. Shows seen included *Tell the Truth*, with Bobby Howes, at the Saville, Ivor Novello's *Party* at the Gaiety and *Firebird* with Gladys Cooper.

Alone or with friends, they patronised many Lyons Corner Houses and also watched the famous judges in procession at the opening of the Law Courts, courtesy of Stan Slade, who worked with Justice Farnwell. They visited the judge's room and saw his gowns and the black cap which judges wore when pronouncing a death sentence. They also went to the Lord Mayor' show but Stanley was unimpressed.

Stanley watched Surrey and Yorkshire at the Oval. The home county, with Jack Hobbs, who had already scored more than 100 hundreds, succumbed by three wickets. One disappointment was that Sutcliffe was run out for six: earlier in the season, he and Holmes created a new Yorkshire record opening partnership of 555 against Essex, with the former contributing 313 not out.

On 11th November, Stanley went to the Cenotaph service and then on to the Unknown Warrior's grave and the Field of Remembrance. In the evening he and Maidie listened to the service on the wireless. "It was impressive and beautiful. We were happy together and quite content to let the weeks and months drift slowly by." However, the old problem of money recurred. He had saved a reasonable amount but was troubled by the fact that Shell would not pay him his full leave pay until had worked for another three months. He was home for five and a half months, off pay. Furthermore, the Income Tax authorities were demanding £32 which, at that time, represented more than six weeks gross pay. Stanley thought that he had been out of the country for more than two years so was not liable to tax but he had miscalculated and had just fallen short of the necessary period. The officials were sympathetic and allowed him to pay £5 with a promise to pay the balance when his leave pay was received.

A letter from Shell on 15th November induced more anxiety. He was to join the *Pecten* at North Shields as second officer. "I was really shattered. I had served as chief officer for just under four years but what was really catastrophic was that my pay, at £15-9-7 per month, was my lowest for nine years and this, just after being married." A loan on an insurance policy with the Prudential, which had arrived on 19th October 1932, helped during the last few weeks before he returned to sea. This could have been an unhappy time but he had a new wife, and, unlike millions of other workers, he had definite employment. That year, there were hunger marches to London by the truly hapless. Some 20,00 marchers, from all over the country, gathered in Hyde Park London, having been organised by the communist-led National Unemployed Workers Movement.

1932 was, undoubtedly, Stanley's happiest to date but Shell's house magazine, *The Pipe Line,* reflected the increasingly significant political and economic events in the outside world at a time when, of course, there was no television and even the ownership of radio sets was limited. The internal publication carried pleas by senior executives for free trade to be sustained and one relatively junior employee had his pamphlet, on how to achieve this, publicised in the magazine. In the 6th July, edition, he wrote "there are abundant supplies of all necessities of life stored in all parts of the world but millions of families are short of foodstuffs and governments are in financial difficulties. The whole of civilised humanity is in a state of continual anxiety."

Sir Henri Deterding, then chairman of Royal Dutch Shell, told readers that, "we have reached a situation that is nothing less than grotesque by reason of the muddle headiness from which it has arisen and of the apparent impotence of the responsible men in dealing with it. There is under-consumption, or almost none, of most of the commodities that are indispensable for the maintenance of human life-there is only one commodity which the whole world appears to be chasing and that commodity is gold." An autocratic Dutchman, Deterding was one of the few foreigners to be knighted but, whilst he was widely credited with sustaining the Shell Group in difficult times, he did not inspire affection. He retired in 1936, as the age of 70: some historians maintain that Hitler was one of his friends. In August, JB Kessler jnr, son of the founder of Royal Dutch Shell and a senior executive, sought a solution for the "world oil crisis" through international co-operation to restrain over-production.

The magazine did not ignore more immediate matters. Sea-going staff commencing their leave could buy or hire a car from the St. Helens Court Stores which would purchase the vehicle back at the end of the mariner's leave. The "Shell shop" was to survive for about three more decades. A boarding house in Westcliffe on Sea offered accommodation for 7/6 a day. Surprisingly, the publication also contained advertisements for a Mapin and Webb' cutlery set at £12-15-0, road tankers (!) and a newspaper delivery service offered by WH Smiths. Lensbury, the Shell social club on the Thames at Teddington, reported annual income of £1,970-9-5 and wages cost over £4,000. The expenditure on coal, coke and fuel oil was £560. Girls started to play cricket at the club and the photograph of one of them was captioned "Miss Doris Buggs, first 'man' in." Free copies were available to distributors "for propaganda purposes".

CHAPTER 6

Back to sea and a happy event

At 5.11 am, on 18th November 1932, on a cold morning, having travelled overnight from London, Stanley joined his new ship near Newcastle. On learning that the *Pecten* would be in port for four days, he promptly invited his wife to join him, thus restricting their period apart to just 24 hours. Stanley was frightened about the future: if the ship went to the East, he could be away for three years. This was an unnerving prospect for someone, recently married, who had enjoyed a happy and secure home life, for the first time, for but a few months. Fortunately, this did not happen and the couple were united again after five months.

"Our first parting, as husband and wife, away from home, was on a cold wet morning on Hebburn-on-Tyne. The streets around the shipyard were bleak and cheerless. As I carried my wife's suitcase towards the station, my heart was heavy and sad. We kissed briefly in a shop doorway and as I turned away my spirits plunged to a new nadir. She was the centre of my world."

By 3.00 pm on 23rd November, the vessel was off Dungeness and he was leaving behind all that "means life to me". At the end of the month, he was depressed, very cold, feeling unwell and thinking of the couple's glorious times past and those still to come. Not for the first time, he was cheered by a letter, of 15 pages, the first from his wife and he soon sent her his first as husband. "How happy she makes me: I feel exultant". The next time that this adjective appears in his notes was when he described his reaction, as a prisoner-of-war, to news that thousands of Germans were being killed.

On 8th December, Stanley remarked that England beat Australia in the first Test by 10 wickets at Sydney. Australia scored 360 and England responded with 524, with Sutcliffe scoring 194. Australia reached 164 in their second innings, leaving England to score just a single for victory. The series, which became notorious for England's bodyline tactics, prompted bitter recriminations and the series was nearly abandoned when some injuries occurred in the third match. England, captained by Douglas Jardine, won the series four-one.

Within a few days, Stanley received a bundle of newspapers from his new wife and she followed this with a 13 page letter. Nearer Christmas, when in Genoa, he was pleased to have two more letters, 12 and 17 pages long, and more were received in Istanbul.

Away from the grim economic conditions and the sense of helplessness that they induced in millions, the world tried to continue as normal in 1932. The Olympic Games were held in Los Angeles, air conditioning was invented and air transport was developing fast. Amelia Earheart flew the Atlantic solo, for the second time, having been the first woman to achieve this feat, in 1928, but, less happily, the child of Charles Lindbergh, who first flew the Atlantic in 1927 in the *Spirit of St. Louis,* was kidnapped. In the entertainment world, the newly married couple might have listened to Paul Robeson, Duke Ellington, The Boswell Sisters, Louis Armstrong, George Formby, Cicely Courtneidge, Eddie Cantor and Henry Hall and the BBC Dance Orchestra on their new wireless set.

Mahatma Gandhi, the Indian Nationalist leader, was jailed after the breakdown of talks between India and Britain. British scientists split the atom, Franklin D. Roosevelt won a landslide victory in the US Presidential Election and 70,000 people were killed in an earthquake in China where major floods had caused havoc in the previous year. Two 20th century icons, Australia's Sydney Harbour bridge, and the 102-storey Empire State building in New York, were opened. The USSR and Germany signed a non-aggression pact.

The *Pecten* was comfortable and Stanley soon made friends but it was not a happy ship because the captain was unpleasant. Stanley reasoned that he would soon be on another vessel, so it was best to ignore it. He was to leave the *Pecten* in June 1933, before becoming chief officer on the *Trigonia,* formerly the *Marinula*, a Royal Navy oiler. His monthly income was now £22-15-5. The vessel visited Constanta, ports in the Mediterranean and Curacao before returning to Rotterdam after five months. Would Maidie be there to meet him? His wages, after deduction for the pension fund contribution, were just £14 per month and the fare from London to Rotterdam, that May, was about £6. Nevertheless, the 23 year old wife made her first trip abroad to meet him. Two days later Stanley had sailed but "somehow I sensed that our future would be happy and that despite the inevitable setbacks, together, we would overcome everything". Soon after this, the vessel drydocked on the Tyne for repairs and he was pleased to learn that he was now number 55 on the ranking list of 57 permanent chief officers. One rung of the ladder remained to be climbed.

In the wider world, in 1933, nearly half of the United States banks had to close because of losses in the Great Depression and by August 1934, Adolf Hitler had assumed the title of Fuhrer and begun the task of building up his nation's military power. Two months later, the first concentration camp was opened at Dachau. The struggle for democracy was becoming more obvious even if some nations chose to ignore the unmistakeable signals.

Stanley's next appointment, as chief officer, which he took up in Rotterdam in June 1933, was to the *Trigonia,* which

Shell had acquired after the war. This was to be his home for nearly three years. All the accommodation was on the main deck which made it uncomfortable as the slightest bad weather, when the ship was laden, flooded the decks and forced the closure of the port holes and the engines were unreliable. Perhaps this persuaded Head Office to route the vessel, mainly, to the West Indies to load and to discharge in Northern Europe.

After one voyage, the master departed for leave and his amiable successor claimed that after assisting the Mexican government, he had been given a free two-month holiday. His description of the people and places was impressive but Stanley later found that all his information had come from a guide book in the ship's library. In Las Palmas he promised Stanley a meal and the two set out for the town with an interpreter. The first destination proved disastrous but the second was acceptable. Then the captain promised him that they would visit a count he knew. "We went down a quiet road with pleasant but unpretentious houses, prompting the thought that this particular count was not very wealthy. My colleague knocked on one front door which was opened by a slatternly, heavy middle-aged woman. We were ushered into a pleasant lounge and sat down, awaiting the count's arrival. The captain expressed the hope that the count's two nieces would be able to meet them. Apparently, they were out but expected to return soon. The pictures on the walls were of attractive young girls, minimally clad." The captain whispered to Stanley that the woman who had let them in had been a very good madam. "Soon the nieces did return and I decided that I had to go back to the ship."

The next time in Curacao, Stanley was called at 2.00 am by the second officer with the news that the captain had cut his face after a fall. Stanley cleaned the wound but the victim wanted it sewn up. Stanley, the second and third officer all refused, insisting that he must see a doctor. "Hearing this, he said that he would do it up himself. Clearly, he did not want anyone to think that he had been drinking. I did as he wished and the brave man did not flinch. I was secretly rather pleased with my surgery because after the wound healed, there was only a very faint scar." The master's problem was caused by his addiction to rum, which was plentiful and cheap in Trinidad.

Maidie joined her husband when the ship called in at Hamburg. The elderly and middle-aged Germans were friendly and polite but the younger ones were aggressive and unpleasant, particularly to English people. This was the time when the Nazis were outlawing democracy, rounding up political opponents and setting up the first concentration camps. Apart from one trip to a café, it was thought wiser to stay on board. The next port, Rio de Janeiro, had an impressive harbour entrance, dominated by a huge figure of Christ perched on the peak of Corcovado and by skyscrapers and luxurious buildings. Santos, a quiet and small town where everyone seemed to be asleep or silent was next and it was here that the fourth engineer sold his radio to two locals. Unfortunately, the "money" he received was advertisements taken off tins of milk.

Thence followed Stanley's longest sea trip, of 34 days, across the South Atlantic, around the southern tip of Africa, then across the Indian Ocean, making first landfall, to the North point of Sumatra. He was excited to be returning to the Malacca Straits, where he had spent so much time in small ships. Crude oil was loaded for discharge at Paulliac, near Bordeaux in France, where Stanley hoped to see his wife again, for the first time for five months. He was not disappointed and was pleased to find that his schoolboy French allowed him to order poached eggs.

On the next voyage, when the vessel was still four days from Curacao, a Chinese steward died and his colleagues wanted him to be buried there. Making a coffin was a problem because there was little demand for wood on a tanker. Consequently, it was constructed of thick planks used for storage but there was no time to plane them down. "The carpenter and I measured the body and, as I was afraid to make the coffin too small, I put a few inches on the measurements.

Later, I was appalled to see that the coffin was far too big. We were in the tropics and it was very hot. We covered the body in lime and awaited the arrival of the authorities. They refused permission to bury the unfortunate man in Curacao and one of them even put his hand under the lime coating to prove that the body was still there. We could have buried the body at sea, wrapped in a canvas shroud but, by this time, the captain and I did not fancy the task of handling the corpse any more. He was in a coffin so that was enough. We added some metal to the coffin, drilled many holes in it, so it would fill with water, and nailed it down. We stopped the ship, one of the Chinese said a few words and with a heave, the coffin was consigned to the water, making a splash as it hit the surface. I expected it to fill with water, but it floated. If it eventually went ashore, on to a West Indian island, some eager native would have an unpleasant shock."

A fatigued Stanley eagerly anticipated his leave. He had been on the vessel for 30 months and had had only a few days off. The *Trigonia* had been generous to the married couple and as he left the tanker on 26th February 1936, he hoped that all would go well with the old ship. Leave, of about four months, was enjoyable and there was no financial problem as he was paid at the beginning of his furlough. "We didn't do anything special: we were happy enough to be at home together. Towards the end of the leave, Maidie was confirmed as pregnant. We were both so happy we were dazed. We had lunch and then went to Hampstead Heath. We sat under a tree, thinking how clever we were. It was hard to leave my wife but, in a way, it was to be easier. Before long, she would not be alone."

In the wider world, between 1934 and the end of 1936, the Nazi party had consolidated its grip on Germany and its troops re-occupied the Rhineland. The Spanish civil war began and the Nationalist government was set up. In Italy, Mussolini announced a Rome-Berlin axis and in the Soviet Union the brutal dictator Stalin was responsible for millions of deaths as he sought to impose his policy of collectivisation of agriculture.

Stanley took up his next appointment, as chief officer on the *Circe Shell,* on 29th June 1936 at a monthly income of £25-15-00 plus £2 in lieu of overtime. Soon after sailing from Rouen, the captain, with whom Stanley had sailed before, told him that a doctor in Singapore had informed him that his heart was suspect. At that time, the ailing mariner was ranked officially as a chief officer but, knowing that he would be taking command in Rouen, he ignored the doctor's advice. Every vessel carried a copy of the *Ship Captain's Medical Guide,* which Stanley had studied closely over the years, and which recommended amyl-nitrate phials for heart problems. So, whilst hoping that they would never have to be used, he had ensured that some were in the medicine chest.

The vessel loaded at Baytown in Texas for Curacao but, when in the Caribbean Sea, on 25th July 1936, the radio officer shouted out that the master had collapsed. Stanley hurried aft, grabbed and broke the glass phial and held it under the captain's nose. "His face was purple and he showed no response. We sent out a general call on the radio for medical advice and one American hospital and several ships responded, recommending what I had already done. Fortunately, this was one of those voyages when we had a padre on board and together we carried the captain to his room but he was dead." The following day, the padre and Stanley sewed up the corpse in a canvas container and added two iron bars to make it sink. Later that day, the burial took place. Those not on watch gathered around the corpse which was laid out on a wooden platform, covered by the Red Ensign. The ship was stopped and the padre began the burial service. Stanley's thoughts were with his colleague's wife as he knew that she was pregnant. "Soon the only sounds were of the waves slopping against the ship's side, the cries of a few inquisitive seagulls wheeling overhead and the solemn words of the burial service. Then the platform was raised and the body slipped from under the ensign into the sea, and within a few seconds, was lost to view. The engines were restarted and the voyage to San Francisco was resumed."

Stanley packed the captain's belongings and moved into his quarters himself. This was his first command, at £45-0-0 a month, but there was no satisfaction in the way in which it had happened. Soon the *Circe Shell* reached the Panama Canal, first used in 1913 but only officially completed in 1920. The French had begun work on the project in 1881 and more than 20,000 lives were lost before the Americans bought the canal zone, including a strip ten miles wide, for $10 million. The canal impressed the stand-in captain who was seeing it for the first time. "Across the narrow neck of Panama are several freshwater lakes which are joined by the canal. These lakes are nearly 80 feet above sea level so they built a series of locks to lift the ships from sea level to the level of the canal and then, of course, to lower them when they reach the end of the canal. The ships are towed in and out of the huge locks by very powerful electric engines that they call mules. There is no confusion, nor noise, the pilot on the bridge signals on a small whistle and his signals control the whole operation." Later, when in the prisoner-of-war camp in Germany, Stanley and 67 other master mariners unanimously agreed that the Panama Canal, with its locks, waterways and harbour facilities was one of the greatest marine engineering feats.

The *Circe Shell* proceeded to France and then to Cardiff for drydocking. Stanley had to attend an enquiry conducted by the Board of Trade, which handled all shipping matters, about the death of Captain Albert. He was questioned closely by a government doctor who was satisfied with his response and assured him that he could not have done more. After a few days at home, Stanley went to the Tyne to the *Sepia*, a 9,000 ton ship nearing completion. It was now October and a very pregnant wife, who was due to give birth in the December, followed him there. He was to be chief officer and the monthly rate of pay was £24-15-0 but this was increased to £27-10-00 six months later and then to £36-0-0 plus £2 for overtime on 1st July 1937. The accommodation was above average and the saloon and smoke room were adorned with reproductions by Dutch artists and a shell bearing the vessel's name. This was Stanley's first brand new ship and he took pride in maintaining it at a high standard. Sea trials took place in the North Sea but, as it had not been handed over officially, Stanley and colleagues were merely onlookers. All went well.

The *Sepia* sailed to Curacao and then loaded for Shellhaven in Essex but as it was now early December 1936, it was not wise for the pregnant Maidie to travel. However, colleagues agreed to take Stanley's watch so he arrived home on a Saturday afternoon, only to have to return 24 hours later. "The journey from Fenchurch Street station in London was cold and it was raining and there are more exciting places to be than on a tanker discharging at Shellhaven: all my instincts were to stay at home and to remain there until the baby was born." Then it was back to Curacao and thence to San Francisco. "When we reached the Pacific, I felt as if a barricade had been erected behind me. Was the baby late? Was all well? I was thousands of miles away. I was relieved and happy to learn that, on 23rd December, 1936, I had had a son. When would I be able to see him?" The new father was in good mood at the turn of the year and it was not just the fine weather. "I have a wife and a son at home, waiting for me. I'm feeling very happy and excited…"Another reason for the optimism was that it was likely that the new vessel would soon be routed back to the UK for the guaranteed drydocking as it was customary for checks for faults and any subsequent repairs to be carried out in the yard where the vessel had been built.

Sadly, Stanley's hopes were shattered. The vessel was routed to Singapore, Borneo, Hong Kong, where the inspection would take place, and Japan. Worse still, he had only served one year and three had to be completed before he could become eligible for leave. "When shall I see my son? How are my beloved wife and new son? This is terrible!" A few days later, the black cloud had lifted but his immediate hopes of receiving mail were dashed, when, on 9th January 1937, the vessel reached San Francisco. The only correspondence from home was dated 22nd December, the day before his son joined the human race. The weather was cold and wet and depression returned, especially when there was no more mail for him.

Early in February 1937, his spirits recovered although he notes that Australia beat England by 148 runs in Adelaide. Australia's first innings ended on 288, with Barnett contributing 129, to England's total of 330. Australia managed 433 in their second innings, with 212 from Don Bradman, before England slumped to 243 all out. This meant that Australia drew level in the series, having previously been two-nil down. They went on to win the series at Melbourne.

The arrival of a letter when the ship reached Kobe induced a much better mood and by the end of February, he had received the first photograph of his new son. "At first, I laughed. He looked such a funny little chap. Not at all good looking but very sweet and lovely." A week later, the proud father admits to being hypnotised by the photograph: "I look at him a dozen times a day and he is a fine little chap."

The vessel continued to trade between the US and the Far East. One compensation was that Eastern wage rates were much higher than home rates. In Japan the silk was cheaper than cotton, which had to be imported, so Stanley bought silk items, shirts made to measure and pyjamas, both with monograms on the pockets, kimonos, dressing gowns, scarves and shawls for family and friends. His purchases at the end of March, in Kobe, including his dressing gown, a kimono for his new son, a scarf and two shirts cost a total of 36 yen, then equal to £2-2-2.

Nursing home expenses, presumably from Philip's birth at the end of 1936, accounted for £22 (£1,000) and unspecified bills for the doctor took another £12-8-0. On the first of May, after having suffered from "a touch of fever," he was cheered by the news that his pay was to go up by 35/- a month. Although still feeling far from well, he was able to heed what was happening in the outside world: on 12th May 1937 George V1 was crowned and Neville Chamberlain became the UK Prime Minister on 28th May.

One voyage from Kobe to San Francisco was the most uncomfortable Stanley had ever experienced. Enveloped in

93

thick fog, the engines were put at "standby", so the engineers would be prepared to stop the engines instantly if required. The ship's steam whistle was sounded every minute and, in the still and eerie still, "it resembled the agonised moan of a stricken marine monster. Then, for a short while, the ship drifted along, alone in a white and ghostly world, as we strained our ears for the sound of another ship." Early one morning, with visibility below 200 feet, Stanley, on watch, was startled to see a Japanese fishing boat appear right under his vessel's bow. It had not signalled and soon disappeared in the fog. "As the fog vanished, we ran into more severe weather. The ship rolled, pitched and shuddered as each mountainous wave came roaring down on us, threatening to engulf all in its path. It was impossible to walk on the deck and watches were spent on the bridge, huddled into a corner holding on to a stanchion. Gradually nature relented and the sun appeared and we emerged into a bright new and pleasant world."

The remainder of 1937 was dominated by thoughts of home, especially on anniversaries. On his own birthday, in September, he wrote "All I can think of is my wife and my desire to see my little son. Phil's babyhood is slipping away and his dad is not seeing him." There were anxious waits for letters and, particularly, for photographs, often followed by instant and sometimes short-lived euphoria. Despite the length of the letters, one was 27 pages long and two others reached 24 pages, he wrote, "sometimes I feel that I am cut off, imprisoned, with no way back to my two treasures".

In March, he learned that the ship had been adopted by the County Secondary School for Girls at Streatham and later he wrote a ten page letter to the school, describing typhoons and a day in the tropics. When the vessel had to stop for engine repairs, Stanley indulged in some shark fishing and he managed to pull three, each about five feet long, to the rail before his line broke. On 5th July, the fireman's boy became ill. On the next day the youth sadly succumbed to a heart attack at 9.30 pm. Twenty four hours later, Stanley had sewn him into a canvas coffin and consigned him to the deep. In

October, a voyage to Vancouver enabled him to visit Katie, a friend, and her family. He showed them over the ship but this reminded him that his own family was thousands of miles away and depression returned. On 2nd November, he received a letter from Arthur, his brother, probably asking for money. Stanley described him as a "rat" and asked "why can't they leave me alone?"

Occasionally, his depression was lifted by listening to music. "There seems to be something about us that is immortal for us to have these thoughts that music can inspire. We cannot be just a candle, burn during our brief little interludes and then be extinguished. No more, nothing. If there was nothing after this, we wouldn't have these thoughts and we'd just live for the day and never have what love and beauty give us." A passion for music and its ability to inspire helped him survive the long and difficult days to come in the prisoner-of-war camp. On Christmas Day 1937, he heard a woman sing "Only a rose" on the radio. This was a particularly evocative song for him and he became very emotional. Books read during the year included *Heavy Weather* by PG Wodehouse, (funny), *The Moon and Sixpence* (Somerset Maugham, good), *The Great War*, volume two (Winston Churchill, good) and *Watch on Deck,* (Commander Dearden, RN, excellent).

The news from the rest of the world continued to be depressing in 1937. In the Spanish civil war, the nationalists forces were supported by the fascists of Germany and Italy and the republicans were backed by the communists of the Soviet Union. The Basque town of Guernica was destroyed by Nazi bombers and the German fleet bombarded the Spanish port of Almeria and Franco's forces captured Bilbao. Stalin shot 12 generals and Great Britain and Germany signed a naval pact. Buchenwald concentration camp was opened by the Nazis and Belgian safety was guaranteed by Hitler whose friends welcomed the Duke and Duchess of Windsor.

1938-1939

Some ten years had elapsed since Stanley had first served as chief officer so, on arriving at Tarakan in February 1938, he was delighted to learn that he should go to Singapore for his first command. Usually, it was customary for a new master to be appointed to a small or even an old ship but to his surprise, on 6th March 1938, he was given command of the *Elax*. This type of vessel, built in 1927, was usually reserved for senior captains but he realised that he had been chosen because there was a vacancy and he happened to be in the region.

The new master's first test was to take the vessel alongside the wharf at Pladjoe, in south east Sumatra, without a pilot or tugs. "In the examination rooms, I believed that I could tell the examiner how to take the Queen Mary alongside at New York, but this practical test was rather different." He had not been to Pladjoe for several years but the operation was accomplished smoothly. His income was to reflect his new status. As a chief officer, Stanley's pay was £36 a month, plus £2 in lieu of overtime: now he was paid £50, which was a good rate in 1938.

The vessel began trading between Abadan and Suez. Walking around a village near Abadan, he watched silversmiths at work, crouching on the stone floor with blow lamps and small hammers, a procedure doubtless unchanged for centuries. Stanley ordered six hexagonal serviette rings, made from one rupee pieces, with each side having a different scene engraved on it. Dhows, camels, or palm trees were on one side and a sixth side bore the initial letter of each recipient's first name. They scratched or cut the picture into the silver then rubbed black liquid over it before baking it in the fire and removing the surplus black. He collected the rings on his return from Karachi. Two of the rings survive, 70 years on.

Eventually his command was routed to the Mediterranean, calling in at Alexandria, Malta, Tunis, Algiers and Bone, prompting hopes of visiting home and seeing his new son.

After seven months on the *Elax*, he was to load at Constanta for the UK. He was overjoyed at the thought of seeing his wife again and the prospect of meeting his son, now aged 22 months, for the first time. Having rounded the southern tip of Greece and whilst threading its way through the Greek islands, the *Elax* had new orders. "Proceed to Port Said and Abadan and then to Madras and Calcutta for discharging." Bitterly disappointed, Stanley wrote to the company from Abadan, requesting leave as he had served 28 months and had not yet seen his son, now, nearly two years old. London sympathised and he returned to the UK from Singapore as a passenger on a Dutch tanker which chugged along at a slow 11 knots.

In 1938, despite the German annexation of Austria, which violated the Treaty of Versailles, agreed at the end of the 1914-1918 war, there were still hopes that a new conflict could be averted. The UK Prime Minister, Neville Chamberlain returned from negotiations in Munich with Hitler, Mussolini and Edouard Daladier of France to brandish a piece of paper, which, he claimed, guaranteed "peace in our time". Italy, France and the UK agreed that a part of Czechoslovakia, the Sudetenland, should be ceded to Hitler. Winston Churchill, who had warned the UK on the threats posed by German re-armament in the Thirties, led a protest against Chamberlain and the pogrom against the Jews in Germany gained momentum. By the end of the year, the Spanish civil war was virtually over, as General Franco and his allies defeated the Republicans after more than half a million people had lost their lives. Japanese advances in China meant that the invader controlled the six largest cities in the country, Canton, Hankow, Nanking, Peking, Shanghai, and Tientsin.

Crucial as this was, Stanley must have been pre-occupied with the thought that he would soon see his new son. On 19th January 1939, Stanley was met at Liverpool Street station in London by Maidie. She was alone. Where was Philip? Apparently, it would be better for him to meet his son for the first time at home. "He was a sturdy good-looking little chap with no inferiority complex....There was an awkward moment when he saw me the following morning, pointed a finger at me

97

and said 'butcher boy'." This claim was not investigated but, as the infant had only met uncles thus far, Stanley was addressed as uncle-daddy. That phase soon passed. In the 10 weeks leave, the proud father noted some of the comments made by his son. On being offered baked apple, he took one look at it and said, "for God's sake". When rushing to the window, to see a passing aircraft, he opined, "My god, I'll have to be quick." Asked by his mother, what was wrong, he said, "Philly's gone screwy."

After ten weeks' leave, the happy father was shocked to learn that he was booked as a passenger on a ship for Singapore. He had just completed two years out East and now was to return with the prospect of not seeing his wife and son for a long time. During an angry confrontation with a senior Shell official in London, he said he would prefer to sail as a chief officer on a home ship. He was told that he could stay at home for as long as he liked! Both men then cooled down and it was agreed that Stanley could remain at home for two more weeks. After that, he was to be appointed as supernumerary chief officer, on the *Agnita*, a home vessel, which was to load sulphuric acid in Amsterdam for Curacao and then on to Houston to load butane for France and Holland. A contented Stanley joined on 26th April 1939 and was made master the following day. Was his resolve being tested? His pay was to be £50 per month and by 1st July, he was granted permanency as a captain, so his pay rose to £53. He was then number 64 on the ranking list, out of a total of 79 masters.

The 4,700 dwt *Agnita*, dwt, built in 1931, was unique in that it was the first ship to be constructed specifically to carry butane and propane. Inside each of the usual port and starboard tanks was a cylindrical tank and its top was eight feet above the deck level. Because of her unusual cargoes and appearance, the pioneering *Agnita* was well known in shipping circles.

Stanley's accommodation was very comfortable and the prospect of seeing his wife every trip, in Holland or France, made him happy. Oddly, his notes did not show any

98

recognition of the prospect that these two countries might soon be engaged in deadly conflict. Before long, the ship dry-docked in Birkenhead and his wife and son joined him. After a few days, he was granted leave and "as we were crossing on the ferry, my wife suggested to Philip that he should say 'goodbye to daddy's ship.' A shrill childish voice rang out and I pretended not to hear him". There were ominous signs of impending war and it was decided that it was preferable for the family not to return to the ship.

CHAPTER 7

Another bloody war

Six days later, when the *Agnita* was well into the Atlantic, war was declared on 3rd September, two days after the Germans had invaded Poland with a force of 1,250,000 men. Neville Chamberlain, the UK Prime Minister, broadcasting to the nation, after a programme discussing recipes based on tinned food, said that he had sought an undertaking from Hitler to withdraw his troops from Poland. "I have to tell you now that no such undertaking has been received and that consequently this country is at war with Germany."

The Manchester Guardian of Monday, 4th September, conveyed the news thus:

BRITAIN AT WAR WITH GERMANY
France's Entry follows: Mr Churchill in war cabinet

Britain and France are now at war with Germany. The British ultimatum expired at 11.00 am yesterday and France entered the war six hours later, at 5.00 pm. The first announcement, that the country was at war, was made by Mr Chamberlain in a statement broadcast from Downing Street. A little later, Mr Chamberlain addressed the House of Commons where the fateful words 'the country is now at war' were heard calmly and with a notable demonstration of determination and unity.

Sir John Simon was to be Chancellor of the Exchequer, the Foreign Secretary was Lord Halifax, Lord Chatfield was Minister for The Co-ordination of Defence and Winston Churchill was to be First Lord of the Admiralty. Anthony Eden was named as Dominions Secretary. Prime Minister Neville Chamberlain, who had favoured appeasement, possibly to allow the UK to build up its arms, although he had disregarded all previous warnings, was to resign in May 1940 and he died later in that year. He was succeeded by Winston Churchill, who, over the years, had warned the country, strenuously and repeatedly, to little effect, that Germany was re-arming and that the United Kingdom should react accordingly.

Other front page headlines on that same unhappy day were:

King's call to empire, calm and unity
Germans use gas bombs in Poland: Attacks on civilians,
town set on fire
War against Hitlerism
The Commons Scene: calm, relief and unity

Many people had anticipated war, even if the country had not prepared adequately militarily. One year before Chamberlain's sombre broadcast, 38 million gas masks had been distributed to the population. Within 24 hours of the declaration of war, voluntary evacuation of children, many of whom had never seen the countryside, from the main cities began. By the end of September, about one million children and some mothers had moved to potentially less dangerous areas, including Devon. Some moved only a short way, from central London to Windsor. Later, the total rose to more than four million, although many returned, but had to move again when the blitz started.

The Channel Islands, effectively abandoned to the Germans, were occupied from July 1940. One German project on Jersey, part of the long-term plan for the island, was the military hospital which was constructed by Russian civilian slave labour. When the Germans won the war, the island was to be developed as a holiday resort and an outpost of the German empire. Over 25,000 people, about a third of the population, registered to leave the islands, just days before the Germans arrived in late June but about 11,000 actually departed. Those who remained suffered from starvation and many were deported to German concentration camps. Hundreds, some of whom had been denounced by collaborators, were murdered by the army of occupation.

On the mainland, Anderson shelters had been erected in gardens from spring 1939 and air raid sirens were tested in June. One letter to *The Times*, on the 14th began "I do desire most strongly to protest against the tone emitted from the sirens as a warning of approaching hostile aircraft....the wailing vibrations broadcast from the sirens, however, are in my opinion, dismal and distressing. I submit that, under war conditions, the morbid note of the warning siren would produce a terrifying effect and one which is likely to add to, rather than allay, any panic which might occur. As a constructive alternative, might I suggest intermittent high and low notes as the warning and a continuous medium note as the "all clear" or vice versa?"

The country, simply, was not prepared for war militarily and many of the plans, for evacuation, for example, had not been thought through adequately. However, some measures were announced immediately. After existing stocks of petrol had been sold, only one grade, pool, would be available and it would cost 1/6 per gallon. Petrol rationing persisted until 1950. Food rationing was introduced early in 1940 as German U boats threatened imports but shortages had occurred before this. In March, sugar, meat, bacon and butter were rationed, tea followed in July and, in 1941, as German U boat activity continued to threaten supplies, jam, canned foods and cheese, too, were rationed. By November 1942, the weekly meat ration was 1/2. Distribution in the 1939/1940 was rendered more difficult as the winter was the coldest for 45 years and many areas were cut off by snow. Clothes were rationed in 1941 and wartime problems inspired much innovation, as they did in prisoner-of-war camps in Germany. Campaigns of "make do and mend" and "dig for victory" were mounted.

Income tax rose from 7/6 in the pound in September 1939 to 10/- in 1941 but there was little to buy. People worked long hours and there were few labour-saving gadgets to assist in housework. Cinemas, theatres and sports grounds were closed immediately on the outbreak of war but the regulations were soon eased to bolster morale, providing some rules were observed. Similarly, the BBC, having initially confined its output to one station, added another, the Light Programme, partly to provide "competition" for the infamous Lord Haw Haw and his propaganda.

Minutes after the declaration of war, the air raid sirens moaned loudly in London and other cities but this was a false alarm, caused by a plane carrying two French officers to the UK. The contrast with the reaction of the British people at the beginning of World War One was most marked. The news was received not with enthusiasm but resignation and, unlike the early days of the previous war, there was a sense that this would be a lengthy conflict. (In August 1914, such was the enthusiasm, volunteers for the army had risen from 500 a week to 3,000 a day.) Severe restrictions on lights at night caused numerous accidents and during the first three years of the war, more UK civilians than military personnel were killed. Road deaths doubled in the first year of the war.

By the summer of 1940, despite the "phoney war", as both sides seemed reluctant to engage on land, the Germans were in Denmark, Norway, Belgium, France, Luxembourg and the Netherlands, where, later, because of the shortage of food, the inhabitants ate tulip bulbs and cats "disguised" as rabbits. The war on land might have been "phoney" but this was not true for those at sea as casualties mounted. Between September 1939 and May 1940, 286 British ships were lost: by the end of the war the total was 3,910. No less than a quarter of those men who began the war in the Merchant Navy were either killed or disabled. 32,000 Merchant Navy personnel were killed.

In June 1940 the *Agnita* was in Aruba, in the Dutch West Indies, west of Curacao. There was a large black population, many of whom had originally come from Trinidad and the other islands of the British West Indies. Seeing Stanley walking on the main street, they realised that he was British and shouted out, joyfully, the latest number of British troops saved from Dunkirk which cheered him up. Between 27th May and 4th June 1940, there was an extraordinary effort to rescue a total of some 338,000 British and French soldiers, of whom 210,000 were members of the British Expeditionary Forces. They had gone to the continent by the second week in September 1939, to be confronted by overwhelming odds and better-equipped German troops. They escaped thanks to the courageous efforts of crews, amateur and professional, in about 1,000 boats, including several hundred Royal Navy vessels. In total, about 200 craft were sunk by the Germans.

Many small boats carried the men back to the UK whilst others ferried the men to nearly 300 warships. However 30,000 of the allied forces were killed or missing, and more than 1,000 guns were abandoned on the continent, as was much other equipment. The great escape was justly described by Churchill as a miracle of deliverance for which he had dared not hope but he warned that wars were not won by spectacular retreats. Failure would probably have led to an early German invasion and defeat for Britain so Dunkirk was understandably hailed as a victory.

Italy had declared war on the United Kingdom in June 1940 but later changed sides. The Soviet Union invaded Poland in September 1939 after signing a non-aggression pact with Germany in the previous month. In 1940, Russian troops invaded Finland, then, in June 1940, without even bothering to declare war, invaded Lithuania, Latvia, Estonia and Romania. In June 1941, notwithstanding the non-aggression pact between Germany and Russia, Hitler, backed by Italy and Romania, invaded the Soviet Union with an army of 3.2 million men and some 3,300 tanks.

French resistance to the enemy was brief: the country collapsed in June 1940 and the Germans marched into an undefended Paris. France was then divided into two sections. One, effectively self-governing, in the south, was headed by a collaborator, the aged and subsequently disgraced Marshall Philippe Pétain. He was caught on the Swiss border by Free French troops in April 1945 and sentenced to death but this was subsequently commuted to life imprisonment. He died in 1951. The premier, Pierre Laval, was executed in October 1945.

In November 1942 Germany and Italy, then still part of the axis, marched their troops into Vichy France and imposed martial law across the whole country. As a minor indication of their plight, in January 1941, the French were forbidden to burn, discard or destroy certain materials, except for health reasons. They included metal scrap, old paper, feathers, rubber and hair. When the war ended, French collaborators were rounded up and with minimal ceremony or even justice, possibly 5,000 were shot and many more tarred and feathered and generally abused.

The first bombs on the UK that caused civilian casualties occurred in March 1940 but the Battle of Britain, as the enemy sought to eliminate the Royal Air Force and its facilities, began in July 1940 and by September, the valiant efforts of the RAF had forced Hitler to abandon his plans to invade England in that month. As Churchill said, "never in the field of human conflict was so much owed by so many to so few". The Luftwaffe, with some 2,600 planes, had a three to one numerical superiority over the Royal Air Force. On 15th August, the Germans flew some 1,800 sorties and this was followed by another 1,700 the following day. Both sides exaggerated their opponent's losses but it was thought that the Germans lost some 1,700 aircraft. British losses were counted in hundreds and one significant but seldom publicised fact was that some 160 damaged aircraft were being repaired every week to allow the few to continue.

Having been thwarted in his desire to eliminate the RAF, which caused his invasion plans to be frustrated, Hitler embarked on the blitz. One story was that a German bomber pilot, seeking to lighten his burden to speed the flight back to his homeland, dropped his bombs on London. This prompted an angry Churchill to order his men to bomb Berlin. Hitler, who had intended to leave London intact, for his triumphal march through the city, decided that it had to be obliterated which would also lower UK morale. Thus, in the first week of September, the blitz began over London and was sustained for another 55 nights. Between September 1940 and May 1941, many thousands of Londoners were killed and injured. The underground system was to provide nightly shelter for some 170,000 Londoners although 173 lost their lives at Bethnal Green when they fell down the escalators trying to escape from the bombs.

Many horrendous attacks were launched on other cities, night after night, through autumn and winter 1940 and into the New Year. In the spring of 1941, for example, Plymouth became the main target and raids on five successive nights resulted in 750 deaths and the destruction of the town centre and 30,000 homes. In April 1941, Plymouth was bombed on 59 occasions, resulting in the death of 1,172 civilians. Other cities, including Liverpool, Coventry, Birmingham, Bristol, Portsmouth, Glasgow and Belfast, suffered enormous loss of life and damage. *The Daily Herald* of 16th November 1940 front page was dominated by

MIDLANDS CITY IS NOW LIKE A BOMBARDED FRENCH TOWN
COVENTRY HOMELESS SLEPT BY ROADSIDE THIS MORNING

In the last nine months of the blitz, although figures are at best estimates, it seemed that nearly 44,000 civilians were killed and, according to official figures, probably too low, another 88,000 were seriously injured.

Japan's surprise attack on Pearl Harbour on 7th December 1941 and its declaration of war against the UK and US was to change the outcome of the conflict. More than 2,400 people were killed or listed as missing and seven warships were sunk or immobilised. President Franklin D. Roosevelt declared it as a "date that will live in infamy". Until then, US politicians had vowed, since the end of the First World War, not to become involved in European struggles. Roosevelt had frequently told his fellow citizens, "your boys are not going to be sent into a foreign war". In the period from 1941 to 1945, the US produced over 250,000 aircraft, nearly 90,000 tanks, 350 destroyers and 200 submarines. Their drive for material was such that a guilty motorist in San Francisco was able to surrender his bumper rather than pay a fine.

A move to the West Country

Stanley, sensing that war was approaching and fearful of bombing and possible invasion, had moved the family in 1939 from North London to St. Mawes, in Cornwall, where, ironically, the main feature was a 16th century castle, built to repel any invasion intentions from France and Spain. A few months later, the family moved to Preston, between Paignton and Torquay in Devon. Their home for the duration of the war was close to the Oldway mansion, acquired in 1872 by the Singer family, the inventors of the sewing machine. The 17 acre site was used during the war as a training school for Royal Air Force staff. The area was not immune from enemy attacks, although, of course, the loss of life and damage was absolutely minimal compared to London, Coventry and other cities. The blast from one bomb, aimed at Oldway, in 1943, blew Philip down the stairs.

During raids, the family was able to seek protection in the kitchen of their semi-detached home in a Morrison shelter, named after the Home Secretary, Herbert Morrison. These cage-like shelters, free to those earning less than £350 a year, but £7-12-6 to others, had a flat roof, made of steel plate some 0.5 inches thick. The shelters were about 2 feet nine inches high and 6 foot six inches long and the sides were of square mesh units which could be hooked on to the structure.

In 1942 the German air force, having consulted a pre-war UK travel guide, attacked many historic cities, including Exeter, some 20 miles from Torquay. Apparently, the intention was to lower UK morale because many of the targets had little or no military significance. Torquay itself was bombed occasionally and experienced hundreds of air raid warnings. Ironically, the town and the neighbouring countryside and coast might well have become a prime target for the enemy in the latter half of the war as a significant part of the allied invasion forces gathered there. Just before that historic event, a grand total of 1.5 million Americans were in the United Kingdom and many were based in south Devon.

Bombing raids over Torbay occurred about monthly, especially when enemy aircraft were disposing of bombs, originally intended for Plymouth, the most bombed city in England after 1941, before returning home. In March 1942, a German fighter was shot down on the Torquay beach but the pilot died because the barbed wire and fortifications against an invasion prevented help from reaching him in time. During 1943, Torbay was bombed 10 times. Some children who had been evacuated to the area returned home later in the war as the south west became a more frequent target. In total, during the entire war, Torbay was hit by about 1,200 bombs which killed 168 people. The worst attack occurred when a church was hit on a Sunday in May 1943, when 26 people, including a number of children, lost their lives. (See chapter 15.)

At the end of April 1944, 39 bombs were dropped on Torquay, killing 25 people, and posing the interesting question of why the Germans failed to see the men and equipment being marshalled for the invasion. Admittedly, the enemy was encouraged to think that the main invasion force would come from other locations. The UK government had located dummy tanks, landing craft, guns, gliders, aircraft and vehicles in Kent and Essex, suggesting that the landing areas might be around Calais or Boulogne. One theory was that one of Hitler's advisers gave him accurate information on the invasion plans but the information was ignored and informant executed.

CHAPTER 8

The early days of the new war

Although, given its likely routes, the *Agnita* should have been clear of the inevitable attacks by German U boats, Stanley was worried. He had been torpedoed and mined in the First World War. What would befall him in this new conflict? He suffered from claustrophobia and his biggest fear was to be captured and taken on board a submarine.

The *Agnita*, now painted dark grey, loaded at Corpus Christi in Texas and proceeded to Curacao and thence to Kingston, Jamaica after which it was ordered to Halifax in Nova Scotia for a convoy back to the UK. The harbour, full of ships, was an impressive sight. The *Agnita* was next in the line to the old Dreadnought *Resolution* and, whilst it was reassuring to see the huge ship with its 15" guns, it was obvious that it would not be a match for bigger and newer German warships. Although the *Agnita* personnel were handicapped because of their lack of numbers, the Commodore later congratulated them on their signalling and station-keeping.

Having discharged the cargo, the ship moved to Cardiff to be fitted with guns. Pill Boxes of steel, nearly an inch thick with a narrow slit for visibility, were built on each side of the bridge. The starboard pill box housed a steering wheel which could be made effective in a few seconds and a telephone which enabled communication with the engine room, radio room and the two gun platforms. One was a 4.7" 1916 gun, for anti-submarine fire. In that conflict, as a teenager, Stanley had worked with this weapon, being responsible for range and deflection. The other gun was an obsolete 12 pounder, which could be elevated to a high angle for anti-aircraft fire. "I looked at them and wondered!" The vessel also carried steel helmets, gas masks, naval signalling equipment, and six .303 rifles. The chief officer was unimpressed. He felt that both guns were restricted in their arc of fire, especially by the funnel and mainmast.

The Chinese crew offered to assist with the guns. The navy had appointed a retired colour sergeant of the Royal Marines to sail on the *Agnita,* to be in charge of the guns and training the crews. Two sailors augmented the gun crews as the small tanker had insufficient men available and was not carrying any apprentices. An ammunition locker was built into the poop, below the guns, so Chinese volunteers were organised to pass the shells from man to man along the alleyway and up the stairs to whichever gun needed the ammunition.

Several wives were on board and, wisely, it was decided to have an early Christmas party. For some of the crew it would be their last party for many years. The *Agnita* sailed from Cardiff on 16th December, without any lights, for Rotterdam to load sulphuric acid for Curacao. Stanley was apprehensive about Rotterdam as it was close to Germany, vulnerable to possible attacks from E boats and, although the gun crews had been trained, they had not had time to become proficient.

On Sunday, 17th December 1939, 15 weeks after the United Kingdom had declared war on Germany, the *Agnita* was some 10 miles south of Hastings, steaming eastwards towards Beachy Head. The weather was overcast, with low clouds and moderate visibility. "I had ordered a gun drill to take place at 4.30 pm and I went on to the bridge soon after 4.00. I was told that the second officer had seen a strange aircraft with black crosses on its wings and sides. He had not realised that it was a German Heinkel 111 bomber!

"The radio officer then reported that a British ship, the *Sultan Star* had been bombed and machine gunned off Dungeness just a few minutes flying time from us. It was now 4.25 pm, the gun crews were in position and the chief officer and I were on the bridge. I was looking aft when I saw the bomber approaching out of the clouds astern of us and the gun crews saw it too. I started to swing the vessel to port as hard as it would go as the plane became ever closer. When it was almost overhead, some 50 feet above us, the gun crew opened fire with one shell and, although it missed the target, it must have shaken the pilot because, by the time that he released the bomb, we were swinging quickly and the bomb missed us although it was close enough to shake the ship violently. The plane disappeared into the clouds but I thought it would return.

"The chief officer and I half-dragged the old Chinese quartermaster, who seemed almost paralysed with fear, from the wheel into the Pill Box and opened the valve to allow us to steer from that box. The plane approached us from ahead and again I swung the ship but this time I saw the bomb dropping but it was further away than the first time. As the bomber flew over us, he raked the vessel with machine gun fire and I feared for the gun crews but they fired another shell. The bomber disappeared astern but came back yet again. The pilot must have been inexperienced because we were only doing ten knots at most and he was barely 50 feet over head yet he missed us for the third time. As soon as the plane disappeared ahead of us, I altered course to be closer to some neutral ships that were showing all their lights.

"When it seemed as if the bomber had definitely gone, we took stock. The first bomb had fractured pipes in the engine room and steam and water were escaping. The chief engineer thought that if we stopped, the engines probably would not start again so we reduced speed and turned around to go to Southampton. The guns were prepared for renewed action and we distributed brandy. There were many machine gun bullet

112

marks on the deck and when the second officer returned to his room, he found that one bullet had pierced the deck and was embedded in his desk. It required little imagination to realise what would have happened had he been sitting there." For Stanley and his crew, the war was already anything but phoney.

"This was the first unrestricted air attack of the war on a British tanker and we were met at Southampton by officers from the Royal Navy and Royal Air Force. The RAF man told me that if they had received our radio calls, their fighters would have been overhead in minutes, but, of course, our call was not received as the first bomb had destroyed part of the equipment. The Navy, represented by a Rear Admiral and a Lieutenant, asked many questions and seemed to approve the action I had taken. A few months later, we learned that our Royal Marine Colour Sergeant had been awarded the British Empire Medal and I received a letter from the managing director of Shell granting all the staff one month's payment. I was complimented for 'the excellent way in which you handled your ship when attacked by aircraft'". Stanley received £53 (£2,000) and modestly described the attack as "a mild affair".

"At Southampton, all except one of the Chinese crew, and one junior engineer insisted on leaving the ship. After the first explosion, the Chinese ammunition party, who had volunteered their assistance, had deserted their posts and had gathered in the alleyway below deck with their suitcases packed. Fortunately, there were several shells in racks near the gun which had enabled a reply to be made against the bomber."

Engine repairs were expected to take about 10 days and Maidie visited the ship at Southampton. Stanley was granted a few days leave so was able to have Christmas 1939 at home, which was now the cottage, rented for six months, in St. Mawes. It was high above the harbour and "as I left in the ferry for Falmouth, to rejoin the war, I could see my wife, with our son in her arms, both waving good bye. Would I ever see them again? I had been involved in the First War and I did not anticipate that this would be any less deadly." This was the last time that Stanley was to see his wife and son for nearly five years, during which time his very life was in jeopardy, as it was for millions of innocent military personnel and civilians.

In early January 1940, some five months before Holland was invaded by the Germans, the *Agnita* sailed for Rotterdam where the neutral Dutch Navy took away the breechblocks of its guns. "They were carrying out their instructions and presumably obeying international law but I resented this and requested that the breechblocks be returned as soon as possible. I had told the staff not to mention the attack by the German bomber but, within 24 hours, there was an account of the incident in the local paper. I thought that it would attract the attention of the enemy but, of course, they would have known what was happening in Rotterdam."

"We loaded a cargo of sulphuric acid from barges. I knew that it was a dangerous commodity and could erode metal quickly. Apparently it was safe to carry it in our steel tanks as long as it was 93 per cent or more pure. Mixed with water, it became sulphuric acid which could burn and emit a poisonous gas. So, if we were torpedoed, in addition to the hazard of the explosion, and drowning, we could have been burned, poisoned or gassed! Breechblocks returned, we cleared Rotterdam and the North Sea Canal but I did not appreciate a Dutch naval patrol boat turning its spotlight on us and on our funnel. We sailed to the Isle of Wight and subsequently joined a convoy but, once we were well into the Atlantic, the convoy disappeared and we were alone, as we were to be for the rest of our time."

For the next few months, the *Agnita* sailed between Curacao or Caripito in Venezuela to Dakar with occasional calls to Aruba. Dakar was quiet but had few facilities and the so-called night spots lacked appeal but champagne was cheap so the chief officer and Stanley shared the occasional bottle in mutual commiseration. Caripito, dominated by just two wharves and about 20 miles up the river, was a poor place. A

Venezuelan pilot took the *Agnita* up and down the river and he left near Guira, in the Gulf of Paria, opposite Port of Spain. "On this occasion, I was too close inshore and put the ship aground. The British Admiralty charts erroneously indicated that there was sufficient depth of water. After a few hours, we were towed into deep water by another tanker but there was no damage to our ship as the sea bottom was sand and mud."

The news from the war was not good and Stanley, like all those risking their lives at sea, was increasingly concerned by reports of enemy air attacks on the UK, especially as Maidie was expecting their second child in September 1940. France had capitulated in June 1940, so Dakar became enemy territory and was replaced as the discharge port by Freetown in Sierra Leone. The vessel was to be fitted with anti-magnetic devices which involved a system of wires completely encircling the ship, outside the hull. This work took 10 days and whilst it was being carried out, as there was nothing to do, the men of the *Agnita* relaxed in the pleasant and easy-going Port of Spain. The agent took Stanley to the occasional lunch, followed by a drive into the country or a swim on a lovely and deserted beach. "The tropical vegetation, the flagrant flowers and shrubs and the fruit provided a riot of colour. The small children in the villages seemed fat and happy and the people were smiling and friendly. The war seemed so far away."

The stay coincided with the annual carnival. The streets were thronged with men, women and children in fancy dress of fantastic designs, colours and gaiety enjoying the music of the steel bands, and dancing in the streets. "I marvelled at their stamina and envied them their happiness and wished that sanity would soon return to this world." The day before the *Agnita* sailed, Stanley visited an agricultural show and admired the massive cattle, the huge yams and other fruits and vegetables that were new to him. "I felt depressed because there was so much bombing at home in the UK and in Europe and I sensed that I would not see Port of Spain again for a long time. I was also worried about the imminent arrival of our second child so was greatly relieved to have a message from the company that I had had a second son on 20th September

1940. Inevitably, the question was when shall I see him?" Perhaps it was fortunate that he did not know the answer.

In November 1940, the *Agnita* went to New York for drydocking and repairs. Stanley, already depressed that the war was going badly, saw a film on Broadway which contained scenes of London being bombed. The audience seemed stunned. "I was filled with compassion for our people and an impotent rage against the criminals responsible. I resented the easy times that the Americans were having and my unspoken thought was 'get a move on' which, to be fair, was what they were doing." The US entered the conflict one year later, in December 1941, after the disaster of Pearl Harbour.

When in New York, some of the Chinese crew eluded the guard on the ship and the escort whilst ashore. One was caught and the agent told Stanley that the police were holding the deserter and they had to collect him. "At about 7.00 am one morning, the agent and I were shown into a large bleak room, the walls of which were painted a shabby green. The furniture consisted of a desk and a few chairs. The floor was bare. In one chair, with his feet on the desk, was a grimy, unshaven fat policeman with an enormous revolver strapped to his waist. He eyed me without any enthusiasm or warmth and I began to feel that I was the suspect in a fifth-rate gangster film. In a flat expressionless voice, he implied that his sympathies were with the Chinaman, who had falsely claimed that I had given him no money and that he was denied shore leave. I was able to prove that he had received an advance and I explained that he could not leave the vessel and go home until we had either returned to England or he had completed his contract."

"Do you mean that he has to stay on the ship for three years?"

"Yes."

"That seems unfair to me."

"That's the way we conduct our business. A signed agreement should be honoured."

"Presumably satisfied, the policeman said that the Chinaman was on Ellis Island awaiting collection." We entered the impressive building and looked down from a balcony on to an extraordinarily large hall. The agent and I saw groups of bewildered looking immigrants, with their pathetic little bundles, waiting to be interrogated. Eventually, we found the right office and again detected hostility towards us. Curtly, we were told that the police had already taken the hapless Chinese back to our ship and we would find him there."

Stanley was fearful of a mass desertion of the surly and argumentative Chinese crew, who had friends in New York, so arranged with the authorities to sail one day earlier, which information was not conveyed to the potential dissidents. He then anchored off Staten Island for the completion of the necessary formalities before resuming the voyages between the West Indies and Freetown in Sierra Leone.

By now, Stanley had served over 18 months so wrote to Head Office requesting leave, especially as he had a new son whom he had not yet seen. He was told that he could take his furlough if, when next visiting Curacao, he could find a captain keen to relieve him. Eventually, he was successful. Excited and confident, Stanley was told by London to go ahead but subsequently, the other master changed his mind. "For a few moments, my world fell about my head." This decision was to influence Stanley's entire life as subsequent efforts to find a replacement failed. Apparently, captains preferred to take gasoline to the UK, with all its risks but with the prospect of some days at home, rather than being confined to a ship running between the West Indies and West Africa.

CHAPTER 9

Captured

Stanley sensed that the quiet times were ending. At Christmas 1940, as the *Agnita* approached Freetown in West Africa, news was received that ships were being sunk by submarines to the north of his tanker's route. One vessel had been sunk, to the north of the *Agnita,* by a submarine the position of which was broadcast. Stanley's calculations suggested that the submarine could be close to the *Agnita*'s position at dawn the following day but fortunately nothing happened.

"As we sailed from Freetown, we heard that ships were being sunk south of us so they must have crossed our track while we were in Freetown. Occasionally, the Germans or French sent planes from Dakar which flew over Freetown so the Germans knew what was happening. By attacking tankers delivering bunkers to the ships in Freetown they could, if successful, immobilise the vessels waiting for fuel to allow them to reach home. With so much enemy activity west of Freetown, it was surely only a matter of time before we were caught which was why I was so disappointed when we were ordered back to Freetown. Before leaving that port, every master had to report on board the depot ship, the *Edinburgh* Castle, for sailing orders and instructions." The elderly naval officer told Stanley how he envied those who were at sea!

"On 22nd March 1941, some three days and about 700 miles west of Freetown, we were en route, in ballast, for the Venezuelan port of Caripito. The third officer reported a ship sighted right ahead. I saw that it was obviously going south. As our radio needed time to warm up, I had instructed that, whenever another vessel was sighted, the radio officer was to be warned so that he could warm it up ready for transmission if necessary. I told the third officer that the vessel was bound south, possibly to the Plate, but to tell Sparks to switch on and I retreated to have breakfast, having told the officer to let me know if the vessel behaved suspiciously.

"As I sat down, the alarm, a succession of short blasts on the ship's whistle, sounded. I dashed to the bridge and saw the ship heading straight for us. I said, tell sparks to send the message, 'enemy raider,' which would give our position and that we were being attacked by a raider. By this time, the alien vessel, in only a few minutes, had hoisted the German flag, dropped its false sides, revealing its guns, and hoisted a two flag signal which we all knew meant 'stop.' As the raider could move twice as fast as our ten knots, I stopped the ship. Our wireless room was aft but some months before, I had told the carpenter to construct a dummy Bradfield on the bridge. This was a wooden or metal structure about eight feet high which received the wires from the aerial and led them down into the radio room. My intention had been to draw away any enemy fire from the real radio room to the dummy. Briefly, I wondered if my idea had been so clever after all. I expected the Germans could hear our messages going out and I thought that we would soon see shells directed to the bridge.

"The raider was now flashing with his lamp, 'stop transmitting.' We hoisted the 'answering pennant' flag which indicated we could not understand his signal. I told the chief officer to phone sparks and ask him if he had been able to send the raider message. He had, six times, and I ordered him to stop transmitting as the raider, now close, was pointing all his guns at us. To avoid any misunderstanding, I sent the chief officer aft to the crew manning our 4.7 inch gun on the poop, to order them NOT to fire and to get away from the gun. I felt proud of that gun's crew. They were standing by the gun and if I had ordered them to fire, they would have done so, firing one shell before being slaughtered and we all would have been the victims. As I still suspected that the raider might open fire on us, I gave the order to 'abandon ship', which, to my relief, was done in an orderly manner without any mishap. I told the officers to pull away clear of our ship and then to wait. The chief officer shook my hand as he left. Who knew what was going to happen?" The decision not to defend his vessel against absurdly superior odds provoked this unsolicited comment in September 1979, from an old colleague. "I have, and never have had, any doubts that I and the rest of the crew of the *Agnita* owe our lives to your intelligent decision."

Stanley's narrative continues. "I dumped the secret papers in the weighted box and, sombrely watched it sink as the motor boat from the raider approached from the other side. I watched the German sailors clambering on board with their coal scuttle steel helmets, grey uniforms and potato mash grenades, carrying revolvers. I felt that it must all be a nightmare and I would soon wake up. I did when I was brusquely ordered down into the motor boat to be taken to the raider. When onboard, the German captain questioned me and I told the truth or lied as appropriate. I was then taken back to the *Agnita* and told to pack a few clothes and possessions and to be quick about it. Hurriedly, I filled a suitcase with clothes that were handy, my copies of Shakespeare and Palgrave's *Golden Treasury* and then I went into the chief officer's room and filled a pillow case with his clothes.

"A German sailor asked to be taken to the rope store. As we entered the gloomy centre castle, he pulled out a large revolver and kept it at my back. I was too angry to be scared: a few minutes before, it had been my ship and now I was being pushed around at gun point. I hoped that his trigger finger was steady. I was childishly pleased to find that all the storerooms were locked and I told him that the keys were with the Chinese storekeeper, not mentioning that a duplicate set was in the chief officer's room. The German boarding party had laid explosive charges in the engine room and I was ordered back into the boat. The officer in charge lit the fuse and the spark started to travel up the ship's side and along the deck towards the engine room. Oddly, only then did the officer start to count his men."

"On boarding the raider, I was hustled below but I managed to glance at the *Agnita*. She lay, deserted, rolling in the swell. I recalled the 90,000 miles we had sailed together in peace and war, the happy times that my wife and I had had on board, and my small son pedalling his tiny tricycle around the lower bridge. Now the ship lay helpless and soon would be sunk. I was ordered down below but I don't think that I could have watched, even if permitted. The crew, 37 strong, were pleased to see me and a few minutes later we heard the muffled sounds of the explosion on the *Agnita* and then shellfire as the original explosives in the engine room had been insufficient to sink her. We were all very quiet. I think we realised that it could have ended so differently, with some of us perishing with the ship."

"We were taken down forward in the bows, one deck below the main deck. The Chinese crew were put in the next deck below us. There was sufficient space and it was clean but there were no port holes so we had to rely on artificial light. We were allocated hammocks and shut in by a locked steel door. An armed sentry was posted outside. Given time to think, I wondered if I could have done anything differently. Our orders had been to scuttle the ship if loaded with oil, to deny access to the Germans, or, if the ship was not loaded, we should not scuttle it as there was a chance that our navy might recapture it. Later, I heard that the Germans had taken a fully-loaded tanker into a French port.

At first, everyone from the *Agnita* was stunned by the change in our circumstances but glad to be alive. The Germans had previously captured a British ship, loaded with frozen and tinned meat, homeward bound from Buenos Aires, so captors and captives received plenty of meat but the bread and coffee was horrible ersatz stuff but, as we were to discover, this was to be our staple fare. However, at this point, what exercised us was when would our next of kin find out our fate?" Indeed, many months were to pass before his stricken wife knew whether he was alive or dead.

The next day there was an alarm, indicated by ringing bells, and the prisoners could hear the ammunition hoists. They were living above the ammunition stores. Fortunately, this was only a practice drill but Stanley was disturbed to hear the steel door, which separated them from the rest of the ship, being locked. The next day, a friendly lieutenant visited the crew and Stanley said that the prisoners had heard the steel door being locked and suggested that if real action occurred, perhaps the door could be unlocked so that the prisoners might have a chance of surviving if the ship were sunk. The German lied that they always had a sentry and the door was not locked. Stanley persisted. "What if the sentry were killed or left his post?" There was no response but it was clear that the door was locked when the raider captured a Canadian ship, the *Canadalite,* a few days after this exchange.

Stanley subsequently wondered why the raider had not fired on the *Agnita* when they were transmitting "enemy raider signals" in the early stages of the incident. Why had the Germans allowed all 38 personnel to escape, safely? The visiting lieutenant subsequently told him that the tanker's signals were too weak to reach any distance, so, presumably, the enemy did not expect retaliation from any other sources and had decided against wasting ammunition on the tanker as a surrender had been secured very early in the incident. Charitably, Stanley wondered if the German commander, Theodor Detmers, was in a good mood on the fateful day. Months later, in the POW camp, survivors from an unarmed Yugoslav ship, the *Vaebit,* told Stanley that Detmers had slaughtered all but six members of the crew.

Some self-serving German fiction?

One version of the incident, attributed to Theodor Detmers, some years after the war, challenges Stanley's account. Detmers said that he soon realised that the *Agnita* was a

122

tanker. He claimed that there was fog, not even mentioned in Stanley's account, but, presumably, even restricted visibility allowed him to discern the shape of the tanker. Nevertheless, he could only determine whether it was an enemy or neutral ship when the fog cleared 15 minutes later. A canon mounted on the bridge was sufficient to identify an enemy even if, according to Detmers, it was not showing any flag.

The German account claims that, presumably when it was realised that the vessel was a tanker, the *Agnita* was challenged to identify itself, the response came back "immediately". The claim that Stanley reacted immediately, in the fog, to a vessel that he could not see clearly, with the message, "*Agnita,* en route from Freetown to Caripito in Venezuela" is absurd. The British 3rd officer had earlier noted the presence of a vessel, despite the "German fog" and this prompted a suspicious Stanley to tell the radio officer to warm up his equipment lest a message had to be sent. He knew that there were enemy vessels in the area and expected to be caught. He was aware that the Germans, like the allies, occasionally disguised their vessels so he would have been suspicious and would not have sent any messages until he was satisfied that the recipients were genuine.

Detmers assumed that sending this message implied that the British captain believed that he was responding to another allied vessel, possibly a freighter. Such a message was doubtless sent, later, when Stanley was able to see the alien vessel, albeit still disguised, but the assertion that the message was sent immediately casts doubts on other German claims.

The German commander says that, when the *Agnita* details were transmitted, he then ordered the raider's disguise to be removed, the German flag hoisted and the *Agnita* was ordered to stop sending wireless messages. Stanley's account made no mention of sending any messages apart from the crucial one "enemy raider". At this time, presumably in improved visibility, the enemy vessel was heading straight for the British tanker and Stanley contends that, as the raider was obviously faster and better armed, he ordered that the *Agnita* should stop.

123

An instruction from the Germans to cease transmitting prompted Stanley to signal that he did not understand the message, which must have allowed him to repeat the potentially crucial "enemy raider" message. At this time, all the enemy guns were pointing at the tanker which must have influenced Stanley's thinking.

Detmers argued that, initially, the tanker seemed acquiescent but then sought to escape. Would this have been attempted with all the enemy guns pointing at the tanker? Allegedly, black smoke belched forth as the engines were "revved up" and radio messages were sent out as if the tanker were already under attack. Detmers ordered the gun crew to commence firing as soon as the tanker made a first change in direction. According to the German version, a few grenades exploded on the engine room level, implying that the tanker did indeed, change course. "These well-aimed salvoes were sufficient to bring the conscientious captain of the tanker to his senses."

A number of contemporary marine engineering experts, familiar with the technology of vessels built in the Thirties, say that, shutting down the engines under the circumstances described could almost certainly cause black smoke to be emitted. In this case, Detmers may have believed that the *Agnita's* tactics were changed, even if, ironically, such action had been taken to show the Germans that total surrender was being implemented. Did Detmers really believe that an escape was being attempted, although in this situation, the vessel would neither have changed direction nor moved its position? Although the timing of each event within the incident is unknown, it is probable that at least most of the crew had long since been ordered to abandon ship as Stanley knew that this was his only hope for saving lives.

Many aspects of the German account are difficult to credit. At an early stage, Stanley ordered the radio officer to cease transmitting, the gun crews not to open fire and for everyone to abandon ship, specifically to persuade the Germans not to fire. The enemy version suggests that a change in tactics was implemented and, of course, Stanley would have known that this would have provoked instant and deadly retaliation. Why would he have reversed his position and tried to escape, knowing that death was the only outcome?

The *Agnita* was a small vessel with a small engine room. It is likely that a few explosions in the engine room, which Detmers said had caused sufficient damage to justify not taking it to an axis port, would have caused some casualties, even if most of the crew had already began to abandon ship. If men were taking to the lifeboats that would have been very visible and, if the engine room was staffed, some casualties must have occurred.

Stanley made no reference to any casualties, even when he records rejoining his colleagues on Detmer's *Kormoran*. His concern for the ultimate fate of the Chinese crew, when he was himself in a prisoner-of-war camp, prompted him to press the German authorities and the Swiss, the protecting power, for information. It is impossible that, in his report of the encounter, he forgot that someone had been injured. If Stanley had expected to be shelled, is it likely that his detailed account would not have mentioned that this was precisely what happened, despite his sensible tactics?

Allegedly, at this time, the German radio operators were trying to disrupt the *Agnita*'s "loud signals" on the same wavelength. This is odd. The German lieutenant who questioned Stanley shortly after his capture told him that they were not worried as the tanker's signals were too weak to reach any distance. Why did the commander and the lieutenant have totally different opinions on the signals being sent by the distressed tanker?

The German version then claimed that Stanley brought the tanker to a stop, after the apparent effort to escape, ceased sending out radio messages and lowered the boats into the water. The German investigation team boarded the *Agnita* and sent back the details to the raider. Detmers argued that, "this little vessel of 3,561 dwt" belonging to the Anglo-Saxon

Petroleum Company "carried fairly strong weaponry but did not try to defend itself". Does this also imply that it did not try to escape? Surely, if the *Agnita* was trying to escape, it would have used some of its "fairly strong weaponry" to buy a few more minutes of active life?

This claim about, "fairly strong weaponry," seems bizarre. What was it? The tanker carried a 4.7" 1916 anti-submarine gun and an obsolete 12 pounder that could be elevated to a high angle for anti-aircraft fire! In the opinion of the *Agnita*'s chief officer, the guns were restricted in their arc of fire because of the position of the funnel and mainmast and that this "fairly strong weaponry" might have been successful in the battle of Trafalgar over 130 years before.

Because the tanker had been damaged by German fire and was "extremely small", Detmers decided to sink it. The crew, 13 Englishmen and 25 Chinese crew were evacuated on two boats. In Detmers' account there is no mention of any injuries. Then explosives were placed on the tanker but, ten minutes later, as the detonations were made, after the smoke had cleared, the tanker remained afloat as if nothing had happened. The vessel's design, to allow it to carry liquefied petroleum gas, had thwarted the enemy. "A series of shots, fired at the water line, also failed to bring the ship closer to its end. With heavy heart, I was compelled to sacrifice one of my precious torpedoes. It seemed too risky to allow the ship just to float there as it could have been towed away if found." This was the decisive factor and eventually the *Agnita* was sunk.

Stanley would not have expected anyone else to read his notes on the encounter, written in a POW camp. His account makes it clear that he never had any intention of escaping or firing on the raider. He also frequently questioned himself on whether he could have taken any other course of action, other than surrendering immediately, to save loss of life. If he had tried to escape and failed, as he knew would have happened, he and his colleagues would have all been killed. Why should he have described the action so inaccurately to his diary if it was all fiction?

Another mystery is why Detmers decided to sink the tanker, using in the process, as he ruefully admits, one of his precious torpedoes, although he could not have imagined that this would have been necessary. Although the *Agnita* was travelling in ballast, would it not have been a valuable prize? He decided that it was sufficiently important to sink it, rather than to leave it wallowing in the ocean, possibly to be recaptured by the allies, so why did he fire at the engine room when it must have been obvious, early in the encounter, that the tanker could neither escape nor wish to? Was the damage to the *Agnita's* engine room so severe that it was not worthwhile capturing the tanker? That was Detmers' reason for sinking it but it seems inconceivable that the *Agnita* might have been severely damaged and that Stanley omitted any such comment in his notes, not least when he was allowed to return to the vessel to collect a few personal belongings which must have been after the "attempted escape" and just before explosive charges were placed in the engine room.

Did Detmers want to capture the tanker and tow it to an enemy port? Was that why one of his men asked Stanley, in vain, for rope? Was he more interested in hunting and destroying other allied vessels? If he was to remain a lively predator, he had to sink the *Agnita* so had to devise a story that it had been necessary to shell the engine room which made towing the stricken vessel to port an undesirable option.

The German commander also claimed that his boarding party found a chart of Freetown harbour showing the location of the mine fields. Stanley noted that one of his first actions when confronted by the raider was to take secret documents, put them in a weighted box and consign it to the deep on the side of the vessel away from the raider. Would he have left a genuine map of the minefields in his office for the raiding party to find, not least as Stanley had decided, at an early stage, to surrender. Why, if the enemy found such a chart, was Stanley questioned at length on the subject? The friendly German lieutenant, who visited the British prisoners on the *Kormoran* daily, wanted to know as much as possible about

Freetown. If the Germans had discovered a map of the minefields were they trying to establish its authenticity? Stanley had become angry and said "why don't you go and see for yourself? He flushed and told me that there was 'no need to talk like that' and left."

Furthermore, although details are unclear, it seems as if the Germans allowed themselves little time before trying to sink the *Agnita* and Stanley makes no reference to visiting his office again, when under guard by the Germans, although he does mention that he went to the chief engineer's room to pack some clothes for him.

If the enemy version of the capture is correct, it suggests that Stanley had no influence on the outcome of the confrontation but that is hard to reconcile with his detailed account. Finally, how can the German version be accepted in the light of the unsolicited comment of the senior colleague, many years later, who told Stanley, that his intelligent decision had undoubtedly saved all their lives? To have attempted an escape, as alleged by Detmers, would have led to slaughter and Stanley knew that. The German commander was later described by a war historian as a master of deception. The whole truth will never be known but Stanley's more immediate version was free of any intention to bolster his status or morale. He was concerned with saving lives.

The first few days of captivity and the *Kormoran*'s subsequent progress

A few days after the *Agnita* was sunk, the German warship captured the *Canadalite* and, with a prize crew, took the ship to Bordeaux. Later, the *Kormoran,* doubtless aided by its disguise and false flag, won encounters with eight other allied vessels and all apart from the *Canadalite* were sunk. Her captain, chief engineer, radio officer and a Canadian gunner joined Stanley and his colleagues.

Much later, when in the prisoner-of-war camp, Stanley discovered that the vessel that had captured them, the

Stanley at Scout Camp

Young Stanley Boy Scout

Stanley, Boy Scout

Aged 16 in 1916

Hong Kong April 1923

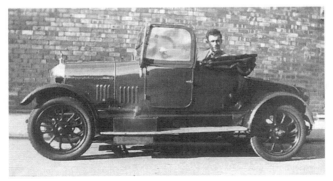

Stanley in his Morris 1929

Stanley and Maidie's Wedding Day July 1932

Trigonia, North Atlantic December 1932

Sepia, San Francisco 1937

Elax, Suez 1938

Caprinus

Agnita, Dakar 1940

Agnita, North Atlantic January 1940

Agnita

TELEGRAPHIC ADDRESS:
ANGSAXPET, LONDON.

ALL CODES USED

TELEPHONE Nº AVENUE 4321.
TELEX Nº AVENUE TELEX 2312 & 2313.

THE ANGLO-SAXON PETROLEUM COMPANY, LIMITED.

MG.

ST HELEN'S COURT, LEADENHALL STREET,
LONDON, E.C.3.

IN REPLY
PLEASE REFER TO "M"/J.W.W.

11th October, 1940.

Captain S. Algar,
    m.v. "AGNITA".

Dear Captain Algar,

      We would refer further to the attack by enemy
aircraft on your vessel in December last, and when despite
the persistence of the raider the "AGNITA" was well defended
and brought safely to port.

      Our Directors have given consideration to the
excellent manner in which you handled your ship on that
occasion, and in expressing the Company's appreciation, we
have pleasure in advising you that it has been decided to
grant you a bonus equivalent to one month's pay, i.e. £53,
in recognition of your valiant effort. This amount is
being placed to your credit in the Provident Fund.

      You will also be pleased to hear that a gratuity
equivalent to one month's wages is being granted in a similar
manner to other members of your vessel's staff on that occasion.

          Yours truly,

        For and on behalf of:
    THE ANGLO-SAXON PETROLEUM CO. LTD.

Tower in POW Camp

Barrack Room for Captains in POW Camp

Fellow Prisoners June 1942

At work on the Trigonosemus 1949

Kormoran, had been called the *Steiemark* between its launch in September 1938 and 1940 before being assigned to the navy. It was a formidable ship of nearly 9,000 tons and had been taken over by the German Navy when on the building stocks and completed as an auxiliary cruiser. It was armed with six 6" guns, two 8" guns midships, torpedo tubes, pompom guns and machine guns and could carry 200 mines. It moved at 18-19 knots. In everything except armour, it was a regular warship, length 164 metres, and carried a crew of between 350 and 400 men. It frequently flew a non-German flag and was disguised as a merchant vessel, often Dutch or Russian, until it was ready to attack. Between January and November 1941, it sank 10 ships with a total tonnage of around 75,000 tons. A week after the *Agnita* had succumbed, the *Kormoran* stopped in the South Atlantic to bunker several submarines and to supply them with torpedoes.

In November 1941, after suffering severe damage after a major clash with the Australian vessel, the *Sydney*, the *Kormoran*, initially disguised as a Dutch freighter, possibly the *Straat Malakka*, was apparently scuttled. (One problem for the German commander was that he did not know the necessary codes.) This occurred after a three hour battle and 60 Germans were lost, 40 of whom were drowned when a lifeboat overturned. Apparently, the German commander had anticipated that its Australian adversary had summoned aid and that it was preferable to sink the raider as its engine room was severely damaged, before it had to face superior odds. In fact, no assistance had been summoned by the Australians.

The *Kormoran* had been engaged in a serious battle but it was a pyrrhic victory for the allies who not only lost the vessel but 645 men in the worst naval disaster in Australian history. Some 320 of the German crew were picked up by a British tanker, the *Trocas,* and taken into custody in Australian prisoner-of-war camps. Their number included the commander, Theodor Detmers who, with colleagues, was adrift in a lifeboat for several days. He was only released in January 1947, some 18 months after Stanley had been freed. Whilst in the camp, Detmers wrote a history of the *Sydney* confrontation, tried to escape and had a heart attack. He was unable to return to the sea and died in Hamburg in November 1976, aged 74.

In March 2008, the wreck of the *Kormoran* was found some 120 miles north of Sharks' Bay, on the west coast of Australia, at a depth of some 8,400 feet. The remains of the German vessel were in two large pieces some 3,900 feet apart, and it seems that an explosion aft detonated a cache of about 320 mines on board the ship. The *Sydney* was discovered about 12 miles away. This undermines an earlier theory, possibly based on Detmer's notes, that the *Kormoran* blew up much later when a mine exploded as the vessel was in pursuit of other shipping, some distance away. However, details of the *Sydney-Kormoran* clash, especially on the timing of the battle, are mired in confusion and doubt, some of which originates from a document found on Detmers when he and 19 other Germans tried to escape from their prison camp in January 1945. The truth will never be known.

To the prison camp

Back on the *Kormoran*, the allied prisoners had to listen to martial music, usually accompanied by the sound of stamping jackbooted feet. One of the favourite pieces was called "sailing against Britain". The prisoners howled an obscenity at one point in the repeated chorus, implying that they did not endorse the overall sentiments. "It was childish, but it made us feel a bit better." On one occasion, the Germans broadcast the latest news and details of the numbers of ships sunk and their tonnages. The information was probably exaggerated but the depressed captives knew that there was some truth in the statistics.

Once, the loudspeaker was playing a female singing "One fine day" from Madam Butterfly. It reminded a very emotional Stanley of a visit to the opera with his wife, prompting the question of whether he would ever see her again or his two sons. Later, whenever he heard that song, he was reminded of the prison ship and some of the most miserable and bleakest days of his life. In the years of captivity, music was to trigger powerful recollections and memories.

Many of the *Kormoran's* crew were young enthusiastic Nazis and, at that stage in the war, nothing had happened to challenge their belief that they were members of the master race. In Stanley's experience, it was only the middle-aged and elderly in Hitler's Germany who showed any small acts of kindness or consideration. After about two weeks on the *Kormoran*, the *Agnita* crew was transferred to a 3,000 ton tanker, the *Rudolph Albrecht*, which fuelled the raider. The British crew stayed on this vessel for a month. When on board the raider, Stanley felt that there would have been little chance of survival if it had been attacked by a British cruiser. She would have sunk, as she eventually was, and all personnel on board would have perished. The new prison ship, too, would not have lasted long if hit by a torpedo or a few shells.

"We were directed to the fore hold where rough wooden bunks had been erected. To keep us confined to our quarters, they had constructed stout wooden fences, interlaced with iron rods. Above the fence was the open hatch and daylight. If the vessel had been attacked, the only hope would have been to break out of the quarters and to try to reach the deck. Potentially weak links in the fence were noted."

The German captain visited the prisoners on their first and last days on his vessel and the chief officer, a sour and unfriendly man, saw the prisoners occasionally. The second officer, seemingly involved in liaison, asked the prisoners every day if anything was needed. He did what he could and was free of the usual Nazi arrogance. Bizarrely, when he was an assistant marine superintendent, Stanley met this man again, after the war. The German was the chief officer of one of the vessels owned by Stanley's employers. There was no embarrassment.

A corporal and two young sailors were the guards. The corporal, who was friendly, had seen action against the Royal Navy at Narvik and had a healthy respect for his enemies. The two young guards were Nazis who maintained that Germany would never be bombed. "What a shock they must have had before hostilities ceased, if, indeed, they had survived."

Because the prison ship's wooden bunks were new, it was assumed that the vessel had only recently left Tenerife in the Canary Islands. One prisoner found an onion behind a plank which inspired a fruitless search for more food. Sometimes, the tanker stopped for hours, which, according to the friendly corporal, was to allow allied convoys or naval ships to pass clear of the prison ship. The British and Chinese captives wanted to be detected by the British navy although they might well have lost their lives, as happened to some British personnel when their prison ships were attacked by UK submarines. Life on the *Rudolph Albrecht* was easier than the *Kormoran* in that the latter was under strict naval discipline, liable at any moment to be involved in action whilst the prisoners were locked in their steel cell.

CHAPTER 10

The prisoners reach Bordeaux
and go to Sandbostel

The British prisoners arrived in Bordeaux in Vichy-controlled (anti-allied) France on 3rd May 1941. Five months later, 100 French local citizens were shot there by the Germans as a reprisal for the French Resistance movement killing two Germans. Fortunately, Stanley did not know that it would be more than 200 weeks before he was to see England again. "We were all pushed into a bus and taken to a prison camp outside Bordeaux. We had to stop several times in the town, because of the traffic, and occasionally, when the French people realised we were prisoners, they waved and some of the middle-aged women had tears in their eyes. We arrived at our destination in late afternoon and were surprised to be put in a military camp occupied by Algerian troops. They made us welcome but we wanted to be with our own people." The energetic Algerians, clearly not demoralised, drilled each day. After a few days, some received modest food parcels from home and generously insisted on sharing their food.

On the first full day at Bordeaux, presumably to deter escapes, the new prisoners had to shed their civilian clothes, which were retained by the Germans until they left the camp, and were offered a selection of second-hand French uniforms, some of which were holed or stained. Stanley was first and the others waited outside the building. "I took off my suit and handed it to a German. Distastefully, I picked out a snappy blue uniform: I felt that I had reached the depths of humiliation. The fancy markings on the collars, cuffs and shoulders failed to appease me. I don't know if I was dressed as a general or corporal and I seethed with helpless rage. I had no idea how to wear puttees but did my best. I had a vague suspicion that I was not exactly a Saville Row figure but I was not prepared for the laughter that greeted me from my shipmates but my dignity had called it a day and gone home.

"I found consolation, when, one by one, my colleagues appeared. All the ranks and branches of the French army must have been represented. Some coats hung on shoulders making the wearer look like a shabby scarecrow and hands were lost in sleeves. Some men had trousers that were tight under the arms or the seats were so slack that they almost swirled from side to side when the occupant walked. Our laughter annoyed one German officer who marched us back to barracks. Next morning we greeted one another with grave salutes and bonjour, mon general etc."

Food, or, more accurately, the lack of it, soon became a serious worry. The daily issue consisted of a piece of bread, enough for about four thin slices, a desert spoonful of watery jam, a mug full of weak soup and three cups of ersatz coffee with no milk or sugar. The disgusting bread was probably made of straw.

"Occasionally, we saw parties of British prisoners and wanted to be moved to their camp. A German officer, reminiscent of a caricature in the British press, visited us. His skull looked shaven, his fat face was red and his neck bulged over his collar. His eyes were cold and one was aided by a monocle." A polite Stanley thought that this would be a good time to ask about a move to another camp, with fellow Britons. "Excuse me sir, I think a mistake has been made and we are in the wrong camp. At the word 'mistake', his face became nearly purple, his eyes bulged and I thought that the top button of his tunic would burst. 'We Germans do not make mistakes.' Clearly, we could not be moved after that as it would have implied admission of a mistake."

Eventually, the British contingent was to move to a camp for British Merchant Navy personnel. As they passed the watch towers overlooking their prison, a Liverpool man, glanced up, saw a guard and unleashed a stream of obscene language at him. The German's response, in kind, was couched in much better English than his critic's. All was going well for Germany at this time and any group of their soldiers, when marching past a prison camp, bellowed out their marching song to add to the inmates' misery. After 12 days of near starvation at Bordeaux, the British Merchant Navy men were told that they would be taken to Germany and that their trip would be really tough. It was.

On the 12th May 1941, they were escorted to a line of railway wagons each of which bore the legend "40 hommes, 8 chevaux". The one assigned to Stanley's group of 30, all of whom were British and came from the *Agnita, Mandasor* and *Canadalite*, had recently carried cement, judging by the thick dust on the floor. A request for a brush was ignored and each man was given a tin of mutton whilst one loaf of bread was to be shared between three men. No drinks were provided and one blanket each was allocated. Hinged narrow seats were arranged around the sides of the wagon and were lowered by chains. The sliding doors were only unlocked when the train was in a station and the men had to sleep on the floor or on the seats. A large metal drum was provided for sanitary purposes and this was emptied only once a day but, despite having a tight lid, it was very unpleasant after 24 hours, especially for whoever was sleeping near it.

During the day, the heat was intense and small holes were cut into the side of the enclosed wagon by the prisoners' penknives, which, surprisingly, had not been confiscated, which allowed them a glimpse of the countryside. A small shutter on the roof of the wagon was opened during the day but closed at night as it became cold. The men tired of tinned meat and dry bread but they were more thirsty than hungry. "When the train stopped at what seemed to be a marshalling yard, I stood on the seat and waved an empty bottle out of the shutter. The French railway workers immediately understood and quickly returned with my bottle full. I was greeted with shouts of disbelief when I said it was full of wine but wine it was. We gradually acquired a few bottles which we filled whenever we could."

After three days, the captives, unshaven and unwashed, arrived at Chalons-sur-Marne, about 460 miles from Bordeaux and about 110 miles to the east of Paris. The train pulled up alongside a platform and the prisoners were pleased to see a row of baths, already full of water, but they were not for them and they were confined to their wagon. Some Red Cross French ladies were in attendance and one moved Stanley by saying "have courage". With memorable under-statement, he noted that he needed that advice. "Our position was far from enviable."

One night was spent in what seemed to be a marshalling yard but at midnight the men were woken by the crash of bombs and, looking through their holes in the side of the wagon, they saw searchlights, the flash of anti-aircraft guns and, encouragingly, the flash and explosion of bombs. They wished the bombers well but hoped that they themselves would not be attacked. As the journey continued, the men took turns to look out of the holes and gaze longingly at the beautiful French countryside bathed in glorious sunshine but the sight of a Nazi flag over a chateau seemed obscene.

The prisoners had left Bordeaux at noon on the Monday and reached their destination, the small station of Bremervorde, on the Friday afternoon after about 900 miles and four days of extreme discomfort, unwashed, unshaven and covered by cement dust. This was the nearest station to the Stalag XB camp, which, in turn, was part of the notorious Sandbostel, where thousands of Jews and political prisoners were to be massacred. The senior personnel, who included Stanley, and those who were not fit, were directed into small buses but one embarrassingly sick Italian was propelled into a truck by a German boot. A young German civilian taunted the prisoners by calling them the master race. Stanley shouted back, "no, you're the master race" but it was doubtful if such irony hit the target.

On arriving at Sandbostel at 08.30 pm, at dusk, the prisoners were herded into an empty barrack in a separate section within the camp and given a blanket each. As Stanley was flinging his few possessions on to a bunk, a voice said "here you are skipper" and a mug of hot ersatz coffee and a large slice of bread was thrust at him by a kind sailor from one of Ellerman Wilson's ships. Subsequently, a room mate offered Stanley a cup of cocoa, made with sugar and condensed milk. This was his first real drink since being captured, many weeks before, and he felt that his benefactor should henceforth be considered on a par with Lister, Pasteur and Curie.

The next day the captives were transferred to the main camp where they were joined by other Merchant Navy prisoners. Stanley was given a metal tag on which was stamped Gefangenennummer 100040. Hearing some of the tales from his new colleagues, he and his friends were thankful to have escaped so lightly. "At first we were relieved to be safe, ashore and alive" but, mixed with their relief were doubts, once again, on whether they could have done any more. "I soon realised that we did all that could have been done and that any other action would have resulted in the useless loss of lives, our lives."

At 11.00 am, on their first day in Sandbostel, the men were given some fish soup, which contained some slimy bits of salt fish, including fins and tails, and potatoes. This was a horrible and nauseating mess but hunger compelled consumption. The next humiliation was a visit to a barrack which had been converted into a bath house, where the captives had to strip naked before being pushed into an area made wet by sprinklers in the roof. There was no soap so the men had to rub the water over their bodies. Soon, the sprinklers were turned off, leaving the prisoners to stand around until they were dry.

137

"There were about 200 of us, the old, the middle-aged, the young, the emaciated, the slim, the fat and the utterly gross, from many different countries. A German soldier sat on a chair and, one by one, we had to stand before him, first facing him and then with our backs to him whilst he scrutinised us for signs of vermin. This was a horrible and humiliating experience for us and one that was not too pleasant for him. Our clothes were put into large ovens and deloused."

The Germans issued each prisoner with British army clothing which had been captured. Each inmate received a battledress, two second hand pairs of socks, one of which Stanley used as gloves in the winter, and two French army grey, cotton singlets. One reached Stanley's ankles so he used it as nightshirt. Boots were not issued so before winter arrived, Stanley saved up his cigarettes, from Shell parcels, and bought a pair from one man who, oddly, had two pairs. These new army boots were too big and he maintained that he had to walk for a few minutes before his boots moved but at least his feet were dry.

As Stanley and his colleagues were the latest arrivals in the camp, their names were last on the Red Cross clothing roster. Consequently, when clothes arrived, they had to watch others being given them so the stock was exhausted before their names were called. It was grossly unfair because the available garments were not allocated according to need. This system also ignored the fact that some prisoners had brought clothes with them from their vessels. What really angered and hurt Stanley was that some men who were given Red Cross boots already had their own and used the "new" ones for football whilst other inmates, including Stanley, were suffering with wet feet. Stanley unsuccessfully challenged this injustice although changes were implemented later to help deserving cases and prisoners also received clothing parcels from home.

CHAPTER 11

To Wilhelmshaven for interrogation

Before the prisoners could settle down in their new surroundings, some were taken to the naval base of Wilhelmshaven, about 60 miles away, ostensibly for interrogation, but, in practice, "to continue our studies in starvation which began at Bordeaux". Stanley was accompanied by the chief officer, chief engineer and third officer from the Agnita. They travelled on an ordinary passenger train and were divided up into small groups: a young and polite German soldier, the antithesis of the arrogant Nazi, led Stanley's group. Before he left his charges, he asked them how long they thought the war would last. They suggested "about three years" to which he responded, smiling, "no, about six months".

"We changed trains at a small country station and, whilst were waiting, several trains passed through, pulling wagons loaded with tanks and heavy guns which was a depressing sight." Presumably, these trains were destined for Russia. Apparently, the Germans had intended to wage war on the USSR in late May, but postponed the invasion for about a month, having opted first to attack Yugoslavia and Greece. Ultimately, in a surprise move, Russia was invaded on 22nd June 1941, despite the non-aggression pact signed by Hitler in August 1939. Stanley and his colleagues, when still in

Wilhelmshaven, heard some German sailors who were clearly excited and, by careful questioning of the guards, found out that Germany and the Soviet Union were at war. In his diary, Stanley recalled the 1939 pact, "when the Russians imagined they could stay out of the war and enjoy the spectacle of the British and Germans slaughtering each other. I had little enough sympathy for the Russians except for the poor people who would suffer most. But anyone who fought the Germans became an ally."

On their way to Wilhelmshaven, a passenger train stopped and a young German officer, speaking excellent English, and doubtless noting that the men were clad in British army uniform, albeit without any badges, asked, politely, who they were and how long did they think the war would last? The prisoners' responded, as they had done before, "three years". He replied "six months" as had one of his colleagues, suggesting that this was the official view."

"At Wilhelmshaven, we were marched through the town. As the march took so long, I thought that the camp must have been some distance from the station but this was probably just to show us off to the local people. A group of Liverpool firemen and sailors in our contingent sang "It's a long way to Tipperary" and the friendly smiles from middle-aged men in uniform who came to their barrack gates suggested that they had heard that song in the First World War. On reaching the barracks, a dozen men were put into a large room with metal bunks, mattresses and blankets.

"We were quite comfortable but what really worried us were our daily rations. They consisted of a piece of black bread, enough for four slices, a piece of margarine or lard, big enough to cover a thumb nail, one desert spoon of jam, a bowl of soup, which usually contained a few potatoes, which we kept for supper, and a mug of ersatz coffee, without milk or sugar, three times a day. We had noticed that the soup dispenser filled his ladle and then deliberately slopped some back into the zinc bath container. To prevent this, we lined up in a queue and, as soon as one person had received his portion, the next prisoner darted forward and immediately put his bowl under the soup ladle before the dispenser could pour any soup back into the bath. This ruse never failed. Any stray pieces of potato in the soup were recovered and then used to augment the slice of bread and lard or saved for supper." Occasionally sauerkraut and some cabbage would be substituted for the soup but Stanley's stomach refused to accept the sour cabbage. A tiny mouse used to visit the prisoners at night, calmly staring at the prisoners. It was told that it was pointless to sit there, waiting for crumbs as the prisoners did not have enough for themselves. "Although it was a German mouse, it must have understood English as it never returned."

"There is much nonsense written about the brotherhood of the sea. Perhaps brotherhood in Germany means something different. The criminals received Red Cross food parcels for us but kept them, saying that we could not do any cooking but everything in the parcels was already cooked and could be eaten cold."

The chief officer became ill so was moved to the hospital immediately below the rooms occupied by his colleagues. One day he shouted out that he could let them have a piece of white bread. "We found a piece of string and, when the sentry patrolling in the street below had his back to us, we lowered the string and hurriedly pulled up the bread, which, although more grey than white, tasted as good as a chocolate éclair." Exercise in a small square was allowed each morning. One day, the British men were sitting on a long seat and a middle-aged German sailor was at the other end. After a few quiet words, he said "this war is no good" and left. This was an impressive comment as the Germans were then doing well.

Each day Stanley and friends were taken, individually, to be interrogated by two Germans. To avoid those who had been questioned communicating with those about to be interviewed, the British had to take their belongings with them, after being interviewed, and join those who had already been interrogated. However, the prisoners defeated the system. After a man had been questioned, he asked to go to the lavatory, where he hid a

141

piece of paper with his questions and answers for the next man to be interviewed.

The captives were given three cigarettes each day and it was here that Stanley noted one of the few acts of kindness in Hitler's Germany. He had arranged with a guard to exchange cigarettes for black bread: the soldier handed over the bread but refused to take the cigarettes. After three weeks and many complaints, one guard gave four of the prisoners a bar of soap but later they discovered that the soap had been stolen from a Red Cross parcel that the Germans had no right to open. During the war, in most weeks, some 2,000 Red Cross personnel packed and despatched 90,000 parcels, bound up with 180 miles of string.

The prisoners, with nothing to do and nothing to read, sat at their window for hours and watched the street below. Every afternoon, some young women walked past and waved and, on seeing a German naval officer with a girl, Stanley wondered when, or even if, that would happen again to him and his friends. Whilst at Wilhelmshaven, Stanley pondered, once again, what had happened to his crew, his ship and, of course, to him. Could he have done anything to have altered the situation? He came to the same conclusion as before and vowed not to consider the subject yet again, but he did.

A subject of greater immediate concern, understandably, was food. It had been sufficient on the German vessels but a grim indication of prospects had become apparent at Bordeaux, when the prisoners had been taken ashore. The Algerian prisoners had been kind to the British but what was provided by the enemy had been virtually a starvation diet. However, after an intensive "12 day course in starvation", the hapless prisoners had been subjected to another 4½ days of hunger whilst travelling across France to Germany and this journey induced fears of what might happen which were confirmed at Wilhelmshaven.

After five weeks in Wilhelmshaven, Stanley and his colleagues returned to Sandbostel, "ready to take an honours degree in malnutrition". The march back to the station took just five minutes, thus proving that the earlier circuitous route had been to show the prisoners off to the public "although I cannot think that a ragged rank of a few Merchant Navy prisoners roused any local frenzy of enthusiasm for the German war effort".

CHAPTER 12

Sandbostel again and Milag Nord

The men, happy to be back with their friends at Sandbostel were less pleased about the lack of food. No Red Cross food parcels meant that they had to exist on German rations but complaints produced "the patently obvious lie" that the prisoners received the same food as the garrison troops. However, the Germans, not having anticipated a long war, were in some difficulties themselves. Their food supplies were fading in 1941-2 and bread, meat, potatoes and fat were all rationed for their nationals and the scarcity of fuel for the local population was such a problem, that from January 1940, Germans were only permitted to bath at weekends. Suggesting that progress was not as the Germans wished, newspapers could not print many names of those who had been killed, to avoid damaging morale. Despite being prepared for war in many ways, the German economy was only truly converted to a war footing after the fall of Stalingrad at the end of January 1943. By 1944, flagging output had been boosted by an influx of some seven million workers from defeated nations.

Eventually, Red Cross parcels reached Sandbostel, but the newcomers had to wait for a few days for theirs. Stanley, on receiving his first Red Cross food parcel, admitted "feeling like a child opening his Christmas stocking". A one pound tin of meat, a tin of meat roll, a one pound tin of rice pudding, a

144

little dried fruit, four ounces of sugar, one pound of biscuits, two ounces of cheese, half a pound of margarine, one tin of condensed milk, a four ounce bar of chocolate, two ounces of tea, and, equally important, a two ounce bar of soap, caused his eyes to "pop out like organ stops and I was deeply thankful to decent people for sending such parcels".

In the first few months of captivity, from July to Christmas 1941, men from the two Shell ships whose crews were in the camp, received small food parcels from the group's company in neutral Portugal. These usually contained chocolate and a small tin of sardines or tunny fish and provided welcome confirmation that the men had been remembered. These regular parcels stopped in early 1942, because of currency and other difficulties. However, Shell employees received parcels of cigarettes or tobacco for the remained of the war and Stanley, who did not smoke, was able to trade cigarettes for extra bread or even eggs acquired from outside the camp. He also gave some to colleagues who were desperate.

The Merchant Navy camp adjoined that of the Royal Navy but a barbed wire fence separated them. All food parcels were delivered to the RN and handled by naval ratings. Tins of food were punctured, under the gaze of the German guards, to ensure that they could not be saved for any escape attempts. Most of the guards were middle-aged men, who had served in the First World War or, if they were younger, they had some physical problem. Their number fluctuated but there were usually at least 20 and more occupied each of the four watch towers in the corners of the camp. There were also some particularly loathsome members of the Gestapo who enjoyed being obnoxious but who, sensibly, vanished just before the camp was liberated. Stanley had a grudging respect for one German who seemed to run the camp. Unlike most Germans, he had a sense of humour. During one early morning muster he turned to one of the ratings who, apparently, had neither washed nor shaved for a week. The German wagged a finger at him and said, "come here my love". On another occasion, an inmate had hung some washing on the line that divided the

Royal and Merchant Navy camps. "It is not permitted to hang washing on the barbed wire, it is NOT the Siegfried line."

A move to Milag Nord

The Sandbostel camp was later to become particularly notorious, even when judged by the bestial standards of German wartime human behaviour. It had been built in 1933 for "undesirables" but, during the war, when it was a concentration camp, some 50,000 were murdered there. The Germans remained consistently cruel to the very end, refusing to surrender the camp and taking shelter behind the starved and emaciated remaining inmates. In 1941, The International Red Cross protested to the Germans that Merchant Navy prisoners, kept in Sandbostel, were not combatants so should not be held in that camp.

Between autumn 1941 and spring of the following year, Sandbostel's Royal Naval prisoners and Merchant Naval personnel were moved to, respectively, separate but adjacent compounds, Marlag and Milag, known collectively as Marlag und Milag Nord. These two camps, separated just by barbed wire, were a few miles from the village of Westertimke, some 10 miles north east of Bremen and 16 miles from the horrific Sandbostel concentration camp. Hamburg was about 30 miles to the south west.

On 4th February 1942, Stanley, packing hurriedly for the move to Milag, planned for the morrow, was moved by a gift of two packets of tea and some sugar from the second cook. The countryside around the new camp was attractive with many fir and beach trees, woods, farms, fields and pasture land occupied by Friesian cattle. The southern half of the camp, where the ratings lived, was on bleak sandy ground but the north end was on higher ground with many fine beech and oak trees amongst the huts. There were several farm houses across the road from the camp and some inmates used to sit for hours, watching the life and movement on the farm and the women and children at play but this simple pleasure ceased when the guards obscured the view with by placing grass matting over the barbed wire. This meant that the only remaining views were to the south and east across open country. Occasionally, the prisoners enjoyed watching tame red squirrels in the trees but the matting on the barbed wire and cats in the camp eventually drove them away.

On arrival at Milag, on 5th February 1942, each prisoner was given one bed sheet and three blankets, one of which had to be returned to the Germans when the captives received a blanket from the Red Cross. Judging by the poor quality of the German offering, Stanley thought that they must have been made of dogs' wool. The most effective blanket was the khaki overcoat. The POWs also received a thick pint mug, a knife, fork, desert spoon and an enamel bowl, not a plate because "the only food a German understands is soup".

Another serious problem was the condition of the living quarters. Evidently, the preparations for the prisoners had not been completed, possibly because the Red Cross had insisted that the prisoners be moved away from the concentration camp as soon as possible. The barracks, partly erected, had been saturated with near-incessant rain or snow and the roofs were hurriedly flung on and felt was laid on wet wood. "Our first few nights were absolute hell. Persistently low temperatures, around minus 12 degrees Fahrenheit and the lack of heating sapped morale which was further undermined by bugs." Solid ice formed in the corners of the room. It was bitterly cold, the rain seemed ceaseless and the ceilings and walls were dripping wet. Even the sour-faced German officer felt obliged, after three requests, to give the prisoners daily, instead of weekly, fuel for their stove until the rooms were dry. The day after the transfer, Stanley's feet felt frozen all day and he was only able to acquire some reasonable quality boots, in return for 100 cigarettes, a week later.

The cold weather persisted and there was a heavy fall of snow on 9th February. The hapless prisoners were forced to stay outside, in the cold, for lengthy periods for muster. Stanley was acutely miserable. There was no immediate improvement. By March, an easterly gale had exposed gaps in the accommodation and it was impossible to keep warm and there was still ice in the rooms. These cold, cheerless days, rendered worse by hunger, were "sheer hell". A case of smallpox, and the need for all inmates to be vaccinated, added to the gloom and Stanley felt unwell. In what must have been a further setback for morale, in April, the Germans searched the camp and confiscated Stanley's diaries for 1939, 1940 and 1941. That day, the prisoners were detained on the parade ground from 9.00 am to 15.00 hours. Stanley was sick after eating sauerkraut but remained convinced that the allies would triumph. On 11th May 1942, he wrote, "although I know that we are going to win this war, I get very depressed. Months are flying by and I'm getting older and it is years since I saw them. I will, definitely see them again and many men better than me will never return home." Later that month, still depressed, he wrote, "it is terrible to be imprisoned here when so much is happening outside. Sometimes I feel a washout as I've done nothing in this war but at least I did not lose any lives when the ship was sunk."

Accommodation

The wooden barracks in which the prisoners were incarcerated consisted of ten large rooms and four small ones, arranged as five and two rooms on each side of a long central corridor. The large rooms were 24 feet by 16 feet and were nine feet high. In the officers' barracks, 18 men were assigned to each room and no less than 22 ratings were crowded into their rooms. The double height bunks were so close that there was only just enough space to enable a man to reach his bunk and, on most days, in the ratings' rooms, there was insufficient light to allow reading. In each room, there were two tables, 6 foot six by two feet each and forms, or benches.

The four end rooms, eagerly sought, were much smaller at 16 feet by 8 feet and were occupied by four men. In the ratings' barracks, they were occupied by the barrack captains, committee men, (camp trade union officials), camp workers and stars of Milag's sporting and theatrical worlds. The officers' end rooms housed captains and chief engineers until smaller barracks were built for senior officers exclusively, after some 18 months. This area, previously used as a parcel office, was altered for the accommodation of captains. Here in 10 rooms of various sizes, lived 52 captains. Inmates of barrack 11 included Stanley who shared a 15 feet by 17 feet room, number eight, with six other masters. His room, which contained eight bunks, two tables and eight stools, also had three lockers and a stove was based in the corner close to the door. There was one window. In September 1942, after a row, Stanley was moved into barrack 26 and felt much happier with his new colleagues.

By October, the cold cheerless weather indicated that another depressingly miserable winter was in prospect. "How I envy everyone in the ships." He spent a miserable day washing out the bunks and killing the horrible filthy bugs. One night he slept particularly badly, being disturbed by the bugs and a rat gnawing at the woodwork. The problem persisted and the bugs came through the walls from the next room. By November, he had to leave his bed to plug up holes in the wall. He used up a tin of insect powder and this seemed to eliminate the problem: fumigation was only carried out annually. The British camp officials lived in barrack number two where the rooms were 16 feet by 12 feet and were occupied by only three men. These rooms, known as "Park Lane", boasted indoor lavatories, warm showers and spring beds. The warm showers during the day were also used by elderly prisoners and invalids.

The winter weather frequently prevented prisoners from remaining outside so the rooms became crowded with the closely-packed bunks, tables and benches, washing hanging across the ceiling, and above the bunks and clothing hanging on nails. Many men, of different nationalities, habits and cultures, were crowded together in a room "with insufficient space to change your mind". Given the over-crowding, men of different cultures and nationalities, it was remarkable that there was so little ill feeling and friction. Because space was so precious, every square inch was used to advantage. Red Cross boxes were converted into cupboards and bookcases and nettings were made and stretched under bunks and ceilings.

Boxes and bags were hung everywhere. The bunks reminded Stanley of an overcrowded Hong Kong sanpan and he wondered whether an avalanche of books, toilet gear, clothes and carefully-horded food could bury a sleeping man.

Many barracks had only a single floor, with no covering, so icy draughts, permitted by the lack of wind-proofing, meant cold feet. Germany was then winning the war so complaints about overcrowding were ignored. However, Stanley expressed his dissatisfaction frequently to the Germans and to visitors from the Swiss embassy. Repairs were eventually carried out on the roof, floors were doubled and room numbers were reduced. Two new barracks were built but left empty for months before being occupied by the inhabitants of the two barracks that had been condemned. They were relatively comfortable and not crowded, but, above all, there were no bugs.

Food

Although some Red Cross food had to be cooked or at least heated, no cooking utensils were provided. Some captives were fortunate in the early days to be able to buy canteens or dixies from some Yugoslavs soldiers for cigarettes but the majority, showing considerable imagination, made tea pots, kettles, pans, etc from empty biscuit tins. "Any plutocrat possessing a frying pan was very popular."

Understandably, the lack of food, and the grim nature of the little that was provided, dominated Stanley's notes until the good news, if not food, started flowing after the invasion in June 1944. Indeed, the allied attacks on the German infrastructure exacerbated the food crisis. For the bulk of their imprisonment, many prisoners suffered from genuine hunger and relied on the Red Cross and, occasionally, other sources, rather than their captors, for keeping them alive. Surprisingly, given the lack of regular and reasonable quality food and confronted by harsh living conditions, serious illness was not rampant. Occasionally, it was feared that, if the fortnightly food parcels failed to arrive, stocks in the camp could soon become exhausted. Sometimes, the prisoners received some food in a bulk shipment from Argentina including solid meat, half a kilo each of pure butter, a large hunk of cheese and even a large piece of soap and the Canadian parcels, too, were always welcome.

The German soup, provided at mid-day, was a weak unpalatable liquid with slimy potatoes and the merest hint of turnip. Some small pieces of potato were rescued to augment a portion of Red Cross stew or meat loaf for later. Each man had a soup card and the day's date was crossed off in ink or indelible pencil as the prisoner drew his mid-day soup. When the flow of Red Cross parcels ceased, between February and April 1942, and the men were desperately hungry, many tricks were tried to obtain a second bowl of soup, one of which was to rub out the date on the card, ironically with soup, and then claim a second bowl.

The culinary masterpiece was then bread pudding. Any bread that was too much of a challenge was saved, cut into small pieces, soaked in water until soft then squeezed to remove surplus water. A few currants and raisins, if available, were added, together with some margarine and a blob of jam if available. This mixture was put in a greased tin if a "cake" was desired and baked in the galley or buried beneath the hot ashes of the stove in the room. The cake, or pudding, when boiled, was popular when the prisoners were relatively strong but later, despite hunger, proved too much of a challenge.

Soon after the move to Milag und Milag Nord, in 1942, rations from the Germans had deteriorated and were "insufficient for a healthy mosquito". Apart from the issue of bread and a concoction seemingly based on potatoes, the prisoners were living off Red Cross parcels. A typical parcel then contained a one pound tin of meat, a tin of meat roll, a one pound tin of rice pudding, a little dried fruit, four ounces of sugar, one pound of biscuits, two ounces of cheese, a half pound of margarine, one tin of condensed milk, a four ounce bar of chocolate, two ounces of tea and, occasionally, a four ounce tin of cocoa and, almost equally important, a two ounce piece of soap.

At this bleak time, the humble potato became a meal in itself. It was so important that it was issued separately, unaccompanied by the other ersatz commodities. The shout along the barrack corridors of "potatoes up" or "kartoffels" provoked not just excitement but also the hope that that they might not be soft and slimy. The potatoes were boiled in the galley in their skins and then issued en bloc to each hut where they were divided up for each room. As the potatoes were of different shapes and sizes, the problem of justice in distribution was overcome by putting eight piles on the table. One captive would then turn his back to the table whilst another would point to a pile and say whose are these? One by one the prisoners' names were called out until all eight piles were claimed. The quality of the potatoes, however they were prepared, was poor but occasionally the inmates were able to buy some, for a few cigarettes, from their colleagues who worked on the farm. Even the skins became valuable.

The bread, heavy, dark brown and stamped with the date on which it had been baked, was the same as fed to the captives on the warship and even to the German sailors. The ingredients, which made the bread taste sour, were unknown but speculation favoured rye, barley, potato flour, or even sawdust and some lead fillings or cement to increase the weight! After an allied air attack on Bremen, some glass was detected and wood was found on more than one occasion. If kept for too long, not that the prisoners had that luxury, the bread became mouldy and sour. After one air raid on Bremen, the bread arrived in the evening, still warm and with the consistency, and odour of warm rubber. More elderly loaves were as soft as concrete and Stanley observed that, after cutting a few slices, the inmates had to sit down for a rest. "The quality of German bread and coffee explains why the Germans fight so hard. Eating such bread and drinking such slush is enough to make any man savage enough to want to fight everybody." As the war dragged on, the German rations deteriorated further, in quality and quantity, and bread became

152

even more valuable. One man, having acquired a loaf, wrapped it in a cloth and used it as a pillow. When he woke, the ends of the loaf had been cut away: all that remained was the part on which his head rested.

Early in the war, the German meat ration was 8.75 ounces per week but this included skin, bone, gristle and other inedible parts. This ration nearly always consisted of some mysterious sausage that was never sufficiently firm to justify the use of a knife: the only tool necessary was a spoon. In his four years in Germany, Stanley needed a knife only twice. Once was when an RAF raid on cold storage plants in Bremen necessitated prompt distribution of supplies so roast meat was to be included in the evening meal. "Some of the meat looked rather depressed and a few fellows were too suspicious to tackle it but I enjoyed using a knife. God bless the RAF. The Germans now tell us that only horse meat will be sent into the camp." Even one fresh slice of meat was seldom provided and the one ounce per day that was supplied was lost in an overwhelming mass of potatoes and turnips, etc. but two slices of beef each appeared on Christmas Day.

The prisoners were only able to collect their "coffee" at the galley. The main ingredients were thought to be acorn, ground-up flower bulbs and burned barley. It was the same colour as real coffee and, when hot and accompanied by sugar it was drinkable. Its appearance was that of small pieces of cork with a sprinkling of sand. It had no taste and it was never consumed until supplies of Red Cross tea and cocoa were finished. The prisoners joked that it was just acceptable when served, really hot, with plenty of milk and sugar but without the coffee!

Sometimes the Germans provided "cheese", made of fish, and, if eaten immediately, when still firm, it lacked any specific taste. Hesitation meant that it melted, disintegrated and became a slimy, smelly mess which was unanimously rejected. A day's issue of cheese was buried outside one barracks and its location was indicated with a cross: the Germans were not amused. Some fruit and vegetables were occasionally available in the summer. Rosters were organised

153

and the lucky recipients acquired a couple of carrots, a dejected lettuce or a turnip. The apples and pears were usually rotten windfalls suffering from "an advanced form of acne". Once, Stanley, having learned that the canteen had tins of tomatoes, immediately bought one which was "delicious".

Eventually, when new barracks had been constructed, and the officers were allocated one dining hall and galley for their own use, a community feeding plan evolved. Officers who joined agreed that all their meat, fish, puddings and fruit from Red Cross parcels would be retained by the galley staff, together with the rations provided by the Germans. In return, participants received two hot meals a day and a sweet in the evening three or four times a week. It was not as generous as it sounded but it was an improvement on an *ad hoc* system.

Later in the war, and in the months preceding the end of the conflict, especially in the winter, the prisoners were desperately hungry. Apart from one or two periods, especially when the RAF were bombing the local railway system and ports, or when the Germans needed to use the railways for military purposes, the inmates received one food parcel a week. However, the flow of Red Cross parcels stopped in September 1944, sometimes for weeks, as the fighting created transport difficulties. The allocation was reduced to one parcel every two weeks. At this time, each morning, when the galley was preparing the day's soup, the peelings were thrown out of the window. A few anxious men waited to grab them and the peelings were then washed, eyes gouged out and then boiled with a pinch of curry powder if available or salt. Such was the starvation level that men of all nationalities and ratings and officers jostled vigorously to secure some peelings.

Fuel

Although the stoves in the rooms were small and economical, the inmates never received sufficient fuel to keep them going all day, so had to confine their use to a few hours in the morning and in the evening. "We used to collect our fuel, usually patent briquettes, in a box, piling them high, but occasionally an obnoxious German civilian would kick the top briquettes off, however we compensated for this by filling our overcoat pockets, two in each pocket, when his back was turned."

In November 1944, all fuel supplies were stopped, and, in spite of German soldiers, with dogs "as big as donkeys", patrolling the camp at night, the trees started to disappear. All the wood fencing, seats, shutters and even structural parts of the barracks were pulled down for the fires. "Now, December 1944, we are being issued with wood, albeit in insufficient volumes and the Germans have decreed that cutting trees down is sabotage and can be punished by death."

One prisoner composed the following parody on the poem "Trees"

I think that there never will be
Left in Milag Nord a tree
A tree whose lovely wood is pressed
Into the bogey's glowing breast
A tree that looks at God all day
And in the evening's whisked away
A tree that may in summer wear
A swing or hammock, neath her hair
Upon whose back is lain
And cut in chunks across the grain
And now the Jerries have told we
It's sabotage to pinch a tree

Various "timber companies" were set up by the ratings who guaranteed to provide wood in return for cigarettes.

Camp administration and organisation

When the camp was first formed, the senior confidence officer for the British was Captain Lewis, who was elected by the camp inmates. He was assisted by Captain Hill but, when the camp was enlarged, a management committee, comprising Captains Hill, Cavage and Notman was formed to take responsibility for the internal running of the camp. Captain Lewis remained as the intermediary between the prisoners and their captives. However, after a few months, he was dismissed by the Germans, presumably for failing to co-operate with them, and was despatched to another camp. Captain Notman replaced him but the prisoners were given no voice in this appointment. To assist the management committee, the officers elected a welfare body of seven members and the ratings followed suit. The function of these two groups was to pass requests, suggestions and complaints to the management committee for consideration by the Germans. Members were elected every quarter and, eventually, the chairmen of each welfare committee were given seats on the management committee.

Each barrack had a captain, usually elected by the men, who was paid 12 marks a month by the Germans. His duties were to distribute the mail and German rations, not an arduous task, and to help the guard to count the number of men on the thrice-daily muster which could be an arduous task.

Captains and senior officers dominated the official positions within the camp organisation. The leading roles were senior confidence officer, camp leader, camp paymaster, camp treasurer, Red Cross clothing officer, Red Cross food officer, (this role required two men), private parcels officer, post office and mails officer and camp grounds officer. Other inmates became managers of the cinema, the theatre and the recreation rooms, which, earlier in the day, were the dining rooms. Some men in the camp cleaned the washrooms and lavatories, collected empty Red Cross tins, emptied ash bins and kept the camp as clean as they could. They were usually paid out of camp funds. The cooks were paid 8½ marks a month by the Germans but this wage was augmented by the camp. Camp funds were secured from revenues derived from letting space in the west hall to operators of roulette wheels and other gambling devices. The Milag Jockey Commission and Milag Greyhound Racing Association also contributed to camp funds as did any profits from the work of the two barbers.

The various nationalities in the camp, including the American, Dutch, Greek and Egyptian, had their own confidence officers who dealt directly with the Germans and the embassy of their protecting power. Every three months, the camp was visited by officials from the Swiss embassy: Switzerland was the protecting power for the British nationals. They interviewed prisoners, in front of the Germans, and received requests, enquiries and protests. These ranged from complaint of insufficient lighting, fuel, disinfectants for the lavatories and cleaning materials for the rooms, to the need for glass to repair broken windows but the responses were feeble and inadequate and calculated to delight the empty minds of faceless bureaucrats. Responses were along the lines of "the German High Command would be consulted, a note would be made, the information would be passed on etc."

On 25th August 1943, Stanley demanded information on the state of health of a Chinese crew of seamen taken, forcibly to work in Germany. By November 1944, there had been no response and no information was forthcoming on the plight of other seamen, taken to a jail in Hamburg. It was assumed later that some of the crew had been killed whilst forced to work for the enemy. The Germans, allegedly, had little information on some of these issues so the embassy visits achieved little.

Health and hygiene

Inevitably, the continuing squalid conditions had an impact on hygiene and on mental health but general health, despite occasional malnutrition, poor sanitation and over-crowding, was reasonably good especially as the prison population comprised many different nationalities. Indeed, many men, some of whom, not renowned for high standards of personal hygiene, contended that using ice-cold water in cold bathrooms was unjustified masochism.

There was little evidence of serious outbreaks of any serious diseases and Stanley recorded only one case of smallpox which necessitated widespread vaccination. For many the worst feature was the total absence of privacy.

"Everything, literally everything, was done in the sight of others. For example, using the lavatory was to see another man, similarly engaged, just a few feet away. Living so close together, in a crowded room, others' habits, mannerisms and idiosyncrasies could easily irritate and obscure their good habits."

Naturally, some prisoners became profoundly depressed by the tedium, the barbed wire, their exclusion from their family and the world and became physically and mentally ill. Several, including those who had attempted suicide, were eventually repatriated with the sick and disabled. It was not unusual to see a man talking or laughing to himself or frantically biting his finger nails or fidgeting and being unable to keep still. One man who walked round and round the camp, belching and moaning, was eventually sent home. A few gave way to acute melancholia and were convinced that they were dying. One Egyptian broke down. He waited near the gate and accosted any camp officials who passed. He wept, telling them that he was a sick old man, who wanted to go home. Eventually, the medical commission for repatriation agreed that he should leave and he immediately packed his few belongings and sat waiting by the gate. On learning that he would have to wait a little longer, he lost heart and died. Another man lost all feeling and did not feel pain, even when standing too close to the boiler.

Between September 1941 and November 1944, 28 men were buried in the little cemetery. Of these, 18 were Europeans and the total included at least one man who had become insane. Going to funerals in such awful circumstances must have been particularly traumatic. On 16th May 1942, Stanley attended the funeral of a radio officer. "We all lined the route to the gate and everybody was silent. There were many wreaths but the height of hypocrisy was reached when the German Navy sent a wreath and the man responsible for his death attended." In June 1942 new captives from a British and from an American vessel reached the camp but sadly one of them, a 22 year-old man died immediately. On 28th December 1942, Captain Nicholson, a room-mate of Stanley's, died of tuberculosis.   At the end of January 1944, one man died and another attempted suicide.

Stanley's health

In March 1942, after he had been vaccinated against smallpox, Stanley felt ill, probably as a result of the injection and a cold. He stayed in his bunk for two days but had not recovered a week later. His diary seldom mentions his physical state but he often remarked on his depression and a need to sleep, probably to shut out the grim reality and sense of helplessness. In May 1942, by the afternoon, he was feeling exhausted and slept. Later that month, he had the first of two inoculations against typhoid and admitted to feeling sore. He also concedes to feeling groggy and that he suffers from occasional giddiness which he attributed to the lack of food. This was followed almost immediately by a sore throat and a headache.

Five months later, on 22nd October, he felt, "really queer after breakfast: my hands and legs trembled and I am on the verge of tears". Hopefully, he soon felt better because there is no further reference to his health until July 1943 when, with others, he was x rayed by a German doctor for tuberculosis. He was clear but, ironically, and this was something that he did not know then, Maidie had contracted the disease.   Just before Christmas, he was confined to his bunk with a cold.

In January 1944, there is a cryptic entry in his diary saying that he went under chloroform and had his finger cut which was "a queer experience". There is no other information. The following month a cold and sores on his face prevented him from shaving. "I feel like something that the dog has chewed and left in the gutter. I'm not feeling too bright." Stanley's weight in battledress reflected his worries and, of course, both the quality and quantity of food. Confronted by near starvation, his weight had plummeted by 25th February 1945 and his health was also being challenged by the fact that the temperature was hovering around five degrees above freezing and no coal or wood was being provided.

The condition of his nerves worried him. As late as September 1944, he attributed his emotions to nerves: "my nerves must be in a frightful state. A few days ago, I saw a chick, a tiny pretty ball of fluff, and the sudden thought of it being slaughtered and eaten made my eyes flood. I must be getting silly". Denied the company of humans outside the squalid world of the camp, watching a squirrel in a tree and listening to a little bird, "singing as it its tiny throat would burst and making me wish I could hold it and stroke it" deflected thinking away from the immediate reality into another world, just for a few minutes.

The hospital

When the camp was set up, the hospital consisted of an ordinary wooden barrack and was run by a Czech, Dr. Spurber. There was only a small, ill-equipped operating theatre for emergency cases: serious cases were sent to another camp. Apparently, as Dr. Spurber left Czechoslovakia after the German occupation, and was captured whilst serving on board a British ship, he was unpopular with the Germans so received minimal assistance. There was no galley attached to the hospital and friends had to cook and take the meals to patients. The service inside the hospital was poor.

In November 1942, the Germans took Dr. Spurber to an unknown destination and he was succeeded by Major Harvey of the Royal Army Medical Corps. By November 1944, the hospital had been considerably enlarged, a new barrack had been built and joined to the south end and a galley and bathroom had been added. The operating theatre was better equipped and able to deal with major operations, mostly appendicitis and hernias, although occasionally, wounded service men, recently captured, arrived for treatment. The hospital also served the adjacent Royal Navy camp of Marlag. In the latter stages of the war, the staff consisted of three senior men from the RAMC and two from the Merchant Service. The secretaries, interpreter and orderlies were all Merchant Navy men.

Harvey played a key role in minimising disease and illness in the camp and managed to deceive the Germans by hiding two men suffering from tuberculosis. Towards the end of the war, he participated in a conference in Berlin, attended by captured allied doctors, representatives of the International Red Cross and German medical personnel.

Dentistry, the Kranken barracks and sanitation

A fully-equipped dental surgery under Captain Warren of the New Zealand Dental corps, assisted by a junior fireman, but a pre-war dental mechanic, was kept busy. Between September 1941 and an unspecified date towards the end of the war, over 10,000 teeth were extracted, 850 full sets of false teeth made and 850 sets repaired.

The men who were deemed either unfit of disabled by the Medical Commission, and who were awaiting repatriation, were transferred to a specific and dedicated barracks. As far as possible, men with the same complaint were put together in the same room. The mental cases, known cruelly as the Kranks, were supposed to have preferential treatment and their food, as well as water and fuel, was delivered to them and they were excused from attending musters. About 150 of these unfortunate men were repatriated on 16th October 1943.

One of the worst features of the camp was sanitation. Initially, for example, the 800 officers had access to only six toilets blocks. More facilities were built later but there was never sufficient disinfectant. The lavatories consisted of small brick buildings with concrete floors through which holes had been cut out to accommodate the toilet pans and seats. There were no partitions and each man sat just a few feet away from, and facing, a fellow inmate. It was unpleasant in summer and bitterly cold in the winter. The liquid waste from the urinals and lavatories was pumped by hand into a cylindrical tank which was mounted on a frame with a wheel on each of the four corners and which leaked occasionally. This sanitary carriage, soon dubbed "Smellie Nellie", was then hauled out of the camp, often by sailors who had upset the Germans, although the men were later replaced by horses, and the contents of the carriage deposited on the fields, just 50 yards away. When the wind was in the wrong direction, living in the camp was like living in a urinal. The solid dung in the lavatories was scooped out with shovels and mixed with soil and sand before being taken away in open carts.

One day, when the Smellie Nellie crew were outside the camp, they decorated the tank and themselves with small branches and leaves and returned to the camp singing lustily "she'll be coming around the mountain when she comes". The Germans, unimpressed, observed that, one day, Churchill would be pulling the contraption. This provoked the instant retort that Hitler would be in it. Just before the visits from the embassy of the protecting power, Switzerland, the lavatories were cleaned and liberal quantities of disinfectant applied but between the visits, disinfectants and deodorizers were conspicuously absent. The pungent stench during the summer and swarms of flies were unimaginably unpleasant. There were no disinfectants or deodorisers in the camp and at night some "filthy guttersnipes" urinated in the gutters just outside the hut doors.

Washrooms and baths

For a prisoner-of-war camp, the washrooms were satisfactory, according to Stanley. The waste was pumped underground and water was supplied by electric pumps. When they broke down, the prisoners, with their buckets, had to queue up at a small tap or walk in parties, with guards, to a farmhouse half a mile away. There was no heating in the lavatories or washrooms notwithstanding the bitterly cold winters. Hot water for washing clothes was obtained from small boilers, between 9.00 am and 12 noon each day. A delousing station and large bathroom, with hot water, was located between Milag and Marlag and served both camps. Bathing parties were taken there and each barrack had a regular time allocated to it, each week, when between 30 and 70 men would attend. All ages, sizes, and ratings of different colours would share the 40 showers. Every month, prisoners received a packet of soap powder, (soda) each, a small cake of coloured clay, which the Germans called soap, and a stick of shaving soap, real soap, was provided every three months.

Fumigation

Fumigation was carried out every summer. Each barracks was evacuated in turn and fumigated with sulphur. This killed large numbers of bugs but their relatives soon returned. Periodically, the prisoners would dismantle the bunks and wash the room but to no avail. Eventually they realised that the insects dropped from the ceiling so they plugged up the seams with string and bits of cloth but more invaded via the wood and straw. When the humans moved to another barracks they were no longer troubled.

Hootch

Before long, the men worked out how to produce home-made alcohol, hootch, and indeed, a doctor from one of the ships represented in the camp made a presentation on distilling! Understandably, some inmates found hootch helpful in shutting out the grim reality they had to endure. The brew was made from raisins and prunes, from Red Cross parcels, which were soaked for at least a week then boiled and the vapour distilled. To initiate the fermenting, some yeast, a piece of potato or a drop of the previous brew was added. Great ingenuity was shown in the making of the stills. In the previous camp, to prevent brewing, the Germans had taken all the fruit from Red Cross parcels and handed it to the galley for cooking and distribution.

Brewing was against camp regulations and any stills found during an inspection were confiscated. However, in Milag it seemed that the Germans made no determined effort to eliminate the dangerous practice as drunken men were allowed to roll around the camp night and day. Occasionally, a drunk would be given a couple of days in the camp jail if he made a nuisance of himself near the gate. The price of bottles of hootch varied from 40 to 120 marks but this was cheap for anyone who had won a few hundred marks from gambling. Christmas was the busiest season for the brewers but on most Saturdays, a few drunks could be seen staggering around the camp, singing *Sweet Adeline*.

Being drunk was not a crime but the medical consequences could be severe and it became so bad that Major Harvey, RAMC, the senior medical officer, warned his fellow prisoners with a notice that was posted in all the barracks. After some drinkers had succumbed to paralysis, insanity and even blindness, the camp doctor, writing in the *Milag Review,* the camp's own newspaper, on 3rd August 1944, warned on some of the consequences of drinking hootch. "In the past few weeks, the following cases have been admitted to hospital: one instance of paralysis of the right arm and leg and this man will never walk again, seven cases of the Dts, two cases of cut throats, both of whom narrowly escaped death, and one case of insanity. Meanwhile, two cases of blindness have been reported from another camp. All these and many less severe cases are directly due to the drinking of hootch. In addition to causing the above immediate results, it is undoubtedly undermining the health of many men in the camp. All those who brew hootch and, especially those who sell it, are morally responsible for the catastrophes."

Earlier in the year, Stanley had noted that one man, involved in a drunken brawl, had had his throat cut and nearly died and another became insane. This warning and the knowledge that the war situation was then improving, had an impact on drinking but some men went home on stretchers as a consequence of their drinking hootch. By November 1944, there was very little drunkenness which Stanley attributed to the warning and the shortage of food parcels. The fact that the allies were now approaching might also have reduced the corrosive depression that had afflicted some men earlier in the war.

Exercise

When the tide of war began to favour the allies, the captives were allowed to leave the camp for a walk, accompanied by a guard, to whom they gave a few cigarettes for prolonging the excursion. In July 1942, Stanley wrote, "every time we go for coal, the Norwegian ladies smile and wave. It's kind of them but I'd rather not see them. They remind me of all the beauty and sweetness I'm missing and makes me hunger for the one person in this world." The reference to Norwegian women is not completely clear. Possibly, they had been taken from their own country and forced to work in Germany, which was a fate that befell millions by the end of the war. Alternatively, they might have been members of the Norwegian National Unity party, which was based on the German Reichsarbeitsdienst or RAD, and had volunteered to work in Germany. However, it is doubtful if those who were to work would have been housed in the country, rather than near armaments factories. A more plausible explanation is that the reference relates to six Norwegian women and a young girl who had been captured on a passenger ship and who were detained in a guard house, close to the camp, outside its gates. They were moved to an unknown destination, four months later, in November 1942. There were Norwegians in the camp and some of them may well have seen their compatriots, collaborationists or forced labour, when allowed out of the camp, possibly to work on the farm. Additionally, of course, if the women had been captured on a passenger vessel, as seems likely, some of their male colleagues would have been detained in the camp.

Allegedly, 50,000 French individuals volunteered to work for the Germans and towards the end of the war, over 7.5 million individuals, including some women, were working for the enemy. Many came from occupied countries and the total includes prisoners of war. At that time, non-German labour represented about a fifth of the total work force.

In March 1943, Stanley left the camp with others, under guard, to acquire some soil for the garden. They grew *inter alia*, beetroots and potatoes. They passed the camp where some of the commandos captured from the St. Nazaire raid on the west coast of France were incarcerated. "I saw several of them. They waved but were handcuffed with a chain two feet long between their wrists. Great lads, full of guts. Thank God we've got millions more like them at home." In early 1942, it had been decided to attack the port which included a dry dock and pens for U boats. The mission was successful but of the 630 men involved, only five returned to England. All the others were killed or captured. The impact on UK morale was significant and five men were awarded the Victoria Cross, the greatest number in any single mission.

On 17th August 1943, Stanley went out with a cart for vegetables and gave chocolates to two little girls, aged about two and three, who, excitedly, ran to tell their mother. "The incident was deeply moving. All this slaughter and hatred and filth but the Germans must be punished." He seems to have been confined to the camp for another year before he went for a walk again. "It was lovely in the woods, clear of barbed wire and war. It made me think of our own English woods and the times that I would have with Maidie."

When the Germans were facing defeat, being allowed out of the camp became a more common occurrence. On 1th September 1944 "ten of us went for a walk. It was good to get outside the wire and into the country. We met a few children playing and gave them some chocolate and changed a piece of soap for apples with some local country men who smiled and were friendly. Whoever wins the war, it would not make much difference to them. They will still have to work hard on the land."

On the 16th November, "a party of us went for a walk and brought back some apples and on our return, we walked through a wood. The ground was carpeted with beech leaves and the trees were every shade of gold, brown or copper. I thought what a pity we cannot all share this, instead of slaughtering each other." The following year, on 29th April, the day after he was liberated, he went for a walk outside the

166

camp and had his photograph taken, outlined against a Cromwell tank.

Nationalities and occupations

Many nationalities were represented in the camp, the population of which usually varied between 2,300 and 3,000. The total capacity was about 5,300 and, according to the Protecting Power, Switzerland, in April 1941, there were 4,268 inmates from 41 nations. Every part of the British Empire was represented and other prisoners came from Argentina, Belgium, Brazil, China, Chile, Czechoslovakia, Denmark, Egypt, Eire, France, Greece, Holland, Italy, Japan, Java, Latvia, Malaya, Madagascar, Mauritius, Norway, Poland, Portugal, Philippines, Rumania, Saudi Arabia, Spain, Sweden, Turkey, the United States and Yugoslavia.

A large proportion of the inmates, most of whom were captured before 1942, were wartime seamen but others were seized whilst travelling as passengers so many trades and professions were represented in the camp. These included school teachers, musicians, commercial travellers, a company director, clerks, a dance band leader, draughtsmen, commercial artists, a chauffer, electricians, a taxi driver, radio experts, barbers, a beekeeper, an actor, a book binder, a garage proprietor, an estate manager and one man who admitted to being a hawker and part-time pickpocket. This variety of occupations enabled the prisoners to have a more fruitful life than might otherwise have been possible. For example, the production of wirelesses, (radio sets) became relatively easy in the latter stages of the war and receiving the news gave the prisoners real encouragement. Music, too, played a significant role in maintaining morale at a higher level than might otherwise have been achieved.

A total of some 182 ships, including 131 British vessels, were represented in the camp. The locations where they met their end included the Faeroe Islands, Baltic, Trondheim, Narvik, English Channel, Indian Ocean, North and South Atlantic, Tasman Sea, North Pacific, Adriatic, Arctic and the

Mediterranean. The *Kormoran,* which sank the *Agnita,* was also responsible for the demise of four other vessels. The *Scharnhorst* sank six ships, and, in terms of location, the most dangerous area was the North Atlantic where 58 ships were lost. Another 31 met their end in the South Atlantic. The most dangerous adversary was the U boat. This was not a new concept: the first had been built in the previous century and in the First World War, in April 1917 alone, they sank 875,000 tons of allied vessels. Now, they accounted for the loss of 64 allied ships whose personnel were in the camp. Of the vessels whose personnel were in Milag, the earliest loss was of a ship owned by the Boston Fishing Company which went down off the Faeroe Islands on 7th September 1939 and the last was lost in April 1944.

Camp activities

Strictly, the Merchant Navy inmates, and, especially, the officers, were not required to undertake "unusual work", under the terms of the Geneva Convention of 1929. However, there was enormous pressure on the ratings to work on farms, factories, in nearby quarries or to construct parts of the camp and occasionally, they were kept on muster until they agreed to work. Once, allegedly, they were given 15 minutes to decide whether they were prepared to work after which those who declined would be shot by the guards, standing ready with their machine guns. One Belgian engineer who had repeatedly refused to work for the Germans was arrested for allegedly having a revolver in his possession. "A crude and obvious bit of trickery, but they're huns."

Ironically, the officers, not required to work, had plenty of time but, of course lacked freedom and relief from hunger. Consequently, they were active in trading through committees and they organised a rich variety of studies, sport and indoor entertainment. They were also responsible for the management of the camp, including the distribution of Red Cross clothing and food parcels, private parcels and mail. Such "social or sporting" work must have been of major importance to the prisoners who were able to forget their circumstances, albeit but briefly, whilst pursuing a hobby, sport or study.

School

Despite many disadvantages, school flourished. In the early days, those studying had to find an empty room but, later, space was allocated in a barrack that had been condemned for living. This allowed two or three classes to function simultaneously and also provided a separate room for private study which was important because having many men in the same quarters was not conducive for studying. One problem was the provision of paper and the Germans were unhelpful so frequent erasing was necessary. However, as usual, the Red Cross came to the rescue with note books and writing materials.

Large huts were allotted for classes in English, French, German, Spanish and other languages and for other topics such as seamanship, navigation, engineering, chemistry, algebra, electricity, mathematics, geometry, history, shorthand, meteorology, ship construction and much more. Enthusiasm for some classes, such as Russian and Hindustani, soon faded. The class for Malay started in 1942 with 40 students but in less than a month, Stanley was the sole survivor so the room was allocated to another subject and the determined Stanley found a Malay sailor to teach him. *Inter alia*, prisoners passed examinations set by the Board of Trade, The Civil and Electrical Engineers Institutes and the London City of Guilds. One very popular course was on first aid and many prisoners obtained their St. John's First Aid Certificates. Stanley tried to keep busy mentally and attended lectures on history and he also made presentations to some of his colleagues. In March 1942, he spoke on "The transport of sulphuric acid" which was well received.

In 1912, when very young, Stanley had studied shorthand and in July 1942, three decades later, he resumed his studies. Now he was the oldest in the class. Five months later, he decided to enter for the Pitman's shorthand teaching diploma

169

and, after three months intensive study, sat the examination in April 1943. The class had attained a speed of 90 words a minute, more than required to pass the exam, but, overcome by nerves, Stanley and the remainder of his class all failed, to his intense chagrin. "It was hopeless. My hand trembled and my nerves were all to pieces, even although a speed of only 80 words was necessary", but he persisted. Three months later he sat the exam again but, once again, nerves ensured his failure and prompted a similar reaction to that he had felt in April. "After working so hard, and experiencing such shaking of my hands, I know that the failure is just nerves." The course may have been popular because it enabled some of the participants to record key news from bulletins.

The library

For Stanley, one of the best "features" of the camp was the library. It began modestly, with each new member being charged a token fee and having to contribute one book. The number of available books soared with more contributions from other prisoners, the Red Cross, prisoner-of-war societies, shipowners and other sources and reached 7,000 volumes of which some 3,000 were non-fiction. There was even a professional book binder in the camp who, in one memorable month, bound 50 books and repaired seven. Borrowings were brisk and in October 1944, the number of books in the library, by category and by percentage of the total in each category borrowed, was as follows:

Political and social subjects	100	18
Essays and art	450	10
Poems	150	12
Plays	110	8
Travel	600	34
Biography	700	32
History	200	35
Science, sport, gardening	450	25
Theology, theosophy	250	39

There were 2,942 books in the technical library. Topics covered included agriculture, architecture, art, astronomy, biology, botany, business salesmanship, carpentry, chemistry, commerce, draughtsmanship, economics, electricity, engineering civil and marine, English, farming, gardening, geography, geology, history, insurance, languages, law, manufacturing, mechanics, medicine, metallurgy, meteorology, mineralogy, music, navigation, physics, plays and poetry, science, seamanship, surveying and trigonometry.

The annual exhibition

For Stanley, this was one of the year's highlights and he marvelled at what could be done with so little material and with so few tools. One engineer made a model of a steamer and some inmates, discovered unexpected skills and became wood carvers, artists and painters. The art work was particularly good and one unforgettable picture was of a prisoner looking out of the window, through the barbed wire, at a bird singing outside, in a tree.

Sport

One problem was the lack of food and when the flow of Red Cross parcels ceased, all football matches were cancelled. Nevertheless, sport played an important role in improving morale. Some necessary equipment was produced by the ever-resourceful prisoners themselves but the Red Cross was helpful. Many different sports proved popular with players and spectators alike and were organised efficiently by numerous committees and boards such as the Milag Sports Organisation (MSO), Football Control Board (FCB) and the Rugby Control Board. Gambling was rampant and bookies attended every football and cricket match, and boxing and athletics events.

Football

Intending players submitted their names and teams were chosen to compete in the first and second leagues. Each team was intended to be as similar in skills and playing strength as possible and bore the name of a famous English side, such as Arsenal, Liverpool or Newcastle. Readers may wonder why Manchester United was not one of the favoured names but that club had a poor period in the 1930s. Chelsea, too, failed to finish in the first three places in the first division during the decade.

Two managers, one officer and one rating, looked after each team and took their responsibilities seriously, especially at half time when they dispensed cigarettes and advice to their players. The league consisted of 12 teams which competed for the championship and a knock-out shield competition was also held.   The football was keen and usually of a reasonable standard but, after three years or more, the men became stale and tempers were easily aroused. At the end of the season, the league champions and shield winners were given medals, made in the camp from silver paper, or highly ornate diplomas signed by the secretary of the Milag Sports Association (MSO) and the camp leader.

In October 1943, at a different level, Stanley played for the masters versus the third officers and really enjoyed it. He retained his place as, four days later, he was again in the masters' team, this time confronting the chief engineers. He played again in November and again in March 1944, aged 45, so must have been reasonably fit, despite the deprivations.

Cricket

A pool of cricketers was formed for the summer months and teams were named after county sides which competed for the championship. In 1943 and 1944, Middlesex won and Yorkshire were well down the league, thus reversing the usual procedure. (In the 1930's Yorkshire had won the title six times.) The greatest interest was stimulated by the Test matches between England and Australia. Although there were only 113 Australians in the camp, mostly from three Australian phosphate-carrying ships, *Triona, Triasta* and *Triadic,* these games were keenly contested. A carpenter in Milag made a wooden trophy of an urn which had a lion and a kangaroo on

172

each side of the trophy. In 1942, Australia won 3-2 and the following year won 4-1. Honour was restored in 1944 when England won 3-0. Elsewhere, the Milag team beat the Marlag (Navy) team twice, home and away.

Rugby

This sport was not very popular because few of the prisoners knew anything about rugby. However, some teams, such as Kingston-on-Thames, Barbarians and United Hospitals were formed and "these fellows enjoyed pushing each others' faces into the mud".

Baseball

There were only 85 Americans in the camp but they enjoyed their games. They acquired baseball uniforms from home and organised baseball and softball leagues in which they were joined by many Britishers, most of them cricketers. Many attended the matches involving Red Sox, Phillies, Detroit etc, just to hear the barracking and wisecracks which played a large part in these games.

Boxing

There were several open air boxing contests held in the summers of 1942 and 1943 and a few winter ones in the theatre. They were very popular but owing to the small number of contestants and the difficulties of training under reduced rations, they were dropped in the winter of 1943.

Athletics

Clubs were formed from the athletes in the camp and inter-club events, involving track and field events, were held each month between "Oxford, Cambridge, Harvard and Yale". Competition was keen in the 100 yard sprints, longer races, up to two miles, relay races, high and long jump and putting the shot. Occasionally teams of officers competed against ratings.

Each summer a sports day was held when proceedings were opened by a parade of the athletes, led by a Highland Piper. Points were awarded for the first three in each event and at the end of the day, the champion barrack, the one obtaining most points, was awarded a cup, to be held for a year. The champion athlete was also rewarded. The prizes were usually "cheap German rubbish" which was all that was available, and the camp diplomas.

Physical training and skating

PT classes were held each summer. The gymnasts spent hours every day struggling with heavy weight lifting, jam jars filled with cement, vaulting over bars and swinging round and round a bar lashed between two trees. Ju Jitsu classes were held but no contests or exhibitions took place. A pond inside the camp, constructed to provide water in case of fire, froze in winter and was used as a skating rink. Skates were made from the long metal hinges of the shutters at the windows. Eventually, the Germans discovered that the barracks which were not used for accommodation lacked shutters. The wood had been burned and the metal had been made into skates.

Indoor entertainment

Indoor entertainments were held in the two dining halls, the officers in the north end of the camp and the ratings near the main square. In the North hall, whist drives, bridge, housey housey, chess, crib took place with lectures or debates on Sunday nights. The ratings' hall was given over exclusively to gambling except for the nights when dancing was held. The two dining halls were then used for whist drives, bridge and bingo, chess and crib and for lectures on Sunday nights. The ratings hall was dedicated to gambling except when dancing was held.

The debates and lectures in the north dining room, attended by officers and ratings, usually were "good". Topics included "With the migratory fruit pickers in the USA", "A sailor ashore in the depression", "The greatest city in the world",

"Taxi driving in Indianapolis", "Life in a submarine", "Pioneering in North West Victoria", "Life in China", "Newspaper reporting" and a "Landlubber at sea". Some debates, on, for example, 'Town versus country', 'Can a man get rich honestly?', 'Can officers and ratings live in harmony?' were "inane but they provided an opportunity for wit".

The Beveridge plan for a post-war welfare state was another topic. William Beveridge, an economist, academic and writer, produced his Report on Social Insurance and Allied Services in 1942: it had been scheduled for release at the end of the war but it was finished early and proved to be a best-seller in London. Interestingly, sufficient detail was, apparently, available in the camp to allow a discussion. The study eventually formed the background to the post-war welfare state.

Horse racing in the North hall, organised by the Milag Jockey Commission was a very popular Saturday night pastime. A long numbered cloth was the race course and the horses, small and made of wood, moved according to the throw of a dice. A winking electric sign gave the number of the winning horse and a long line of clerks, complete with eye shades, took the bets. No private bookies were allowed. The MJC took ten per cent of the bets and a proportion was given to camp funds.

In the ratings' hall, the same type of sport prevailed except that greyhounds were used and bookies were allowed, organised by the Milag Greyhound Racing Association. The course ran down one side of the hall, the opposite side being occupied by bookies with satchels on their stands, shouting the odds, and their clerks taking the bets. Here it was possible to see a chief officer acting as a clerk to a Japanese bookie who had been a fireman on the same ship.

There were two schools of ballroom dancing in the camp and every Saturday night a dance was held in the West Hall. On other nights, the West Hall was filled by wheel men. These men operated wheels similar to roulette except the wheels swung vertically. The outer edges of the wheels were numbered and a pointer indicated the winning number when the wheel stopped.

Bean boards were also favoured. A cloth had 1, 2, 3 and 4 marked on it and men bet on the numbers. A handful of beans were poured out of a tin and then counted off in fours and the number after the last four beans had been counted was the winning number. Throwing the dice was another popular way of losing marks.

Visiting the West Hall in an evening was an experience, especially during a roulette session. The smoke was solid and around the sides of the hall were the numerous roulettes and numbered tables, on which to lay bets, and the wheel operator and his clerk. There was a constant clicking of the wheel, usually from a bicycle, as it was spun, as well as a hubbub caused by the raucous cries of the croupiers, "place your bets", and "then no more bets", and the babble of different languages. Standing around the tables would be men of almost every race and colour and grade and senior officers mingled with Chinese, Egyptian, Indian and British sailors. In a corner, as if playing in a quiet room, there would be card players. It was light and warm and, for many, more comfortable than their over-crowded barracks.

Music

Recitals, always popular, were held in the cinema when it was not being used for films. They had a powerful impact on morale. A gramophone and amplifier provided mainly classical and light classical music but occasionally a full programme was devoted to swing and jazz. Many POWs worked hard to provide entertainment and some of Stanley's most pleasant hours were spent listening to the band from the *Orama*, a passenger ship sunk early in the war. They were only five in number when they arrived at the Sandbostel camp in the early days but eventually the orchestra consisted of 14 good musicians. They mounted *Bandwaggon* and an hour's good music on Sunday nights during those first few months of captivity when many prisoners were feeling the loss of freedom particularly acutely. "If it were possible to have pleasant memories of life in a prisoner-of-war camp, they gave them to me." *Bandwaggon* proved almost too emotional. "Life can be sweet, rich and tender and at the moment, it is so hard, cruel and filthy."

In October 1942, "at the musical hour this afternoon, the orchestra played the *Barcarolle* from Tales of Hoffman. It made me visualise the band in the park on a Sunday afternoon. Decent, ordinary people listening, men and women, happy together, their kiddies running on the grass, as Phil did in 1939, and, when I remembered that these clean simple things are over for millions of people I was filled with a futile rage and hatred against the criminals who are responsible for all this suffering. I glory in the fact that, day by day, they are being slaughtered in Russia and soon, I hope in the west too."

In March 1943, when he had been a prisoner for two years, a gramophone recital aroused Stanley. "As I sat there in the darkness, I was torn by conflicting emotions, of hunger, and longing for Maidie and the clean normal things of life, and a rage against the criminal German race. I remember the pictures I have seen in German magazines, pictures of dead Russians, men who have died defending their own country and all the countless millions who have known misery because of the Huns' dream of world conquest. I exult when I hear of the Russians killing the bastards in their thousands and I think that the death of a German makes this world a better and cleaner place."

On 29th April 1944, some gramophone music reminded him of old colleagues who had been burnt to death when their ships were mined. "Slaughter everywhere. Men, women and children. What kind of world is this? Where is God? (This was one of the few such questions Stanley posed to his diary during the whole war.) What kind of person is to He to allow all this? When am I going to hold them in my arms, to see

177

Rodney for the first time? I feel very near to breaking down tonight."

The Merchant Navy theatre (MNT)

From the very beginning, the theatrical side of camp life was an outstanding success. Notwithstanding the difficulties, the lack of experience and, for a time, money, too, "little short of wonders of innovation have been performed". When Milag was "opened", all rehearsals and shows were performed in the officers' dining barracks but, in March 1943, a "real" theatre was opened in the usual wooden barracks and "since then, we have had some really good shows". The stage sets were superlative and the engineers and electricians in the camp made the excellent lighting systems A professional actor, Henry Mollison, produced and acted in some of the shows but even those in which he did not participate were, according to Stanley, equally good. One of the performers was Tommy Reilly, a harmonica player who achieved celebrity after the war.

Initially, costumes were hired from the Germans, at 10 marks each per night which strained finances. This system was subsequently abandoned and all the outfits were made by skilled thick-fingered sailors. They utilised bed sheets which had been bought, unofficially, from the Germans for cigarettes and the same procedure applied to the acquisition of make-up and other necessities. When the *Mikado* was in production, an appeal was made for Red Cross toilet bags made of flowered material which were converted into kimonos and dresses. "The sudden burst of colour and the opening music transported us away from a grim prison camp to the Japan that many of us knew and it reminded me of the future when I shall sit with her hand in mine to watch a show."

There were even printed programmes, designed in the camp and printed in Bremen, which were modelled on West End shows and incorporated details of all those involved. As this implies, stage productions were taken very seriously and not only challenged ingenuity, but, importantly, contributed enormously to maintaining morale. Such was the applause from hundreds of entertainment-deprived prisoners that some of the players talked of becoming West End professionals after the war but later "they sobered down". The biggest challenge was in playing the female roles. Some of the stage ladies resembled heavyweight wrestlers but others contrived to look like shapely, pretty girls. One inmate joked that he waited at the stage door for one of the chorus girls but discovered that "she" was a fireman. One early production was a variety show, and when the lights went up, they revealed a chorus of six big hefty chaps with hairy legs and chests, wearing grass skirts and heavy boots, dancing in unison. "It was one of the funniest things many of us had seen for years."

No less than 15 different individuals produced the shows and, after a relatively slow start in 1941, when "only" *Bon Voyage* and *Aladdin* were staged, the number of productions increased dramatically. 1942 saw *Snow White and the Seven Twerps, Tonight's the Night, Private Lives, Spotlight on London, Bandwaggon, Vagabond King, Murder on the second floor, Ragtime, Music Hall, Brightlights* and *Panto Pie*. The opening scene of the October 1942 production of *Brighlights* was a railway station with POWs returning home nearly proved too much, emotionally, for Stanley who wrote that when that day came it would be the happiest of his life. *Private Lives* rekindled memories of his honeymoon in Torquay. Another show that moved him was the March 1942 production of *Mine own country*, a drama with music and set in England. "As usual, I am filled with hatred of the criminals who have brought all this misery and filth on the world."

There were 15 productions in 1943 and one, *The Student Prince,* was particularly well received by the German officers. In April, *Desert Song,* like *Rose Marie*, which was to be performed in 1944, induced tears. "I call myself a fool for being so susceptible but day after day, the longing gnaws at me like a living thing." 1944 was another busy year, once again demonstrating the popularity and value of the shows, with one being produced every three weeks. *Present Laughter* prompted thoughts of seeing Maidie again and then he realised that thousands of good men in France would never see their wives or children again. "I could have broken down. I do hope that millions of the German bastards are slaughtered. They don't deserve to live for bringing all this misery on the world." Even after the invasion commenced and liberation drew near, the shows continued. Whilst the allies were fighting bitter battles, the inmates, powerless to assist but so keen to fight, were producing *Blithe Spirit, Smoko* and *George Washington Slept here.* The last show, *Gangway,* was seen on 3rd April 1945, only a few weeks before the prisoners were released back into the real world.

The psychological value of the shows was significant: the prisoners were occupied with innocent projects which diverted their minds, albeit temporarily, from grim reality. The Germans encouraged the activity as it meant that the prisoners were occupied with work that did not threaten them and those involved were excused from attending musters. The impressive number of shows reflected the fact that, at peak, there were three main groups, each boasting its own producers and other specialists. Some 200 men were involved.

Films

There were no films until early 1943 and then they were mainly propaganda and silent films, with a German giving a live commentary, on such fascinating topics as the German steel industry and the Bavarian Alps. These were shown in the officer's dining hall and, unsurprisingly, drew lukewarm support. Later, there were silent travel pictures but these were more popular, especially the one in August 1943, on Bali, which included footage of women naked above the waist. This provoked longing from the prisoners and Stanley wondered how many more years he would have to wait and waste. On 8th September 1943, Stanley's 44th birthday, the prisoners were shown a sickening film, *Flames over Europe.* In July 1944, the prisoners could enjoy an English-speaking American film, *Bringing up Baby.* It starred Katherine Hepburn and Cary Grant and was much appreciated by the enthusiastic audience. "How we laughed, forgetting our surroundings, and recalled a happy incident in the past." This was later followed by three more un-named American films, one of which, starring beautiful young women, stirred his emotions.

Religion

From the very beginning, Church of England and Roman Catholic padres were in the camp. Two members of the Salvation Army, captured whilst returning home after taking evacuated children to Australia, took the Protestant services. Subsequently, a British army padre replaced the Salvation Army personnel, one of whom was repatriated whilst the other was sent to another camp. A party of Roman Catholic missionaries, bound for Africa, were captured on board the *SS Zam Zam* and they became responsible for RC services. When space was limited, services were held in the dining hall but eventually rooms were allocated, for both denominations, in barracks condemned as being unsuitable for living. The Church of England morning service was held in the theatre.

All this may suggest that the camp was more like a post-war holiday camp than a prison. Those who organised these activities, challenged by the lack of necessary facilities, adequate food and freedom and compelled to live in a squalid, unpleasant and uncertain world, provided their colleagues with brief but valuable reminders of the best of the outside world. Sustaining morale at a time when the main question was whether the powerless inmates would ever see England and their families again was an enormous achievement. We may well wonder how so much ingenuity could be practiced at a time when so little was provided and hunger and fear, dominating day to day life, stalked the camp.

CHAPTER 13

Money, trading and the canteen

Before September 1941, prisoners received no money from official sources. Royal Navy men in the Marlag camp borrowed, when possible, from their officers, with the dependents at home repaying the debt through the bank or post office. Others managed to obtain five marks a month, sent from an RAF camp via an army chaplain and repayment was made in the same way. In September 1941, the American embassy, acting on behalf of the British government, began paying a monthly allowance of 20 marks to officers and 10 marks for ratings. This sum, converted at 10 marks to the pound sterling, was deducted from the UK prisoner-of-war detention allowance which, in turn, was paid by the Ministry of Pensions to dependents.

It is difficult to generalise on the financial arrangements made for those MN personnel who were captured: some shipping companies immediately stopped all payments to non-contracted staff who were captured, callously contending that articles of employment had been terminated so there was thus no obligation to pay crews. Inevitably, much hardship was experienced by next of kin. Other, more reputable, employers continued to make some payments which were often in the form of a pension. In June 1941, the government which, thus far, had seemed ungrateful, belatedly responded to the needs

182

of a service that had already made major sacrifices for the country. Following new legislation in 1941, the Ministry of Pensions assumed the responsibility for paying captured Merchant Navy seamen. Allowances were calculated in relation to a seaman's basic pay, from the date on which his vessel was lost, but the pay did not include war risk allowance or an assumption for overtime.

In October 1943, the embassy money, then being paid by the Swiss, was reduced to 10 marks for officers and five for ratings. For most inmates, this cut was no hardship: there was rarely anything worth buying in the canteen and the main expenses were incurred for visits to the theatre, admission cost half a mark for each performance, and, for those who had one, for an orderly. Many inmates did not bother to draw all the marks available to them as a few cigarettes, the real currency, would buy most of the relatively small number of items that were both desired and available.

Trading was actively pursued by prisoners who worked outside the camp, Germans and foreigners working inside and outside the camp, and the German guards themselves. The ratings who worked on the local farms were the main intermediaries between buyers and sellers. Once, Stanley saw an Egyptian being given eggs by a guard. They were wrapped up in a handkerchief and passed through the barbed wire on the end of the guard's bayonet. Ratings were searched on their return to the camp but cigarettes given at the right time proved sufficient to keep matters secret. When searching at the camp gate became too vigorous for the ratings, especially at night, they would throw whatever they had over the wire, to their waiting friends. "Sometimes, I walked along the road inside the camp, hoping to be hit on the head by a dead chicken." It never happened.

The ratings who worked on the farms obtained their merchandise by exchanging cigarettes, coffee, soap etc from Red Cross food parcels and much of the produce from the farm, such as eggs or apples, was traded around the camp. Eggs were priced between 10 to 20 cigarettes or two to five marks each, and chickens cost 150 cigarettes or 50 marks. A magnificent goose was offered for 600 cigarettes but few could afford such prices unless they had been very successful in their gambling. One man won 6,900 marks in 20 minutes so should have been able to eat relatively well for some time.

The bookies were the camp's plutocrats and were able to live off the fat of the German Reich. Some goods from the outside world were sold in the canteen at exorbitant prices. Matches were ten marks, (one month's embassy money), for a packet. Twelve marks or 100 cigarettes had to be surrendered for 1½ pounds of onions and 1¼ pounds of flour cost 10 marks.

Some prisoners sold clothing and articles from Red Cross parcels. A tin of biscuits cost 20 or 30 cigarettes and two ounces of tea were priced at 70 cigarettes. Four ounces of sugar could be exchanged for 20 cigarettes and a tin of condensed milk was priced at 100 cigarettes. The price of cigarettes themselves fluctuated between 8 and 130 marks per hundred, in line with supply and demand. Most of the trading was to secure cigarettes for use in gambling, rather than smoking.

Camp marks, invalid outside the camp, were specially printed but later they were superseded by regular German money which caused trading levels to increase significantly as many German guards had pockets full of marks but nothing to buy until they traded with prisoners who were working outside the camp. The Germans could only buy inferior cigarettes and real coffee and tea were unavailable. A young radio officer carried on a regular barter trade with a German guard whom he used to meet each night at about 11.00 pm, outside one of the huts. Unknown to him, the guards were changed and the new man, possibly panicking, killed him. Prisoners were allowed to visit the lavatories at night and the young man was some distance from the outer edge of the camp. He was buried in the small cemetery outside the camp but nothing more was heard about the incident.

The canteen

In the first camp, at Sandbostel, a small canteen was set up but it was always difficult to obtain anything desirable. The stock had to be bought from the large canteen in a nearby French camp so, after passing through umpteen hands, the prisoners had to pay very high prices. For example, a tin of tomatoes which, in England, would have cost about a shilling, was priced at 1.80 marks, equal to about 3/9 and this bargain was only available when the potential customer's turn was reached on the roster.

When the Merchant Navy personnel were transferred to Milag, the canteen bought stock direct from the Germans but prices did not fall. Shoddy goods, at high prices, included foot powder, head water, face cream, nail files, boot polish that did not polish, talcum powder, dreadful toothpaste, razors and blades, penholders, ink and nibs, ashtrays and beakers. Items really needed, such as writing paper, notebooks or toilet requisites were seldom available and, even then, they were priced exorbitantly for those whose turn on the roster had arrived.

In the summers of 1941 and 1942, the canteen obtained a small amount of vegetables, carrots, lettuces, turnips and a vegetable roster was drawn up. "When your turn came, you rejoiced in the possession of a couple of tiny carrots, a turnip, and a sad and dejected looking lettuce." In the summer of 1943, on two occasions, the canteen obtained some fruit. "We solemnly lined up and paid our 1.80 marks for half a dozen apples and pears which, on further examination, proved to be rotten windfalls." In the hot weather, something resembling beer or cider was made available.

German newspapers and magazines, printed in German, English, French or Spanish were readily available but the supply was curtailed when the "the total war effort" was declared. The most useful function of the canteen was to act as an exchange. A man who had two left boots in his clothes parcel, anxiously asked if anyone was in a similar predicament with two right boots and another man wanted to exchange a size 32 vest for one of size 40. Another wished to swap chocolate for some corn beef. After examinations, the supply of certain text books increased. A Canadian was heard to say, after reading one advertisement where the supplier wanted a significantly better part of the bargain, "that guy would give his waistcoat sleeves away". Most of the advertisements began "Gent."

Gent:

Will give two ounces of tea for three tins of jam
Is willing to give healthy life biscuits for   margarine
Wants to employ a chemistry teacher
Wants to buy a rabbit hutch
Wants to buy a black kitten
Will give a pair of boots size eight for a new roll neck pullover
Will give four ounces of tea for two tins of condensed milk or packet of coffee
Will give two packets of raisins for one tin of margarine but cannot be peanut
Will give a pair of brand new boots, size 10, for two shirts and a pair of socks.
Wants to buy brilliantine but not Star of Asia
Wants to buy a frying pan and, finally,
Wanted urgently: a volunteer to be the hind legs of a horse in tonight's show.

CHAPTER 14

Mail

Prisoners were allowed to send four postcards, of seven lines each, and three letter-cards, of 24 lines, every month. Seven cards, sent to Stanley's sons, have survived and the message was usually similar. He was pleased that they were behaving well, helping their mother and doing well at school. When relevant, he said how sorry that he was for missing their birthdays but that he would make it up to them when he was home, which he hoped would be soon. Sometimes he requested some items. In March 1943, for example, he wanted five pounds of chocolate, one tin of tooth powder, two tins of boot polish and one small nail brush.

There were no restrictions on the volume of incoming mail the delivery of which took between one and three months to reach the camp. Ironically, it often seemed to arrive, frequently in "bulk", just when Stanley was beginning to worry because he had not heard from home for some time. Letters and parcels, especially of food, but also of clothes and books, bolstered morale by reminding the captives that they had not been forgotten and eased their physical condition modestly.

Stanley's secret diaries were his friend in the camp, to which he confided his news, hopes and fears and his incoming letters added an additional and welcome dimension. "Every time that I get letters from Maidie, I'm pleased and find comfort in my memories." In 1942, a letter from his wife assured him that she would not change a thing about him. On 16th March 1944, Maidie's comment "how thankful I am that I married my sailor" reduced him to tears. On 10th October 1944, he received a letter from Maidie, dated 3rd September, which prompted the comment that he was "immensely moved to read her letter and to know that she thinks so well of me. Her opinion is the one that matters most to me. How sweet to read that Philip went to church with his mother. Soon, God willing, I'll be with them."

This was probably a well-timed letter because, just a few days before, he had confided to his diary. "These are miserable days. It is cold and snow and slush lie on the ground. The wind howls through the trees and we walk up and down like animals in the zoo. When are we going to get out of here?" Occasionally, if no correspondence had been received for some time, it was construed in the worst possible way, even although wartime conditions were probably responsible. Curiously, delays in the receipt of letters were seldom attributed to wartime disruption. Usually, it was thought that the correspondent had not made the effort to write, or, more typically, that something serious had happened. In July 1943, when he was receiving little mail, Stanley was bitter and worried. "It only takes ten minutes to write a letter. Still, I'll get out of here one day."

One "clothes" parcel, which weighed ten pounds and included soap and chocolates, could be received by the prisoners every three months. Food and books had to be sent separately. Food could be sent by people in neutral countries but only next of kin were allowed to send clothes parcels. The average delay in delivery depended on the state of the war and could be from three to nine months, although some only arrived after a full year had passed and reached the prisoners after some of their contents had been stolen by the Germans. There were no limits on the number of parcels of books or cigarettes that the inmates could receive.

Stanley, a life-long non-smoker, received 1,400 cigarettes from his employers, Shell, in 1944 and these were exchanged for food or even clothes. Occasionally the prisoners were confronted by near starvation and Stanley's writing conveys the enthusiasm with which food parcels were greeted and he gleefully recorded their contents. A Christmas 1941 parcel from Shell in Portugal contained one Christmas pudding, one packet of crystallised fruits, two packets of assorted biscuits, one packet of chocolate biscuits, one packet of assorted toffees, one packet of raisins, two packets of Quaker oats and one packet of figs. Also included were a scarf and two pairs of socks. On 13th April 1942, Stanley received his October 1941 parcel. Everything was intact and the contents were more than he had requested. "Gosh, how excited and pleased I am and how grateful to my sweet Maidie. She sent a lovely shirt, pyjamas, towels, socks, ties and handkerchiefs. How good she is to me." In the context of the prisoner-of-war camp and the deprivation, these items must have seemed really luxurious. His February clothes parcel arrived on 26th July and, once again, Stanley was moved at his wife's kindness.

Books were very important to Stanley and his fellow officers who, under the Geneva Convention of 1928, were not required to work but had many hours to fill. In early October 1942, he received some shorthand books and this parcel was swiftly followed by another which contained some Penguin paperbacks. Two more parcels came in three days leaving Stanley "really bucked" but more was to come in this significant month. On 17th October 1942 another parcel from Maidie arrived. It had taken a year to reach the camp but the bedside book, an anthology, was just what Stanley had wanted. In December he received a parcel of books from Eva, his half-sister.

As the conflict progressed and as Stanley's diaries became progressively pre-occupied with war news, there was markedly less information about parcels. However, in January 1943, some Malay books arrived and the receipt of a clothes parcel was confirmed in November. However, it had been badly pilfered and only a towel, a quarter pound of chocolates

189

and a pair of very good slippers remained. In March of the following year, 1944, he received his December 1943 clothes parcel and notes appreciatively that this was intact. "I get as excited as a small boy when I receive mail or parcels." On 10th June, his February clothes parcel arrived.

What to write to a POW

What to say to a prisoner required careful thought. A tone of unrestrained optimism was wrong but it was also desirable to cheer up the hapless inmates. Maidie seems to have avoided giving Stanley too many false hopes but he wrote in his diary in July 1942 that, "for the first time, Maidie tells me that the end of our long parting may be in sight". Naturally, this made him very happy at the thought of their reunion. In May 1943, she told him that she thought that he would be home for his birthday in September. He was only released in May 1945.

News about his sons, which tended to dominate correspondence, both cheered and depressed him. He learned that Philip, then aged five, had asked "how long have you had Daddy and did you have him when he was a little baby?" He also heard that his older son thought that Stanley was more important than John, his uncle, who was one of the survivors from the *Lancastria* when it sank in June 1940, off St. Nazaire. It was carrying up to 7,000 troops, survivors from the British Expeditionary Force, and between 3,000 and 4,000 men perished. The troopship, which, according to its master, could carry about 300 personnel, sank in 30 minutes in the worst ever shipping disaster. The government, fearful of the impact on morale, banned press coverage and next of kin were told that their loved ones were "missing in action". However, the story broke in New York in the July, before the US joined the war. Later, Stanley was delighted to learn that his brother-in-law had been awarded the MBE.

Other letters from home conveyed news of the progress of his two sons, the younger of whom had just started at school. "So the only baby I've known was Philip for a few months in 1939." If letters could boost morale, they could also cause problems. If bad news had been contained in the previous letter, it was most frustrating waiting, impotent, often for many months, to hear more and, hopefully, better news. Additionally, information about a death or illness could induce pessimism and, of course, any communication was, inevitably, a reminder of what was being missed as the years stumbled past. So, how much bad news, about family or friends, should be communicated? On 29th April 1944, Stanley received a letter from his relative, Stan Punch, giving him details of his mother's death, some ten months before although the news had already been passed to him, three weeks earlier, by the camp padre. He also had letters from Maidie telling him that their next door neighbour in Muswell Hill had been lost. Similar letters followed. "I am upset. Decent fellows losing their lives and for over two years, I've done nothing."

On 16th May 1944, as recounted earlier, Stanley was saddened by a letter from Maidie saying that she might have to cut his father's allowance because of her poor financial position. This suggested to Stanley, however, irrationally, that he might not be able to provide for his family unless he worked permanently in the Far East, where rates of pay were superior but where leave was only granted every three years. As he had been away from home for nearly five years at that point, the prospect that, effectively voluntarily, he might be parted from his family for long periods, after his release, must have been devastating. Five weeks later he learned that the allowance had been cut.

A letter arrived from Maidie on 23rd September in which she said that Rodney had broken his arm and that Bloss, his mother in law, who was ill, had been close to having a stroke. "I felt like crying when I think of all that Maidie has had to put up with...I suppose that I have a morbid obsession and fear of them ever being in want and I realise that money alone will enable me to be with them often and, finally, retire. Poor old Maidie, she must be just about at the end of her tether."

Photographs could both cheer and depress. Whilst they assured Stanley that he was not forgotten, they were a stark reminder of what he was missing. On balance, however, they improved his morale. On 5th May 1942, having received four small photographs of Philip, he wrote "to think that I am his father, and more wonderful still, Maidie is his mother. He is a fine little chap". Later he received six more "lovely snaps of my treasures" and these were followed by one of Maidie and the boys taken at a garden party for prisoners' children. A photograph sent in 1942 prompted the observation that "Philip seems to have plenty of weight and looks a sturdy and independent little chap". What he did not know, until August of that year, was that his older son went into hospital on 9th July, to have his appendix removed. "I feel so sorry for Maidie as I do for the little chap. All the things she has had to do alone and how tired she must be. He is getting on all right but I am looking forward to having more mail and learning how he is." No letters came for about a month, which, inevitably, worried Stanley but on the 21st August he learned that his elder son was out of hospital. "I nearly broke down when I read this."

This was followed by his first-ever letter from Philip. "Dear daddy, I hope that you are well. I often think about you. I am better now, all my love, Philip." Another photograph of his two sons provoked a frequent thought which reflected his own unhappy childhood and insecurity. "It seems strange that two lovely little human beings should be mine." At the end of December 1943, he admitted to be "eaten up with longing and I'm never far from tears. The last thing at night, before the light is switched out, I look at Maidie's photograph and recall the happiness we have shared. When will all this end and when will we all meet again?" Acute depression was rampant again in January 1945, when he received a photograph of his sons. "They are both growing up strong independent little men and I'm sad that never will I have a baby of my own, climbing on to my knee, asking daddy for a story. What a miserable unnatural life I've had so far, always hungry for things that ordinary men have every day. I'm almost being eaten with longing and now I'm physically hungry as well." In February he thought that a photograph of Maidie suggested that she was too thin. Unknown to him at that time, she was suffering from tuberculosis.

At some unknown stage in the war, a complete album of photographs was sent to the camp. It contained some 100 shots of different members of the family and friends and covered the period 1927-1939. Of particular poignancy would have been the photographs of the wedding, holidays together and, of course, young Philip with his father just before the war. All are meticulously labelled and it must have been a wrench for Maidie to send the album, which had been compiled by Stanley before the war, into Germany, not knowing if it would reach Stanley or if she would ever see him again. However, as some of the photographs appear in other albums, it seems that Maidie ensured that she had copies.

CHAPTER 15

News, rumours and propaganda

In the early days of the war, prisoners lacked real news. For example, Stanley made no reference to the Japanese attack on Pearl Harbour on 7th December 1941, which prompted the US to enter the war. There was minimal reference to the bombing of the UK's major cities, including Plymouth, some 30 miles from the Torquay area, to which he had evacuated the family in 1940. Some children, despatched to Plymouth for safety, were moved elsewhere and, given the later build-up of invasion forces, it was surprising that his new home town was not a major target. Of course, the omission of such news in the diaries does not mean that Stanley was ignorant of such attacks but one tragic incident in Torquay did worry him. This is discussed later in this chapter.

Inevitably, rumours flourished in the absence of real news but occasionally reliable information came from new prisoners but this source dried up as fewer Merchant Navy personnel were captured. Indeed, the majority of the men in the camp had been taken prisoner early in the war. "Every new prisoner was plagued by about 2,000 Rip Van Winkles, all wanting to know how things were in England and most importantly, when did the people back home think that the war would end? The new prisoner's popularity would depend on his reply." In April 1942, a naval officer, captured a few months before, opined that the war would not be over that year and that people at home feared that, if the Russians suffered any more reverses that summer, they might withdraw from the war. His thoughts were not well received.

In the early stages of the conflict, hard labour or even the death penalty had been introduced for nationals and citizens in occupied countries who were found listening to the BBC or any foreign broadcast. Paradoxically, and towards the end of Stanley's imprisonment, there was apparently less concern about radios in the camp. It seemed that the guards were not interested in eliminating all wireless sets or that they were, on balance, not very intelligent and failed to appreciate the tonic that increasingly good news gave to the captives. Some camp guards even co-operated with the prisoners who were "allowed" to listen to the BBC news in the camp office, in return for cigarettes. Eventually, on most nights, it was possible for one "reporter" to listen to the radio in the German office in the camp. During 1942, it was too depressing to make the effort but one night the BBC news was switched on instead of Haw Haw and the prisoners were entranced by a talk given by Admiral Evans.

On another occasion, during the landings in North Africa, a similar mistake was made by the German who switched on the BBC news in Norwegian. The Norwegians in the camp soon told their colleagues all the latest news and on 9th November 1942, Stanley heard the end of the Scottish regional news. Before long, the prisoners soon established a reliable method of keeping in touch with the war. A British sailor who had joined the *Agnita,* to help with the guns, obtained a job in the camp administration offices, situated a short distance from the main camp. He spent all day there, cleaning the office and doing any work required. Slowly, he ingratiated himself with the Germans and the relationship was eased by the gift of some British cigarettes which were prized by the Germans. Having noticed that there was a radio in the office, after slow and careful negotiations with one of the soldiers, aided again by a gift of cigarettes, the real currency in the camp, the sailor was allowed to be alone in the office with the radio on just as the BBC news was broadcast.

When a new guard appeared, there was a hiatus until he agreed to continue the practice. Over the years, the British sailor became skilled at remembering the news and then conveying it to some of his fellow captives. Stanley, the chief officer and chief engineer and a few trusted friends contributed cigarettes to keep the fund solvent. Unfortunately, they could not pass on the news because it was too dangerous. At that time, there were more than 3,000 men of different nationalities, characters and temperaments, so the source of the information might have emerged, causing a major problem for both the sailor and the guard. Some of the prisoners sent to work on the farms, outside the camp, organised deals whereby they could listen to the BBC for a few minutes. These men were extremely unreliable, having either very bad memories or vivid imaginations. Even in the darkest days of 1942, before more widespread access to wirelesses, they would regale their colleagues with news of victories.

In early 1943, Stanley heard Thomas Woodruff, of the BBC, talking about a raid over Berlin. Later that year, the ingenious inmates were beginning to make their own crystal radio sets which, amazingly, allowed them to listen to the BBC in the morning and evening. Parts were occasionally provided by the Germans themselves, who lusted after British cigarettes. Sometimes, however, the POWs were betrayed. The unintelligent Germans, stupidly stumbling around a specific room, looking for the offending wireless, would find it immediately, thus confirming that there was a spy.

One search was carried out by German soldiers supervised by a Gestapo official. A cordon was thrown around the hut where, it was suspected the radio was housed, and a soldier posted at the main door. The guard smiled at one prisoner who emerged carrying a dish of vegetables and said, "going to the kitchen?" The POW also smiled: he had hidden a radio underneath the vegetables. By the end of 1943, there were many receiving sets in the camp, including some bought from outside and smuggled into the camp so the prisoners were well supplied with "real" news. Presumably encouraged by the fact that there were now many wireless sets in the camp, details of any important event were flashed around the camp in minutes. German efforts to find them who continued but, as the war began to move in favour of the allies, their attempts became even more spasmodic and incompetent although one seven-valve set was confiscated. However, it was not a major loss as there were many more in the camp and by December 1944, it was clear that the men received reliable news on a daily basis.

German news, broadcast in English, was transmitted via the loudspeakers on the central square of the camp. One frequent broadcaster was William Joyce, alias Lord Haw Haw. He was an Irish-born American and a British fascist and broadcast from Berlin with the familiar opening line, "Germany calling, Germany calling." Haw Haw was captured near the German-Danish border on 29th May 1945, tried for treachery, and hung. In January 1940, one in three people in the United Kingdom listened to him but later it was deemed unpatriotic and the BBC scheduled more attractive programmes to compete with him. His audience dwindled, too, as the allies made progress in the war.

In the early part of the war, the prisoners were incensed and then, eventually, entertained by Haw Haw's rants. Obviously, it was propaganda but the prisoners found it interesting, especially when the tide of war began to turn and even the traitor found it difficult to conceal a major reverse. One night in February 1943, just after the Germans had lost Stalingrad and some 100,000 Germans had been taken prisoner, one inmate, arriving late in the transmission, asked what Haw Haw had said. A fellow British prisoner reported that he had claimed that the Germans would fight to the last kartoffel, which remark upset the German guard who was posted to listen to any comments.

For some time, the POWs were able to buy German newspapers and magazines, published in English, but this ceased as economic pressures increased on the Hitler regime.

However, the Germans issued a weekly newspaper in English called *The Camp* for the prisoners. It consisted largely of ludicrous propaganda but it deluded few of its readers who were merely amused or annoyed and it was even a joke to the guards who distributed it. In November 1941, an article contended that all that remained for the German army in the following spring was to mop up the remnants of the Russian army. The inmates also enjoyed the comment that, following the allied invasion, the German troops on the channel coast were "burning with eagerness to be sent against the enemy".

Finally, some news might have been gleaned from letters received by the prisoners but this is very unlikely. In many instances, the authors would not have known some key facts because of the UK government's policy and the strong self-censorship of the newspapers and BBC. Furthermore, even when the writer had some information, conveying it to a POW might have undermined morale, proved valuable to the enemy and rendered the writer liable to prosecution.

Fiction and fact

There are many references in the diaries to military progress or setbacks. It is easy to understand the reason for such passionate interest and, as so many diary entries are correct, it is clear that access to wireless sets, inside or outside the camp, was possible. However, several stories from the early days, when the prisoners seemingly lacked wirelesses, were also accurate. As early as January 1942, Stanley wrote, correctly, that the bad news was that the Japanese were taking Manila. No doubt such bad news was provided by the Germans. Sometimes, and this doubtless reflects confusion on the dates, or merely the availability of spare pages in his notebooks, Stanley was significantly ahead or behind actual events. Occasionally, too, stories were inaccurate, possibly because of British propaganda. Initially, the diaries are full of rumours doubtless born of frustration, but, gradually, such entries give way to "more-reliable" news.

On the 12th February 1941 Stanley noted that Singapore had fallen to the Japanese, although this only happened on 15th February. On 29th June, "the camp is alive with buzzes, all of them fantastic. Turkey and Sweden are in the war." (Sweden was to remain neutral, as it had in World War One, and Turkey stayed neutral until 1945, when it decided to support the allies.) Another popular rumour was that there had been an assassination attempt on Hitler. There were several such efforts, the first of which was in November 1940, but the most serious one occurred on 20th July 1944. This was a narrow failure: some 5,000 people were arrested and hundreds were executed, some by hanging from butchers' hooks, with nooses made from piano wire. Hitler later enjoyed watching their slow deaths on film.

On 4th March 1942, there were rumours that there had been landings in France. "If only it were true." Although most prisoners discounted such "news" immediately, there was always just that slender hope that some of the stories might be accurate. At this time, the UK government was also making up rumours which may or may not have reached the camp. One was that Hitler had gone mad and, according to his colleagues, was in the habit of chewing the carpet and another was that the British had invented a device which could set the sea alight, thus preventing an invasion. One popular belief in the UK was that German spies had landed by parachute, dressed as nuns. A.P. Herbert, writing in May 1940, had cautioned: "Do not believe the tales the milkman tells, no troops have mutinied in Potters Bar, nor are there submarines in Tunbridge Wells. The BBC will warn when there are."

At the end of June 1942, a rumour, possibly based on German radio broadcasts, suggested that the axis expected to reach the Suez Canal in three days. "If this is true, it's really bad news. Millions of men are at home, trained, doing nothing, and yet we have reverse after reverse." Rumours of an allied invasion spread through the camp on 5th August 1942 but perhaps the cruellest rumour, two weeks later, was that some prisoners were to be repatriated. "I dare not believe it: it would be too good to be true."

Some entries were patently wrong: on 24th August 1942, Stanley wrote about "great news of a commando raid of a division on Dieppe. They were ashore for nine hours and succeeded in all they set out to do." Unfortunately, the raid, which took place on 19th August and which was mounted by some 6,200 Canadian and British troops to test amphibious assault tactics, was a spectacular disaster, with 60 per cent casualties and no gains. One hundred allied aircraft, sent to provide cover, were shot down. All that can be claimed is that the experience was presumably useful in relation to the 1944 invasion. That said, the allies were reluctant to concede the extent of the disaster whilst Hitler, notwithstanding how few allied troops had been involved, chose to call it an invasion.

On 1st October 1942, Stanley wrote that "the Russians claim to have slaughtered 360,000 Germans. Day after day the world is becoming a better place". Just two weeks later he was very depressed. "There seems to be no move by our people to get on with the war. It seems to me as if we must wait another year and Rodney is two years old and I haven't seen him yet. My life seems to be a constant hunger and ache for things a normal man has." An irritation at the delay in opening a second front is a regular feature of the diaries but equally, there is an acknowledgement that the sacrifice would be great and that his thoughts were selfish as they were influenced by the prospect of freedom.

One year later, similar comments appear. A second front was "the only thing that can get us out of here in a few months. It seems that we are condemned to stay here for another winter. It is hard to be unselfish and uncritical and it is so easy to forget the sacrifice we must pay for a landing and forget everything in the desire for freedom. The last few days have been terrible." Just one day later, the mood has changed after hearing that the Russians had resumed their offensive. "I really think that they may get us out of here before Christmas. Why doesn't God take a hand and stop it all?" He did not know that there had been considerable pressure at home for the opening of a second front as early as March 1942.

Churchill, facing significant political opposition in the UK, was not impressed. Indeed, those expressing pessimism in public could be fined.

Stanley wrote that, on 8th November 1942, Lord Haw Haw announced that American and British troops had landed in Vichy-controlled Algeria. This was true but they were joined by Free French forces, a fact that Haw Haw failed to mention. That night the prisoners-of-war eagerly awaited more news from the traitor but it was Hitler who spoke. Three days later, there was gossip to the effect that the allies had taken 100,000 prisoners in North Africa. "I hope that it is true and that many more were slaughtered." Two days later, there were persistent rumours that between 40,000 and 200,000 enemy forces had been captured and that the axis had been slaughtered. "It is impossible to wipe out too many of them." (In early November, the second battle of El Alamein ended in a victory for the allies under General Montgomery.)

On 17th November 1942, the diary entry recorded that the Americans were advancing towards Tunis where axis troops had landed, and that the French traitor, Pétain had demanded resistance to the allied troops but failed to secure loyalty from his military force. (In fact, the allied invasion of North Africa had begun on 7th November, as Haw Haw had conceded). By 24th November 1942, there was news that our troops are well on the way to Tripoli (which was captured on 23rd January 1943), and that the Americans, French and British troops have driven axis troops into the town of Tunis. (The British 8th Army entered Tunisia on 4th February 1943.)

Another rumour in November 1942 was that the Russians had surrounded a large number of Germans west of Stalingrad. This was true but the battle of Stalingrad was only won by the Russians in February 1943, when Field Marshall von Paulus and 100,000 survivors of his 6th Army surrendered. The German losses were around some 400,000 and about 750,000 Russians perished. In addition, another 450,000 Romanians, Hungarians and Poles lost their lives. On 27th November 1942, a mentally sick inmate told Stanley that the BBC claimed that the British and American air force strength was 324,000 planes. "Some men actually believe such tripe." In the same month, Vichy France, which had been sympathetic to the Germans, was occupied by German and Italian troops. In a broadcast heard in the camp, Lord Haw Haw, who occasionally was assisted by British prisoners-of-war, claimed that the French navy had scuttled over 70 of their own ships, equal to more than 230,000 tons, including a battleship, two battle-cruisers and seven cruisers as the Germans entered Toulon. The port was mined, preventing escape and the French admiral, who had come over to the allied cause, had promised that, if there were any chance that his fleet could fall into enemy hands, he would scuttle it. Many brave men perished with their vessels causing Stanley to lament the loss of life of so many courageous mariners. On the last day of the month, according to the diary, thousands of bombs had rained down on Rome.

Understandably, as the European conflict would determine the POWs' future, there was relatively little news in Stanley's diaries about the war in the East. However, he noted in November 1942 that in the battle for the Solomon Islands, "the Japs have lost several ships and 34,000 of them have been drowned". It seems likely that the total was around 12,000. On Christmas Day 1942, rumours suggested that 35,000 of the enemy had been killed on the eastern front. "It is Christmas Day yet I am sorry that the figure is only 35,000. They have proved a menace to humanity." A few days earlier, he had written "soon it will be Christmas day. Christ was born and yet I am glad to know that 50,000 Germans have been killed. 50,000 human beings but they are evil and pollute the world which will be sweeter without them".

In March 1943, a rumour flashed around the camp that the allies had landed in France. This, of course, was some 15 months before the real event. Some men claimed to have details of places and casualties and one even confessed to having heard the news himself. Another startling rumour was that the Russians had advanced very swiftly and were on the German border. All this was obviously a fantasy but as Stanley noted, it was easy to believe that there might just have been something in it.

On 8th May 1943, Stanley noted triumphantly that Tunis had been captured: however, the official surrender was on 12th May. German radio said that (losing) Tunis gave them another six months to prepare defences in Europe. Just one day after the offensive on 16th May, Stanley noted details of the successful RAF attack which burst the Mohne and Eder dams in the Ruhr valley. There had been colossal damage and many people had been drowned. "A 10 metre wave of water went racing down the valley. Only eight planes lost. A terrible thing to do but what has Germany done to others?"

On 1st July 1943, Stanley heard of Churchill's pledge that he would strike before the leaves fell. He felt really relieved to hear this as "I know now that the end is in sight." Nine days later, news that allied troops had landed in Sicily was correct which proved that genuine news was now being received regularly. This allowed Stanley to note allied progress which must have been very comforting. The improving accuracy of news was reflected in the entry for 26th July 1943. The previous day Mussolini had resigned to the King of Italy and was subsequently executed in April 1945. On 8th September 1943, at 20.00 hours, Stanley heard "the amazing news" that Italy had surrendered unconditionally, seemingly shortly after it had happened. On 29th December 1943, Stanley records details of the sinking of the German battleship *Scharnhorst* by the *Norfolk, Belfast, Sheffield, Jamaica* and *Duke of York*: it had happened just three days before.

In January 1944 accurate news was received that Leningrad, after a two year siege, had been relieved by the Russian army. About one million people died and another half a million had been evacuated. At the peak, 10,000 were dying each day and such was the hunger that they even scraped wallpaper off the walls to suck the glue. Finally, news of the allied invasion, on 6th June 1944, was known immediately and was confirmed by the camp commander.

The Torquay bombing

On 14th July 1943, Stanley was very concerned to learn that Torquay had been bombed on 1st June. That was all that he knew. Apart from the date, it happened on 31st May, the news was accurate. The last letter to arrive, on 9th July, had come from Stan Slade, his mother-in-law's friend. It was dated 7th June. "At least all was well then" or was it? Would he have withheld crucial information, leaving it to Maidie or Bloss or even official sources to convey bad news? Would the communication of any bad news have been censored? Would Slade, living in London, have read about the attack, which was reported in *The Times?*

Twenty one children and five teachers were killed when a church was attacked during a Sunday School session on the afternoon of 31st May. By the standards of the London blitz and attacks on other cities, this incident, albeit horrific, was very modest. The local inhabitants, unaccustomed to such disasters, were devastated not least as some days elapsed before all the children, or their body parts, were recovered. Some victims were already orphans: they came from a local home for those who had lost their parents. One enemy plane hit a spire of another nearby church and crashed into the road, killing the pilot, but some local residents died when German aircraft machine-gunned pedestrians on the streets and sea front.

On 16th July, Stanley was very depressed: he had not received a letter from home. On 19th July, nearly seven weeks after the attack but five days after he first heard the news, he was becoming very worried as he had not received any mail from home for a month. His agony was to last for another nine painful days before he had a letter saying that all was well. "I am overjoyed. They are all well and Philip thinks that he will pop with excitement when I arrive home. Dear little chap. Really delighted at mail and to know that all is well."

How did he know that Torquay had been attacked and why was there a delay of about six weeks in his learning the sad story? As previously discussed, there were several ways in which prisoners learned what was happening in the outside world. Some stories were related by incoming prisoners but, at that time, there were relatively few new inmates and, if they had been the source, Stanley probably would have had more information and indicated the origin of the story. Another possibility was that he had heard it on the wireless, either in the camp office or on one of their own sets. The gap of nearly seven weeks between the event and his learning of it suggests that this was not the source. Why would the Germans have delayed revealing the story for so long?

Had the BBC broadcast the story belatedly? Given all that was happening in the world, it was unlikely that there would have been such a long delay in covering a sadly typical story. Would they have used the incident to show the character of the enemy who had attacked a church on a Sunday? Even if this were true, it is unlikely that the precise location of the bombing would have been revealed. Official sources offered minimal information about air attacks and it was the UK government's policy not to disseminate any detailed information that could assist the enemy: for example, the German aircrews might not have known which town they had attacked.

Why was there such a delay in Stanley finding out what had happened?

Would the Germans have investigated whether any of the inmates had lived in Torquay and then cruelly pass on the news as a form of mental torture? That seems most unlikely: the guards were few in number, frequently outwitted and unintelligent, although some were sufficiently unpleasant to have done this. Additionally, if they had wanted to use the information as particularly nasty propaganda, would they not have given more details, including the fact that pedestrians had been machine gunned as they walked in the town? Why would they have delayed conveying the news?

Perhaps the infamous Lord Haw Haw had used the story in one of his broadcasts to the prisoners? Stanley was scrupulous in noting details of such presentations and if this had been the source, his natural scepticism of what he heard would not have induced such depression. Clearly, Stanley accepted the story which he would not have done unless it came from a relatively reliable source or seemed authentic.

During the war, UK newspapers acted largely under a system of censorship, imposed by the government and the press itself. However, there were some odd inconsistencies. For example, *The Picture Post* railed against The Ministry of Information and a system that denied them the chance to reproduce the leaflets dropped by the RAF over Germany or photographs of downed Luftwaffe aircraft. The UK press did not publish the specific location of a raid or any details of a target within a town, lest that gave valuable information to the enemy. This meant that there could have been many vague references and some relatively unimportant details could have been deliberately muddled. However, newspapers could report some of the details if they knew that the enemy already had the story. On the 1st June, the day after the attack, *The Times* carried a story headed:

Raiders kill 20 children: Sunday School bombed: Attack on S.W. Town.

The article gave full details of the attack and added that one teacher had been killed and that up to 15 more children were missing. Of the 15 enemy fighter-bombers which made the attack, four were destroyed and one aircraft crashed into a street in Torquay. Streets and the beach were machine-gunned. The Air Ministry and Ministry of Home Security recorded the attack but, as far as the location was concerned merely noted that occurred at "a place on the south west coast of England". How was it that the newspaper was able to reveal that it was Torquay that had been attacked? Such details could be published if the news had previously been confirmed by the Germans and *The Times* noted that "The German News Agency, quoted by Reuter, stated last night that Torquay was the town attacked."

It seems clear that the German News Agency was using the story and this must have been the source for the captives. What remains puzzling is why the news was not released much sooner. Ignoring Lord Haw Haw, it might have been broadcast through the parade ground loudspeakers but this seems unlikely given the long delay. The most likely explanation is that the story appeared in *The Camp* which was a weekly newspaper, written in English, containing fact and fiction, produced by the Germans. The fact that it took about six weeks to reach Stanley suggests that it might have been the newspaper as deadlines would have been less demanding than those for daily broadcasts and the Germans may have felt that the story was not particularly significant and only merited inclusion in the newspaper when space allowed. In one surviving copy of the newspaper, which was published in Berlin, some stories were up to four weeks old.

The Camp

The edition for 23rd July 1944 cites comments from an Associated Press report about the new German "secret weapon", presumably the flying bomb or V1, as the "Big Bertha of World War Two". Herbert Morrison, speaking in the House of Commons, forecast that the attacks by the new German weapon would probably increase and he also warned that it was most likely that the Germans had more new weapons. A colonel told *The Daily Telegraph* that he had never seen such intensity of fighting as occurred in Normandy and the Bishop of Marseilles condemned Anglo-American bombing of French cites, which had "shocked human conscience". *The Catholic Herald,* apparently, was surprised that some British Sunday newspapers were astonished by British estimates that more than half the population of Normandy had no wish to be liberated and that 60 per cent trusted neither the British nor the Americans. According to the

Germans, *The Catholic Herald* opines "We shall not be very popular. We are bringing war to France for the fourth time whilst the Germans were the administrators of four comparatively peaceful years".

Some photographs of victims of allied air attacks on German cities were included but, having shown the prisoners films of gloating German pilots attacking London, this manoeuvre doubtless failed. Meanwhile, according to a paragraph allegedly taken from the *Daily Herald*, church ministers in Torquay were complaining not just about the use of sex in advertising but also the strong role that sexual attraction played in marriage.

Rumours of repatriation?

On 3rd May, 1944, a justifiably sceptical Stanley heard a rumour that Anthony Eden, then foreign secretary, speaking in the House of Commons, had claimed that arrangements had been made for the repatriation of prisoners who had been incarcerated for three years. "At first I felt a rush of hope but soon became sensible again. I cannot believe that I shall be home before the end of the war." He had been captured in 1941 so, if the report were true and the plan was implemented, Stanley would have been freed. Some five weeks later, on 12th June 1944, just after the invasion had begun, the morning muster took on a special significance. The names of those who were to be exchanged for German prisoners were read out. The unimaginable tension must have been horrendous. Would it be imminent freedom or prolonged imprisonment, an uncertain future or even death in the final battle?

Captain Tommy Webster was one of the lucky ones and both men were really moved when they shook hands and Stanley wished him luck. They had been together for four years and he had been a good friend, particularly since they were captured. "I was pleased to see that some fellows would be leaving for home but I was terribly depressed not to be one of them." Cruelly, some of those who had initially been told that they were leaving, later learned that they were to remain captives but Webster was to leave Germany. "I am really pleased: he may be home in a couple of weeks. How excited Maidie will be to hear news about me. There are persistent rumours that more of us are to be exchanged for German prisoners and some even suggest that we might all be going home. If only that could be true." After nine days of suspense, those who were to be repatriated left the camp on 21st June 1944. Later, Webster wrote to Stanley after visiting Preston.

Efforts to arrange an exchange of prisoners with the Germans had been a major difficulty for some years. According to the Canadian Journal of History and other sources, one British proposal was that any prisoner, aged at least 48 years on the 1st March 1943, and who had been captured before 14th April 1940, should be released. A later suggestion was that those aged 42 and imprisoned for more than 18 months should be released. Talks had begun in 1940 but the British had not captured as many Germans as the latter had taken into their camps. Where would the released prisoners go to ensure that they played no part in the war? Neutral Switzerland had already received many escaped British prisoners so it would have been difficult to determine who could return to the UK and who had to remain in Switzerland. Germany would not allow its released prisoners to be confined to a neutral country and the Soviet Union feared that those who were liberated might take up arms again. Officially, Merchant Navy personnel were not regarded as combatants and therefore, when released, lawfully, could participate in the war. The Americans were unhappy about mass repatriations based on age and duration of captivity because many of their prisoners were young and had not been captives for long and the The British Admiralty feared that returned German seamen might be re-employed on the U boats where manning was becoming a substantial problem.

In October 1943, an agreement had been implemented by which some sick and wounded prisoners had been sent home but this did not lead to mass repatriations. Pressure from the International Red Cross, UK prisoners, their families and politicians on the British government had little impact. When greeting returning prisoners in Buckinghamshire in May 1945, Lord Leathers, then Minister of War Transport, and formerly a director of the shipping company, P&O, when Winston Churchill had also been on the board, explained that numerous but unsuccessful efforts had been made to induce the German authorities to agree a system of repatriation.

CHAPTER 16

Air raids

Allied air raids, especially after the invasion, inspired the POWs and encouraged the hope that the end of the conflict and freedom were in sight. However, admiration for the air crews was mixed with great sadness when an allied plane crashed within sight or hearing of those in the camp. In January 1942, Stanley had heard two bombs being dropped, and machine gun fire, nearby, but saw nothing. Two weeks later, he noted that there had been a heavy RAF raid in the evening and before the end of the month, apparently, such activity was routine. There were RAF raids nearly every night. There was no further diary entry relating to air raids for some time but this may have been because the lack of food and bitterly cold weather dominated his thoughts. On 4th May, there was a "huge raid at 14.00 and terrific explosions shook the hut. It was about the biggest I have heard so far."

Precisely one month later, the Merchant Navy personnel were awakened by an air raid alarm at 04.00. "Immediately, a terrific air raid started, mainly over Bremen. The huts shook like a ship hit by a heavy wave and the air vibrated with the heavy barrage and the tremendous explosions of the bombs. We were all cheered by the raid and hoped fervently that it was as bad as the one on Cologne a few days ago." (That raid, carried out by 1,000 bombers, destroyed the centre of the city.)

Not for the first nor last time, Stanley was confronted by a moral dilemma. "How grotesque is it for civilised people to exult at the destruction of human life? Yet I do exult and hope that the enemy loss of life is enormous. I think of Coventry, London, Rotterdam and other cities and the broadcast I heard from Berlin of a German pilot gloating over how he bombed a block of flats in London. It was good fun then but how they squeal now that it is being repaid. I do not want this war to end too soon. Let them be paid for all they've done to the world."

Now, decades later, his words may seem callous, even inhuman and politically incorrect to those who have enjoyed freedom because of the sacrifices of so many all those years ago. It is difficult, from our comfortable position, to imagine what it must have been like to experience the cruelty, the lack of dignity, freedom and food and misery endured by men who did not know if they would survive or ever see their families again. Stanley, like thousands of other prisoners, had been subjected to sustained propaganda, stories of German atrocities and tales of the mutilation and deaths of many colleagues and friends. His delight at the damage inflicted on the enemy is understandable, not least because of the impact on morale and the realisation that successful air raids would hasten the end of the war.

At the end of June 1942, a third heavy raid in five days (probably carried out by 1,000 RAF aircraft on Bremen) prompted the thought that no country could withstand such attacks for long. The focus of the attacks had expanded by July. "Terrific raid in early morning. All round the horizon. They are becoming very frequent." A few weeks later, the air raids had become frequent throughout the day and the prisoners received news of terrific damage and casualties caused by the bombing. "The hun does not like it and openly says so. It was good sport, however, when they were doing it."

On 17th August 1942, there were three raids during the day and this was followed on the 18th by a heavy raid in early morning. A similar raid in the early hours of 5th September made Stanley hope that the deaths and destruction were in proportion to the noise. Thereafter, for some time, the diaries contain fewer comments on other raids except that, in October a heavy raid occurred to the North West. News about the war, recorded in detail, took over from more immediate and local events but another big raid over Bremen was noted on 9th November. The year ended on a marginally more cheerful note. "A British plane dived down out of the clouds and roared over the camp and, some four minutes later, dropped some heavy stuff. A cheering sight."

On 30th January 1943, the RAF celebrated Hitler's birthday by launching terrific raids over Hamburg and Bremen. A few days later, a significant air raid lasted two hours and "everyone in the camp was feeling full of beans and saying 'it serve the bastards right.'" On 18th February, the RAF bombed Wilhelmshaven and, although raids took place every night, the biggest was on 4th March when Hamburg was ablaze until 14.00. (One report suggested that 45,000 were killed in Hamburg in 1943 and the Germans ordered the remaining 1.2 million, mainly old men and women, to leave the city.) Two weeks later, "the huns are squealing all the time about the brutal and barbarous bombing. What short memories they have." Another heavy raid was mounted on the 28th on Bremen and Hamburg. "The planes were very close. With true hun bravery, they try to take it out on the prisoners by insulting us. Still, they get a few appropriate replies." The "best raid so far" occurred on 30th March when Wilhelmshaven and Bremen were attacked. "Later we learned that Berlin, too, had been bombed."

At muster at 13.00 on 17th April 1943, "we heard bombs dropping and then a few minutes later, I saw an inspiring sight. Three large groups of Allied planes, high in the sky, coming from the direction of Bremen. How we laughed and cheered and we felt encouraged. When the ratings were called to attention, they whistled and imitated the sounds of bombs dropping. How great it was and how often we heard the comment 'I hope the bastards get hell.'" The prisoners were also immensely cheered at 09.30 on 13th June 1943 by the sight of 100 allied bombers flying over the camp. "There were no German fighters and the bombers flew in formation as in a peacetime manoeuvre. A marvellous sight."

There was another terrific raid over Hamburg on 25th July. "The air hummed with the passing bombers and later flashes, flames and explosions lit the sky. It looked like the heaviest yet." (This was part of an operation which was carried out over four nights and which resulted in the deaths of 42,000 Germans and injuries to another 37,000. Hundreds of factories were destroyed.) "The following day, the Germans looked very glum. Yesterday's raids on Hamburg, the largest so far, were carried out by the Americans who dropped 2,300 tons of bombs." Tales of horror in Hamburg reached the camp from the workmen. "Do they recall Warsaw, Coventry, Rotterdam etc.?" On Wednesday 28th July, there was another heavy raid over Hamburg and more followed every few hours for three days. These attacks continued and in less than a week, the POWs believed that 7,000 tons of bombs had rained down causing even the Germans to admit to indescribable destruction. "How soon they forget what they have done to others."

"On 3rd August 1943, at about 01.00 we saw the greatest air raid of the war. It was as if Hollywood sound effects men had gone mad. The noises were like frequent thunder, the drone of the planes passing overhead, the rumbling of the barrage, the occasional terrific crack of a nearby mobile gun, the bursting of the bombs, the whole sky was aglow with the shell flashes and flairs from the planes, star shells and sudden red flames from bombs and the lighting silhouetting the huts, trees and countryside. It was nerve wracking here but what must it have been like in the town?"

Bremen was the target at 15.00 on 8th October as swarms of flying fortresses flew over the camp but the prisoners saw two planes shot down. This raid was followed by another at night. At 13.00 on 26th November, the prisoners saw an "inspiring sight. Squadron after squadron of bombers flew overhead and, as they passed through the clouds, they left a wake of white, fluffy vapour. There must have been hundreds of them and German fighters kept away."

In late February 1944, there was another significant raid, probably undertaken by the United States, that lasted from about 23.30 to 04.00 the following morning. "Wave after wave passed over the camp and the sound of bombs exploding and gun fire was almost continuous. Bremen seemed to be the main target and there were several big fires. I hope that many Germans lost their lives. New prisoners, from an Empire boat and an American ship, arrived from Wilhelmshaven and they told us that Bremen was still blazing when they passed through late in the afternoon."

That same month, a German war bride, living in Bremerhaven, near the POW camp, visited the area where her own house once stood. "All we found was ashes and rubble....The day after the bombing, I heard that an enemy aircraft had been shot down and that pieces of the aircraft were scattered where our house had been. I saw the wreckage and in it a human torso, probably the pilot, burnt beyond recognition. They said it was a British plane. I felt nothing. Later, when working in the garden, I found a human arm lying there between the dung heap and the cabbages. It was a man's arm, quite hairy, with the hand still attached. Probably what was left of the crew. That shocked me deeply."

One day, in March 1944, the captives were being inspected by a German general whilst allied planes roared overhead, en route to and back from Berlin. "How foolish he must have felt." (This may have been the first significant US daylight raid: over 700 bombers and more than 800 long-range fighters were involved.) On 18th May, Stanley saw much aerial activity and was pleased to learn later that a plane he saw crash was German. The following month, after the invasion, the inmates saw "crowds" of American bombers, escorted by Lightening fighters. On 27th July, at about 01.00 a plane dropped a bomb about two miles from the camp and "the huts vibrated like a ship struck by a heavy wave at sea. If one bomb creates such a fuss two miles away, what does a big raid do?"

The night sky of 18th August 1944 was illuminated by searchlights, coloured flares, the flash of bombs and guns and the glow of fires in Bremen and the air vibrated to the dance of death and destruction. Stanley saw only three planes caught in the searchlights but they escaped. The following day, "reports from Bremen say that the chaos is unbelievable. Buildings are on fire and factories destroyed. I am sorry for the children but they should not be there." One month later, there was a raid over Westermunde near Bremerhaven and the fires were reflected in the sky. On 26th September about a thousand American bombers flew over the camp at 13.00.

In a different mood, on the 10th April 1945, as liberation approached at last, Stanley noted that there was frequent machine gunning of the road and one plane fired on a road just 200 yards to the north of the camp before roaring, low, over the camp. "Gosh, what men they are!"

CHAPTER 17

Clinging on

Today, national boundaries are irrelevant as technology allows us to contact friends and colleagues around the world, and to find out what is happening abroad, virtually immediately. From our privileged 21st century perspective, we cannot really imagine the enormous frustration felt by prisoners, shut away from all that they knew and forced to rely on spasmodic mail and, later in the war, on a clandestine radio. Reminding themselves that they were part of a more civilised world and that they had not been forgotten by loved ones required faith, discipline, imagination, hope and courage, on an unimaginable scale, dredged from dwindling inner resources.

Even during the bleakest days, defeat, which would have conjured up a vision too horrific to contemplate, was never mentioned. "Somehow, we knew we would eventually triumph: it was the time factor that worried us. We became selfish: our future would only begin when we were liberated and back amongst our own people." Inwardly, some men sensed that they might never see their loved ones again or that they would never be free. A few prisoners, their optimism fatally undermined, became insane and others died when their efforts to secure an early release, on grounds of ill health, failed. Perhaps, if the period of incarceration had been known, faith might have crumbled, leading to more suicides.

The fear of defeat was apparent early in the war. The sinking of *H.M.S. Repulse* in December 1941, the fall of Singapore in February 1942, described by Winston Churchill as a heavy and far-reaching defeat, and the loss of Tobruk in June 1942 and the German advance into Russia all contributed to the melancholy. "Surely to God, we'll get out of this and there's no doubt that the allies will triumph?" This optimism reflected the mood at home where Mass Observation recorded that there was seldom any real doubt that the war would be won. However, anyone speaking in public about a defeat could be fined up to £ 50 or sent to prison.

Better war news helped to sustain morale in the camp, but, as the tide turned, there was increasing frustration. Why had the invasion not been launched? This understandable attitude was accompanied by the guilty realisation that thousands of men would lose their lives when it did come and the prisoners' impatience was inspired by their desire to be free. What gnawed away in the POWs' minds was that they could not contribute to the allied efforts to overthrow an evil enemy. This misplaced sense of guilt was reinforced by the realisation that they were alive, albeit in harsh circumstances, whilst many friends and colleagues would never return home. Kindly comments from home doubtless assuaged some of the guilt.

Letters and photographs from family and friends, crucially, assured the captives that they had not been forgotten and that they were still part of a world from which they had been so cruelly withdrawn. They also reminded them of happier days, which, surely, must return. Parcels of food, clothing or books played a modest role in alleviating some of the hardship. Understandably, mail was always eagerly awaited but delays were seldom attributed to an infrastructure damaged by war but to the belief that next of kin were in trouble.

The prisoners deployed different measures to deflect thoughts away from their plight. For Stanley, music and literature helped but the arts were not just a welcome diversion: they also stimulated memories and deep emotion. "One night, at a concert, a man sang *Toselli's Serenade* and the words 'will my love ne'er come again, oh come shall we waste the golden hours of youth apart', proved too much and I was glad we were in the dark." When leaving his ship at gun point, and as the Germans were preparing to sink the *Agnita,* he had taken his copy of *Palgraves Golden Treasury* with him. This, and books acquired and borrowed from the library, frequently helped him to recover some composure. Stanley used to walk around the camp, alone, quietly reciting all he recalled of Grays Elegy, "the most moving and beautiful poem", then the Rubaiyat of Omar Khayyam, which, "to me at least, contains many a quiet chuckle and also a calm philosophy of the inevitability of life." One library book, *Why love must wait,* was about Matthew Flinders, a prisoner-of-war of the French, in about 1800, held on an island in the East. He was well-treated and lived in comfortable surroundings but was a prisoner for about eight years. One of his letters to his wife was included in the book and "many of us in our camp could read it with a complete understanding of the poor man".

Humour and outwitting the Germans

Humour in the camp, rarely sophisticated, nevertheless offered an opportunity to bolster morale, especially when the guards were targeted. The Germans, seemingly, were unable to count beyond their total number of fingers so musters were an opportunity to improve spirits. Their task was rendered more complicated by prisoners' desire to move around. "We Merchant Navy prisoners were the despair of the German officers who were very keen for us to form straight lines. Naturally, we took a perverse pleasure in denying them the Prussian precision they desired. Our ranks undulated, hands were put in pockets and saluting officers was rare. We lined up in ranks of 10 to assist counting. If one rank consisted of only nine, somebody from the rear, from a rank already counted, would obligingly fill the final place and would thus be counted twice. Considerable amusement would then ensue as the guard argued on the accuracy of the numbers with the senior officer. On one occasion, a prisoner asked if the date had been included."

After losing Tunis, in May 1943, some German soldiers, digging in the camp, were displeased on being asked if they were looking for Tunis. On another occasion, a Gestapo officer, loathed for sawing a treasured cricket bat in two, was walking outside the Royal Navy camp. A naval rating, washing, looked up, saw the Gestapo man and made an obscene remark. The enraged German immediately called a muster of all the men in the nearest barracks. He failed to identify the culprit and finally spluttered that he wanted a man with a hairy chest. One Brit asked, in a squeaky voice, "will I do?"

Some British commandos in the camp, awaiting transfer, were not allowed to communicate with the MN personnel so a dog was sent into their barracks with messages tied to its collar. This, too, may now seem trivial but anything that outwitted the Germans was welcomed. Periodically, the camp was visited by high-ranking, supercilious, arrogant and smug German officers but, as the war turned against them, their attitude changed. "Early in 1945, we just grinned at them and they turned on their heels and went, never to return."

An undated and anonymous poem shows some of the indefatigable spirit that allowed the prisoners to remain human beings. It was probably written between mid 1941 and spring 1942 in the Sandbostel camp.

See them on the square, always formed in fives,
Swarming here, swarming there, like bees around their hives,
Battered men and tattered men, all in one straight line,
And the smartest bunch of prisoners is barracks forty nine.

We have khaki coats and sky blue coats and mine in bottle green,
And the hats we wear, upon the square are the funniest ever seen,
At 9 o'clock and 5 o'clock you will see us there,
All colours of the rainbow, on Sandbostel barrack square.

Herman Bissen is our guard and he is very proud of us,
He gets us marshalled in the yard with quite a lot of fuss,
He's learning bits of English which Germans speak like this,
Barracken Neunund Viergzig, (1945) achtung,
B-off, dismiss.

This prison camp is aptly named, because it's built on sand,
And we collect it in our boots as on parade we stand,
And at the cookhouse when we go, each in our little groups,
We always bring a ladle full, in every pail of soup.

It fills our eyes, it fills our ears, we spread it on bread,
And I dare say that in one day we'll eat a pound per head,
When we get home, our friends will say, "my word, you do look fit."
And we'll reply, with one long sigh, "why, sure, we're full of grit."

In May 1944, just before the invasion was launched, the Germans issued leaflets calling for volunteers in the camp to join the British Free Corps to fight with the Germans against the Bolsheviks. These provided some humour for the prisoners. One pamphlet claimed that "as a result of repeated application from British subjects from all parts of the world wishing to take part in the common European struggle against Bolshevism, authorisation has been given for the creation of a British volunteer unit." This "thoroughly British volunteer unit, conceived and set up by British subjects from all parts of the Empire who have taken up arms and pledged their lives in the common European struggle against Soviet Russia... condemns the war with Germany and the sacrifice of British blood in the interests of Jewry and International Finance, and regards this conflict as a fundamental betrayal of the British People and British Imperial interests."

It desired peace in Europe, closer relations between England and Germany, and the encouragement of mutual understanding and collaboration between "the two great Germanic peoples". It would not fight Britain nor support any action detrimental to the interests of British people. This insignificant group of British fascists had 27 members at the end of the war and it is thought that only one individual saw military action. The movement had been founded in 1942 by John Amery, the son of Leo Amery, a Conservative government minister, who found favour, initially, with Hitler. John Amery spent much of the war in Berlin and was subsequently hung.

Towards the end of the war, often on Saturday mornings, hundreds of American Flying Fortresses passed over the camp. "One morning, after hundreds of flying forts had passed over the camp, heading east, a solitary German fighter flew in the opposite direction, inevitably prompting impotent shouts advising the pilot that he was going the wrong way."

Most prisoners, when captured, were told by the Germans that, "your war is over." When the Welsh Guards liberated the camp they raided nearby farms and threw chickens and ducks over the barbed wire to the prisoners, one of whom was seen walking away with a live duck under his arm. He was telling the duck, "for you, the war is over".

War news and dreams

The greatest boost to morale came from improving news about the war and seeing allied aircraft attacking enemy towns, partly because that suggested that, sometime, an invasion might be mounted. More immediately, there was gratification that the Germans were receiving treatment similar to that which they had inflicted on citizens at home and which had prompted much German glee and boasting. Between 70,000 and 90,000 UK civilians were to die during the whole war.

Life for Stanley became a collection of memories of the past, aided by photographs, which he looked at on waking and just before closing his eyes at night, and hopes for the future. The present, too unpleasant to ponder, was excluded. Life in a harsh and physically squalid male-only community was crude but overt homosexuality was rare, possibly for physical reasons and because many men were religious. All were dominated, physically and mentally, by the ever-present, cruel reminders of war, which they could not influence, and the accompaniment of an understandable yet corrosive hatred.

Hours of darkness offered some temporary respite as dreams of hope and memories replaced the awful reality of deprivation and horror. How grim it must have been to return to the horrors of the prison camp, and the prospect that a normal life may have gone for ever, after visiting a world where all is civilised, agreeable and peaceful. Doubtless like many prisoners, Stanley had vivid dreams of home life. In October 1942, for example, he was troubled by dreams and visions of the past. In one, he was on the ship and Maidie suddenly appeared near him. "I didn't believe that she was real and repeatedly touched her face and then I woke up to this." Another dream two weeks later, again about Maidie, was more comforting: he awoke, confident that he would again enjoy a better life. On 4th February 1943 he dreamt that he had arrived home and on meeting Philip said delightedly "why, he's still only a little fellow".

Later, news of the war increasingly dominated the diaries. However, in December 1944, probably influenced by the success of the invasion and increasingly encouraging prospects of liberation, one dream reminded him of the happiness that he had experienced and could anticipate again. The following night he dreamt that he was "shopping in Muswell Hill and buying cakes with my lovely cheeky smart Londoner".

Diary entries

Stanley's dairy became his friend to whom he was able to convey his thoughts and emotions, which were never far from the surface. He hungered for so many small things that were "so commonplace in civilian life". "I have one five year old son and I have seen him for less than four months. I have never seen my second son. Some days it becomes almost an intolerable ache and a longing that shuts out everything else. I think of home and family and all that it means until I stumble in my walk around the camp, my eyes blurred with tears and then I rebel against such weakness and curse the people responsible for such misery."

Dairy entries for the first day of each New Year were revealing. In 1942, Stanley saw in the New Year, "thinking of them and wishing for victory and a speedy return". One year later, he attended morning service and then repeated the comment he had confided to his diary one year earlier. Then, in words that would be repeated on 1st January 1944, he added "surely this year will see the end". One year later, he allowed himself to write "SURELY it must be the year. Thinking all day of my three treasures." By then, the tide had turned and an early entry in 1945 records that there had been two more air raids and that the POWs had seen two RAF fighters shoot down a German. "He seemed to offer no resistance and just dived to earth in a terrible crash. Serve the bastard right but I wish that all this slaughter was over and we could all live as human beings again. Still, it must end this year."

Birthdays and anniversaries stimulated memories and hopes. In 1942, on Maidie's birthday, he wrote, "I hope to God that we shall see each other before her next." On 9th July, recalling his marriage, he wrote, "ten years today it was a glorious sunny day. How vividly I can remember every little incident and how wonderful life can be. Now we have two sweet little humans to whom we have given life." On 20th July 1942, he noted that he joined the Anglo Saxon Petroleum Company 20 years before. "In some ways, a wasted life but at least Maidie and the boys are comfortable." In contrast, his own birthday, on 8th September 1942, passes without comment but, two days later, noting his mother-in-law's 59th birthday, he refers to her as "his old pal". Ten days later, it is Rodney's birthday and he wonders when he will see his second son for the first time. In December 1942, on his elder son's birthday he wrote, "he is six and how I wish I was with them. I remember when I was six. What a difference between his childhood and mine."

On Maidie's birthday in 1943, he reminisces about the same date four years before. "We spent a glorious day together. We went for a walk in the West End and in St. James Park then home to tea, put Philip to bed and then to the Palladium, but even sweeter days must lie ahead. I'm not feeling too bright today, the longing becomes so intense." A few weeks later, on his wedding anniversary, he is depressed. "Eleven years ago. What a waste of time when we have been separated. First of all two years out East and then four more since 1939. If only I could go home and never leave them again."

He was similarly melancholic on his own birthday on 8th September. "I can't but be depressed. My birthday. 44 years old. It seems absurd that, in another few years, I shall be 50. What have I had out of life? A few happy camping holidays with the scouts, to sea at 15½ and tankers for ever after, two days in port, after long days at sea. An oil wharf, tanks, dirty native villages and leave after three years. The only life I know is Maidie and a few months with Philip and yet, if I make life as easy as possible for them, if I give the boys the happiness and affection that I missed, then my own experiences will have served some purpose. And we are both still young enough to find happiness and excitement and romance with each other. At 30, 40, 50 she will still be my sweet Maidie, and still the most beautiful, wonderful lady in the world to me. As long as I have her, life can be a sweet desirably precious thing."

On 20th September, Rodney's birthday, he noted that he was three and had not yet seen his father. "Still, surely, I shall see him soon." The diary entry for the 23rd December revealed his sorrow at not having seen his first son for so long. "Our little Phil's seventh birthday. Four years ago, I was with him. In the last few weeks I think that I have reached my lowest ebb. I walk around feeling as if I had a lump of lead in my stomach. Last Christmas I was happy, thinking that it would be my last in captivity. Yet I am still here. I am eaten with longing for home and the clean lovely things of life but, most of all, for my wife." On Christmas Day 1943, Stanley went to morning service and then enjoyed a dinner of cold tinned salmon, a small piece of fat pork and Christmas

225

pudding, most of which originated from Red Cross parcels. Some inmates were rolling around the camp, "drunk on home-made booze and stuff from outside. Thinking all day of those at home".

On 19th March 1944, Stanley noted that it had been "three lost years" since he and his colleagues had been captured. This year, Maidie's birthday coincided with the news that his mother had died and there was no reference in the diary to his wife's birthday. By 9th July, the 12th wedding anniversary, some optimism had returned but he laments their continued separation. "My poor old Maidie. Year after year, alone, but still, it seems that a few more months will finish it off. Very impatient though, for the end of it all and to see Maidie and the boys." Doubtless pre-occupied by the invasion and the progress of the allied troops, the only other reference to birthdays that year is to Rodney's on 20th September. "It is our little baby's fourth birthday. Four years old and I have not seen him. Poor little chap. He must think that his daddy is an odd chap. Not feeling too bright."

In December, he recalls that five years had passed since he last saw his wife and son. "I'll never forget passing the window and seeing his little face pressed against the glass and she standing at the door. My inside felt frozen. I must have known I was leaving for so long." In May 1944, he recalls his first leave, decades ago, and "going in for my first exam, worried at the outcome and troubled by my family. How miserable I was: all they were interested in was to see how much they could get out of me. Just when I was wondering if I was going to find anything worthwhile, on 26th February 1926, I met her and I knew she was the answer to it all." In 1945, his last year of captivity, he allows himself some optimism on 5th April, Maidie's birthday. Although he did not know it then, he would be free within six weeks. Some seven months before the long-awaited liberation, in November 1944, Stanley wrote the following poem, entitled *How Long?*

How long, four weary years the answer I seek
The trees are bare and the winds are bleak
Four dreary times I've seen the leaves fall,
Oak, fir and beech, but the insistent call, how long?

How long must we walk in an endless parade
Like beasts 'mong the trees in Whipsnade'
Useless men in an enemy land
Discarded by war, neath the gentle hun's hand?
How long to exult at raids, bombs and the reddening sky,
At thousands of women and children, doomed to die, When
will all this slaughter and destruction cease
And a shattered world return to peace?

How long to take our place in the world of men
To lead a normal happy life again.
The voices and laughter of children-our own,
Sweet friends before, now strangers they've grown?

How long to return to simple things of life,
Country walks, companionship with one's wife
Fireglow and shadows in the fading light
Tea and cakes, curtains drawn on the gathering night?

How long to walk again in a London street
To see familiar sights from a bus front seat,
The Embankment on a summer night, St. James Park
The Strand, Trafalgar Square, Piccadilly after dark?

How long relation and friends must we mourn,
The lost years, the child not seen since born,
When will we be with our families to rejoice,
And find happiness and sweetness in that lovely voice, How
long?

An un-named army officer wrote something similar which, presumably, reached the Merchant Navy inmates:

After the war, won't it be funny
To hear the chink of silver money
To sit on a chair that isn't hard
To go for a walk without a guard
To eat off a plate that isn't iron
To have a comfortable bed to lie on
To go to a show, to ride a bike
To speak to people you really like
To wear clean clothes, to speak by phone
To have a room, your very own
To send a letter away by post
To have a reply in a week at most
Won't it be funny, won't it be bliss
To get back home again, after this?

CHAPTER 18

The invasion and liberation

On 6th June 1944, a euphoric Stanley wrote, "there is amazing and wonderful news. The invasion is on. Our lads, after a terrific air and sea bombardment, landed between Le Havre and Cherbourg. Gosh, I may see Maidie and the boys in a few months. Too excited to settle down to anything." Some prisoners were sceptical because it was the news for which they had waited for so long but now it really was happening, as the Germans conceded in a notice posted in the camp that afternoon.

GERMAN NOTICE FROM CAMP OFFICER 6TH JUNE 1944

WE HAVE BEEN OFFICIALLY NOTIFIED that the invasion has started and certain new regulations have to be enforced, the main one being:- EVERY PERSON MUST BE IN HIS BARRACKS BY 10.00 PM AND REMAIN THERE UNTIL 5.00 AM. Anyone moving in the grounds after 10.00 pm will be shot WITHOUT WARNING BY THE POSTERNS OUTSIDE THE WIRE.

Stanley noted wryly that he could not see how shooting a few POWs would repel the allied invasion but observed that the Germans were not always logical.

In the UK, the news was conveyed at 10.00 am when Workers Playtime was interrupted with the dramatic announcement. Philip heard the news at school and he and his class mates diligently wrote in their exercise books, with little real understanding of what was to happen, "Today, 6th June 1944, is D Day". Some of the enthusiasm was dented when, within a week, it became clear that the Germans had a new weapon, the flying bomb, which was to cause so much death and chaos. At the peak of attacks on the capital, 500 Londoners were killed each week. It was followed, on 8th September, by the first rocket bomb, known as the V2. The Germans were producing these sinister weapons at the rate of 900 a month. Initially, UK officials reluctant to admit the new reality, blamed the widespread fires on "faulty gas mains" but the grim truth soon emerged. The last attack came only at the end of March 1945, just a few weeks before the end of the conflict.

Many troops and equipment had commenced their potentially perilous journey from close to the family's rented house in Preston, Devon. The usually quiet seaside town, like others on the south coast, had been transformed by the arrival of thousands of allied personnel, many of whom came from the United States, and the grim but impressive paraphernalia of war. One of the visitors to Torquay was General Dwight D. Eisenhower, the supreme allied commander who was to become the US president in 1952. Francois Mitterand, later destined to become French President, was in Kingswear in Devon just before D Day.

Hundreds of different types of vehicles, from tanks, guns and jeeps to Bren gun carriers to trucks and ambulances had been parked near the coast ready for the battles on the continent. Many ships left from the south coast of Devon and on the River Dart, near Dartmouth, the vessels were moored so closely together that it was possible to walk across the river by stepping on to each craft. In total, there were 485 moored in the river. A few weeks before the invasion, in May 1944, there were 2.876 million military personnel in the UK and over 4,000 vessels were ready for the crossing.

It was a sobering and humbling experience to live there at the time and realise that many of the visitors would never return home, whilst numerous others would be handicapped for the rest of their lives. Secrecy was of paramount importance: the area was host to many Americans and US martial law was active. Before the invasion, residents had to carry certificates proving that they lived in the area and visitors were not allowed. In the week before D day, people were banned from going to within ten miles of the coast between The Wash and Lands End.

On the fateful day, some 4,000 ships carried about 150,000 men across the channel to 12 landing points along 135 miles of French coast. They were supported by another 31,000 personnel in the air. Some 1,500 tanks and 10,000 other vehicles made the crossing on the first day. 30,000 men were to die in the effort to secure a landing, including 10,000 who perished on the first day. More than two million more men were to follow their colleagues to France.

On the 6th August 1944 the prisoners in Germany saw over 1,000 allied planes fly over the camp. This was to be repeated the following month and Stanley felt very moved "to think of all those brave fellows up there and I'm filled with hope that their bombs slaughter thousands of these bastards". In November, he saw a German fighter make a forced landing just south of the camp. It had been in action, one of its engines was damaged and the men were wounded. "I wished that they had been killed." On the last day of 1944, there was much local aerial activity. The prisoners saw several American bombers burst into flames and their crews baling out. One crew member dropped only a few hundred yards away and another American just cleared Marlag. "His parachute split and the poor fellow was dead."

"During the earlier years of captivity, some men had sunk into a fatalistic torpor, knowing that release would not come

231

for years but now we were alive again, and eager for each snippet of news. By this time, even the Germans seemed to realise that they were going to lose the war. Our guards were not aggressive arrogant Nazis, they were middle-aged men, or younger men, handicapped in some way. There were several Gestapo men, who had been a nuisance or worse, but even they seemed to be losing their pleasure at harassing us and, of course, sometimes we harassed them. We were unreasonably downcast at any reverse of our troops and anything that slowed their advance. This may seem selfish but we had been in the camp for years and some inmates had been away from their families for years before they were taken prisoner."

In November 1944, as hopes rose that the war was finally coming to a successful end, Stanley listed some of the outstanding memories of his enforced stay in Germany.

The terrific stench from the smelly-Nellie manured fields
The mighty battle with the bugs
The lavatories-German culture, foul smells and habits

The home-made, heavier than concrete bread puddings
Hungry days: no food parcels: black bread, marge, kartofells & sauerkraut
The one bright day of the week when the Red Cross food parcels arrived
The meagre German daily rations
The often-heard remark: "Gosh, how I'd like a good feed"
The great Christmas dinner of 1943 and two slices of meat requiring a knife
The excitement at receiving clothes parcels, new gear, soap and chocolate

The sad news of good shipmates gone under
The funerals, the ensign-draped coffins, the ranks of silent, bare-headed men
The long cold depressing winters and mud, snow and slush
The endless marching on the square, like caged beasts in a zoo
The welcome cry, "coal up", extra bricks in our pockets

Armed guards and barbed wire, always present in our enclosed little world
Bringing in soil for our gardens, hoping we'd be gone before the harvest
The delays, sometimes anxious, between letters
Eggs, apples etc and cigarettes as a means of exchange

Optimism in summer 1943 then dwindling invasion hopes as the leaves fell
Christmas 1943, surely to God the last in captivity
A muster in the rain
The intense longing for the outside world, the clean decent things of life
The room-eight bunks and tables, stools, lockers and stoves
The washing on the lines round the bunks
The wooden meal table, pint pots, tins of Red Cross jam and black bread
Sunday services: hasten the time when we shall be with those dear to us

The library and books
Lectures
Football matches in the cold
The occasional bright interlude by the MN Theatre
The Orama band and the Chordites choir
The community bath party
The summer Test matches, England versus Australia
The voices and laughter of children outside the wire
The New Year concerts
The voice at the door. Anyone want a ticket for a raffle?
The persistent offer of "shall I sing?" "NO!!"

The fall of Stalingrad: will the Germans fight to the last kartoffel?
The endless discussions on how to end the war quickly
The squealing German radio and observations that it served the bastards right
The inspiring sight of hundreds of American bombers
The pyrotechnic displays over Bremen and the red sky as Hamburg burned

The flash of bombs, and shells, rockets and flares
The excitement of the landings
The infrequent walks in the open countryside, barbed wire out
of sight.

It was now 1945 and the inmates seemed to receive all the
news. "We even enjoyed listening to Lord Haw Haw via the
camp loudspeaker in the square announcing that the Germans
were retreating 'according to plan' or 'to shorten their line'. It
made us laugh: we had heard so much of their victories and
now we could enjoy our turn." By now, British and American
planes were flying over the camp almost daily and it seemed
that Bremen was being bombed continuously. The prisoners
saw an American plane being hit and the crew bailing out and
on the 1st January 1945, two allied fighters overhauled a
German plane and shot it down near the camp.

On 15th January 1945, the physically and mentally sick
prisoners were allowed to go home. So, too, were some of the
Americans and whilst the remaining prisoners were happy for
them, they were bitter that "the American government had
exchanged their seamen and allowed them to go home as
civilians whilst we rot here". Later that month, stories reached
the camp that thousands of German refugees were streaming
along the roads and dying in their thousands. "Just what they
have done to the rest of Europe. I'm sorry for the children but
the adults deserve all they get."

A party from the camp went by lorry to Bremen, each day,
to collect bread. Previously, it had been a privilege and much-
sought job but now, as Bremen was becoming the focus of
allied attacks, it lost its appeal. "Sights in the streets of the city
were becoming very unpleasant. One of our bread lorries was
machine-gunned by an American plane a few yards outside the
camp, causing our men to dive into a ditch. Happily, none was
hurt. Because of the bombing, our food parcels ceased and we
became very hungry but, this time, this was tolerable as we
knew that the war was ending." Stanley spent his remaining
cigarettes on buying food. "Twenty cigarettes for a Red Cross
box full of potatoes and seven cigarettes for a dozen prunes.

Supper consisted of half a cup of cocoa, one slice of bread and margarine, and, when in funds, (cigarettes), a couple of cold potatoes. I was always hungry as were the other prisoners."

March saw waves of Lancasters attacking Bremen. "Terrific explosions. Found out later that ten-ton bombs were used and I can easily believe it as the explosions shook the ground and the huts." That same month, notwithstanding the chaos and fighting, Stanley received a cheerful, encouraging and timely letter from Shell, saying that the company was looking forward to welcoming him back to England.

As April approached, the excitement rose as allied troops drew nearer to Bremen. Occasionally, a lorry load of Red Cross food arrived from Sweden or Denmark and this was very welcome as no other food parcels were reaching the camp. German rations were cut yet further and even a slow walk around the camp made Stanley sufficiently tired to have to sit down. "We were all hungry but we were buoyed by the thought that it would soon be over and, after an eternity, we would be back with our families and that our privations would soon slide into the past." On 5th April, Maidie's birthday, ignored in the diary and giving way to more momentous and immediate events, Stanley boldly wrote that "in a week we may be free again." On 9th April, 30 captured British paratroopers were brought into the camp and their stories made Stanley feel proud to be British. On the following day, the Royal Navy personnel, in their section of the camp, were told that they had to leave before the advancing allied troops could liberate them but that the Merchant Navy prisoners were to remain to be handed over to the advancing allied troops.

The RN contingent were to be marched to Lubeck, some 70 miles away, but several hundred of them, unimpressed by this plan, managed to move into the adjacent Merchant Navy area. The Germans were angry but, thanks to the ingenuity shown in hiding the RN men, none was found. "Some navy men walked around the camp in borrowed MN uniforms and others remained in hiding, some under the barracks in the dark. Because the German dogs would not venture under the barracks, it was assumed that nobody was there. Later we were told that the dogs were reluctant to go under the barracks as they could see the shining eyes of the cats that the RN men had taken in with them." Feeding the greater numbers from their own miserly rations, albeit for a short time, was an unpublicised act of heroism and self-denial when many prisoners were close to starvation themselves. "We watched the (other) RN men march off and wished them well. Subsequently, it transpired that three of them were killed on the road when an allied plane attacked them."

"As April advanced, the camp seemed to become the centre of the fighting. Our planes were near us all the time, machine-gunning anything that moved on the road and at night dropping flares all around us. Painted on our roof of our barracks was 'Merchant Navy still here'. One of our fighters machine-gunned some vehicles in the village and a car just 150 yards from the camp, and it roared over the camp, rolling its wings in salute, his cartridges fell amongst us. I picked one up and it was still hot. We were on parade in ranks, but we waved and cheered. It was marvellous." It is, surely, difficult to fully feel the ecstasy that this simple and thoroughly decent pilot's manoeuvre must have generated. Now, at last, the allies were winning, the end of the war was in sight and this one fighter pilot's gesture indicated that the prisoners' presence was not just acknowledged but that freedom beckoned.

By the 13th April, the prisoners expected the imminent arrival of the allied troops. Some German children, anxious to receive chocolates and sweets from the inmates ventured up to the barbed wire around the camp. "Poor little mites. They are the only Germans I feel sorry for." On 17th April 1945, a group of about 200 Russian prisoners, clearly exhausted and too weak to march, were shuffling past the camp. One British inmate shouted abuse at the German who was urging the prisoners, some of whom were wearing dirty bandages and who had open sores, with the butt of his rifle and demanded that he should allow his charges to rest for a few minutes. Surprisingly, he obeyed and the Milag inmates rushed to find anything that could be given to the Russians who scrambled for bread, pieces of chocolate and cigarettes which were thrown over the barbed wire. That same day, a notice was posted in the camp office:

Captain Wilson, RN, has been informed officially by the Korvetten, Kapitan Rogge that he has taken over the camp Milag und Milag from Freggaten-Kapitan Schmidt, the late commandant. Kapitan Rogge says he intends to remain here to the end and surrender the camp to the British Army on their arrival.

Signed R.F.Notman, Captain MN, Milag.

Rogge had served in the First World War on one of the destroyers scuttled at Scapa Flow and had spent some months in a British prisoner-of-war camp. He and his colleagues were regarded with some respect by the prisoners although they came close to starving when Red Cross parcels were unavailable.

Two days later, on 19th April, the prisoners, mustered on the square, were told by Captain Wilson that the Royal Marines were to patrol the camp, that the British army was only about nine miles away and that they would be released that night or early next morning. "At 2.00 am the next morning we were nearly shaken out of our bunks by two bombs and machine gun fire. Later, we learned that six Polish and Rumanian prisoners, who had occupied the RN camp, a few hundred yards away, after the navy had left, had been killed by one of our planes. We assumed that someone must have exposed a light which attracted the plane's bombs and gunfire. Gun fire, bombs and machine gun fire all round but where is the army and when will it arrive?"

Six long days later, Field Marshall Montgomery and the battle were drawing closer. "Last night, an excited audience watched the fight for Bremen. Constant thunder of bombs and shells, flashes, tracer bullets, flames, a glowing sky, and frequent shaking of the ground. All day long we watched the Tempests and Typhoons diving and blowing up roads etc. A flash, smoke and flame almost all around the horizon.

237

Sometimes, the fighters roared overhead and gave us a roll and we cheered, waved and shouted. I felt immensely proud and then insignificant as I think of my own war record."

On the following day, 26th April, the guns were approaching. "The sky is thick with our planes and we saw a wonderful attack of rockets by Typhoons, on the wood just north of camp. Heart-rending sight of refugees streaming across the fields. Tiny children, cripples, old people running from the guns. I saw a horse and cart being driven across a field. There was a flash and explosion as the shell landed and when the smoke cleared, there was nothing left to see. I remembered the film on the bombing of Poland that the Germans had shown us and some of my pity left me."

Mist and poor visibility on the 27th April prevented flying. There were German troops all around the camp and three of their tanks opened fire from the edge of the village, just 75 yards from the camp. "I was afraid to miss the fight and yet I had to dive into a trench when the climax was reached. I watched a German soldier fixing a mortar and he went about it calmly and casually as if he were engaged in a small job on a farm, rather than intending to kill some fellow humans. He looked as if he had seen plenty of action and this was a job he had done many times but I thought it strange that the whole purpose of his activities was to kill humans, which was an odd thought after nearly six years of war. I suppose my susceptibilities were sharpened because it was my people who might be killed.

"Machine gun bullets hitting the barracks, shrapnel falling in the camp, explosions shattering the air, a German multiple mortar, south of the camp, sending shells across, whining and making a terrific row. Finally, at about 6.30 pm all hell was let loose. Terrific excitement, as our troops closed in, and we were all ordered to go to the south side of the camp, the furthest point away from the action. Machine guns clattering, tracer bullets spraying, the occasional heavy bang from a gun and people ducking into trenches. How I wished I was 20 years old and in amongst it. Slept in the camp office, but not

238

for long. Lager 3 was on fire and I saw our tanks outlined against the flames."

Saturday 28th April was the crucial day of days, the one for which Stanley had prayed since March 1941 and which, at times, must have seen as if it would never dawn. Freedom beckoned. "At 12.30 am, the first British soldiers arrived, in a tank. A Welsh Guard from Newcastle was the first man I saw. Someone opened our door and shouted out 'our troops have arrived'. How we welcomed them! There was a stampede to meet them, the culmination of years of waiting and I was amongst the first in the crowd. By the time that I had reached the north east corner of the camp, more troops had arrived and a tank had breached the barbed wire. Eager hands helped, dragging the first soldiers through the wire. A prisoner called out 'what regiment?' A non-Welsh voice responded. 'The Welsh Guards'". Later, some sources maintained that the Scottish, Welsh and Irish Guards, all involved in the fighting around Bremen and the camp, lost more men there than they had since landing in Normandy. Certainly, many men were killed in their efforts to liberate the camp and capture the surrounding area.

"Another voice. 'Where are you from?' When the answer was Willington Bay, on the Tyne, there was a shout of delight from the Tynesiders. We were delirious with joy: our years of captivity were over. We tried to shake their hands, to pat their backs, and my eyes overflowed. The soldiers understood and took our demonstration cheerfully. At 8.30.am, the main force arrived led by a Cromwell tank with a cheerful and smiling major in its turret. How we cheered each vehicle! Tanks, jeeps, Bren gun carriers, radio cars, the procession seemed endless.

"At 11.00 am we paraded on the square, hoisted the White Ensign and Red Ensign, secretly made earlier in the camp, and gave three cheers for the king. We were addressed by a paymaster commander RNVR who, in peacetime, was the superintendent in the North Shields shipping office so many of us knew him. He told us what was going to happen and about our repatriation, our reception camp in England and how we

239

would be helped home. The whole organisation was wonderful. During the day we saw the village of Wilsted go up in flames as the Black Watch reached it and smashed the opposition. We heard the BBC news from a jeep and listened to stories of the fighting and choked at tales of heroism so nonchalantly told."

Sunday, 29th April. "What organisation! Just 24 hours after liberation, 1,000 British, American and Canadian prisoners left for home. The lorries brought supplies for the troops and left with the former prisoners, destined for the nearest airfield, Diepholtz. It was amazing how the hospital was cleared of patients so quickly and the ex-prisoners were treated strictly in rotation, first in, first out."

"In the evening, I went for a walk, without a guard, outside the camp and had my photograph taken against a Cromwell tank. Then I saw the Scots Guards Division going into action against the village of Tarmstedt. My god, what men. I passed Lager 3 and 4, the camp's administration's offices, and saw dead German soldiers lying at the side of the road. For the first time in my life, I saw a dead body without a flicker of feeling. Such people are better dead. As our tanks had advanced, they had sprayed the hedges and ditches with machine gun fire and one German was slumped in his tiny slit trench. He was about 50, a short slight figure with grey hair and did not look like an arrogant Nazi and I felt a pang of pity for him. Nearby, a German soldier was hanging from a tree and a placard across his chest read 'deserter' (A German fought for his country or was executed. Indeed, any Germans found guilty of either defeatism or of being too far from his unit without an adequate explanation was killed.) I saw the destroyed houses of Kirchtimke and three smashed German tanks. They looked as if their gun turrets had been pulled out and flung by the side of the road. I exulted at everything I saw except the sight of two small children playing in a shattered room.

"One German shell had killed several remaining sailors and wounded others, in Marlag, and another struck a tree near the gate of our camp, some 150 yards from our room. I was at the

240

window at the time and saw our fellows flinging themselves flat on the road. Stores were flooding into the camp and the white bread was the first that I had seen for years. A lorry carrying a few German prisoners drove into the camp and a West Indian sailor held up his white loaf and taunted the enemy. We could still hear intermittent gun fire and the occasional rattle of machine gun fire as another sniper was killed in the woods. In the evening I watched the pall of smoke and death over Tarmstedt.

"During the morning of 30th April the band of the Highland Light Infantry played for us on the square. After all that had happened on that square over the previous few years, it was strange and truly wonderful to hear a British army band playing selections from *Maid of the Mountains* and the *Chocolate Soldier*. Each day, now, our numbers are being reduced but on some days only a few leave because of other demands on the lorries from troops at the front. On the radio, I had heard the Germans singing their triumphant martial songs and stamping their jack boots, then on the warship, then in France and for years, when the marching troops were near our camp. Some disconsolate German prisoners passed our camp, escorted by a British soldier with a rifle. I could not restrain myself and shouted out 'now boys, what about a song?' Unsurprisingly, there was no response. The last few days, waiting for transport to take us from the camp seemed an eternity and by the end of April, only 400 of us were left and each day waiting seems like a year."

On 2nd May, Stanley, despite his lengthy incarceration, was still in the camp, feeling bitterly disappointed because there was no transport available but the news was wonderful. "The Germans are surrendering everywhere but all I can think about is getting home." Doubtless, in the chaos, he did not know that Hitler had shot himself and that Admiral Doenitz, the commander in chief of the German navy, now the new Fuehrer, contended that his task was to save the German people from annihilation at the hands of Bolshevism. For that reason, he would continue the war against Britain and the United States for as long as they hindered this objective. Even at the time, this seemed empty boastful rhetoric as the next few days would show.

On 3rd May, Stanley was excited to see a large party leave for home. "Gosh, my turn tomorrow", but he was to be massively disappointed. "No transport and I feel terrible. A few more days after 5½ years away should be nothing but I'd slumped badly and am terribly depressed. All the English newspapers show photos of lovely English women and I feel desperate. Some fellows are beginning to talk wildly of leaving the camp and walking home."

Eventually, his turn came, after a few days in a British military camp, and the released men climbed joyfully on to the truck which was to take them to Diepholtz. "I could hardly grasp the fact that, at last, we were leaving our prison. I thought of the long, weary months and years, the disappointments and heartaches, the bleakest period of my life, and I hoped fervently that the world never again would suffer such a catastrophe. Many of the small towns and villages through which we passed still had white sheets of surrender hanging from the windows." Meanwhile, the prisoners' erstwhile home had a sign up, "This undesirable sight (sic) to let."

Stanley's final contribution to his war log, compiled whilst in the camp, was eloquent. "And so ends this little book, an attempt to describe the life of a Merchant Navy prisoner-of-war, through the most vital years in the world's history, when he was compelled to play the part of an impotent spectator. No pen could describe accurately the longing for one's home and family and the ordinary decent things of life that one takes so much for granted in peace time. Some will retain mental scars of the last few years and a certain amount of bitterness at friends found wanting. Others will return with an increased zest for life and a deeper appreciation of the real things. For some, the sense of desperation and frustration at the passing empty years will remain a nightmare. For others, those years will make them determined to make the future compensation and all have experienced hunger in its every form."

CHAPTER 19

Going home

In the early morning of 7th May 1945, about one week after Hitler had committed suicide, General Alfred Jodl acknowledged Germany's defeat and signed a document accepting unconditional surrender. The following day was decreed to be VE, Victory in Europe, day. Newspapers told their readers "Victory in Europe: proclamation today." The Ministry of Information decreed that 9th and 10th May would be regarded as holidays. The following day Mr. Churchill, soon to be removed from office in the General Election, by an electorate that thought of him as a wartime leader, received a "tumultuous welcome".

May 9th dawned over London with grey clouds and drizzle but cities and towns across the country, and on the continent, soon were crowded by joyous people deliriously happy to be able to celebrate peace. Tens of millions of human beings around the world were denied this experience. They had been killed. Stanley was still in Germany on VE day, in a British military camp, but there is no information on how he spent the day. That may well be because his whole being was dominated by his impending return home, to see his wife and first son, for the first time since 1939 and his new son, whom he had never seen. Furthermore, he was in a defeated and shattered nation where some seven million of its people had been killed.

243

On 10th May, he and other returning POWs were flown in a Dakota to Brussels, which had been liberated on the 3rd September, another fateful date, in 1944, after being occupied since 17th May 1940. "It was my first flight and it was fascinating. The friendly RAF pilot took us over the recent battlefield pointing out the signs of battle and the destruction on the banks of the Rhine. On landing at Brussels, we were disappointed to learn that we had just missed the last plane home for that day. We stayed in a hotel but after a short walk I seemed to have had enough. All I wanted was to be in England and to be with my family. A delay of one hour was more than a disappointment.

"The following day, 11th May 1945, we took off in a Lancaster bomber for home. We sat in two long rows facing each other. It was hot and cramped and, as I looked along the interior of the aircraft, and thought of it being over an enemy town, being fired upon by anti-aircraft guns and possibly fighters too, and then being hit! Suddenly I realised the terrific strain on our bomber crews. I would have preferred to go to sea on a tanker laden with aviation fuel." Soon the plane lost height and the returning prisoners were over England, approaching the Dunsfold aerodrome, five miles from Godalming in Surrey. This little airstrip was to welcome some 47,500 returning prisoners from Europe and further afield in just a few weeks.

"My heart was beating quickly: the moment for which I had lived since 1939 was now so near. We landed smoothly. I was home and now everything seemed to move very rapidly. As we scrambled out of the plane, I looked along the runway and saw another landing just behind us. They seemed to be arriving as frequently as trains and, as one plane disgorged its passengers and moved away, another took its place. We were greeted by smiling men and by women volunteers from the Women's Auxiliary Air Force, WAAF, and ushered to a building. I saw a huge sign in one of the hangers, 'Welcome home'. The building we entered was small and the floor seemed to be dominated by many low wooden benches. I was told to lie down and spread out my arms and legs. I was too confused to know what this was about but when what looked like a giant syringe was pushed up each trouser leg and then sleeve, I did ask. "Delousing" was the reply. I grinned and said 'welcome home.'

We then moved to a hanger where we were given tea, real tea, with milk and sugar, and swiss roll and other cakes, real cakes, for the first time for four years, and sandwiches." The WAAF, under pressure to cut the loaves, used a bacon slicer for the task. The Lloyd loom chairs had been sent by hotels on the south coast. "We were all badly dressed and some of us were deeply emotional as we waited for a lorry to take us to our reception camps. There was a happy hum of conversation and a relaxed air. We were home. There was nobody to shout and snarl at us, no worrying about food or when the next Red Cross parcels would arrive, no anxiety about when, if ever, we would see our families again. It was no longer a matter of months or years: it was but hours. Our lorry arrived and 14 of us, including three Canadians, climbed on board." Thoughtfully, the authorities gave the former prisoners some money so that they could buy any snacks they wanted on their return journey home.

"It was the 11th May 1945, the war in Europe was over and we were in England, home again after an exile of 5½ years. As we drove through Surrey into Berkshire and then Buckinghamshire, it seemed that the fates had decided to give us a memorable home-coming. The weather was perfect, the sky was blue, the sun was warm and the countryside truly beautiful. The neat fields, confined by low stone walls, seemed unbelievably green. We passed through typically English small towns and villages and saw the occasional thatched cottages, the narrow roads and streets, the ancient church in the square, the small gardens with their trim privet hedges and a profusion of gay flowers and shrubs and the friendly smiling people who waved at us. We talked but little, silenced by the occasion.

"The army driver lost his way and had to ask for directions, as the signposts had been taken away. (They had been removed in May 1940, when an invasion seemed imminent.) I did not mind: we were in England and that was all that mattered. We skirted around Windsor and the castle, dominating the surrounding country, looked marvellous in the distance. By early evening, we reached our destination, a country house near Chalfont St. Giles. A major welcomed us and after depositing our little luggage, he took us to the bar for a drink. The house was large and comfortable and it seemed fantastic to have a bedroom all to myself. We had a pleasant dinner but I was anxious to ring my wife. I could not get through so called Rita, my sister-in-law, who passed on the news. It was strange and exciting to be talking to one of the family.

"After breakfast the following morning, we were pushed through the various departments at the reception camp and were thoroughly examined medically and then taken to a clothing store where we were issued with a suit, raincoat, hat, shirt, underwear, socks, handkerchief and a small case in which to carry them. My trousers were about six inches too long but one soldier found some safety pins and used them on each leg. We were given ration cards, an identity card, a railway ticket home, and some pounds in advance. It was all so thorough: nothing was forgotten. Then it was on to Amersham station, en route to Liverpool Street station in London. The weather was warm and sunny and I sat looking out at the English countryside slipping past. We arrived in London and it was time to say goodbye. My shipmates and I had been through a lot since 1939 and there was something moving about our quick handshakes. It was not a final goodbye: we knew we would meet again.

"Having an hour to spare, I phoned my sister-in-law, Rita who met me. She had bullied a friend into using some scarce petrol to drive her to the station and I was delighted to see her. She had thoughtfully brought some spam sandwiches and an orange. I hadn't seen one for years, and, meeting her really convinced me that I was home. I had to go to Paddington for the train to Paignton in Devon and we went there as quickly as possible because I felt that it would be another step closer to home. On learning from the telegraph office at the station that it would take hours for a telegram to reach my home, I told the clerk that I had not seen my wife for over five years. He relented and assured me that he would send the telegram immediately. The journey home seemed endless and I wondered what I would find. My elder son, just over three when I last saw him, was now nearly nine. My other son, whom I had never seen, was five.

"There were several people in the carriage but I just sat silently, looking out of the window at the passing country. On arriving at Paignton my fears and imagination began to race but, after a moment or two I saw my wife. I was, of course, immensely relieved to see her but I was shocked that she was so thin and she looked worn and tired. After all our years apart it seemed possible at first to talk of anything but trivia, like the two strangers that we had become. I think that she was a little shocked, too, at my appearance.

"I was impressed by my two sons but they were shy and we all seemed awkward with each other. I was saddened to learn that my wife had tuberculosis and tentative arrangements had been made for her to go into a sanatorium. I suspected that, like many mothers, she had neglected herself to give more food to the boys. I hoped that, now I was back home, matters would improve and, when subsequently, I visited Curacao again, I brought a considerable amount of food home. However, her condition was to remain a source of worry to both of us for some years." (Bread was rationed in the UK in 1946 and meat rationing was to persist for some years.)

There are no totally definitive figures for military and civilian deaths during the Second World War. Germany probably lost at least three million combatants and some 3.7 million civilians. UK military losses were about 330,000 and at least 70,000 civilians were killed. The Soviet Union suffered greatly. Probably nine million of the military lost their lives whilst about 17 million civilians died. US deaths totalled at least 300,000. Japan lost a total of some two million military personnel and civilians. Additionally, at least 5.7 million Jews

247

were murdered by Germany. In aggregate, it has been estimated that the total number of deaths was probably as high as 60 million.

On the 6th and 9th of August, the United States dropped atomic bombs on Hiroshima and Nagasaki, causing probably 150,000 immediate deaths. Many more were to die later because of their horrific wounds. The Soviet Union declared war on Japan on 8th August and immediately invaded Manchuria. The allies were alarmed lest the USSR might become involved in post-war Japan and some historians maintain that this helped to influence the decision to drop two atomic bombs in four days. Japan, having seen so much carnage and damage to the cities, announced its surrender on 14th August and this was revealed to the tired nation by Clement Atlee, now the UK prime minister, following the major electoral defeat in July suffered by the war-time leader, Winston Churchill. The Conservatives won 210 seats but Labour triumphed with 394. VJ day, announced by the new prime minister, was declared on 15th August. Stanley was at home with his family.

CHAPTER 20

The new life

Many returning servicemen found it difficult to resume their marriages, feeling like intruders in their own homes. Stanley adjusted well but his incarceration was hard to forget. An English girl, fraternising with a German prisoner near the beach at Preston, where massive barricades had been erected to delay any enemy invasion, incurred his wrath but Stanley showed commendable restraint when buying a new hat. "The elderly gentleman who condescended to serve me picked up my hat to determine the size. He handled it as if it were contagious and then muttered disapprovingly, 'issue'."

Senior Shell executives in London welcomed Stanley back: "it was a heart-warming experience. After 4½ years, as a prisoner-of-war, one's self-esteem is low." The Shell group had lost 87 ships, with a total tonnage of 869,661 tons, during the conflict and nearly 800 British and Dutch officers and ratings were killed. Stanley was depressed to see so much bomb damage but enjoyed mingling with the crowds, soldiers, sailors, airmen and civilians from so many different countries, happy people, freed from tension and strain. A Lancaster bomber was on display in Oxford Street and he told his two sons that it was a Lancaster that had brought him home from Brussels although they seemed more interested in the trams.

In early September 1945, Stanley joined the 12,000 ton *Miralda*, which had been converted into a Merchant Aircraft Carrier. These vessels, carrying up to three small planes, operated in the part of the Atlantic that was outside the range of aircraft from the UK or from the US and Canada. There was substantial spare accommodation so Shell offered passages to ex-service men and women, returning to Jamaica and Trinidad, and also company employees going to Curacao or Venezuela. "It was pleasant to see couples, sometimes pushing a pram, strolling on the flight deck and it was difficult to realise that the vessel was a tanker. Quoits, deck hockey and even dances, to the music from the radio, were organised."

In May 1946, Stanley went on leave, happy that the food purchases in Curacao had improved Maidie's health so it was no longer necessary for her to go into a sanatorium. The next appointment, to the *Acavus,* was in October. By now, Maidie was pregnant and Stanley had seen his first son only when he was three and the second when he was nearly five. When would he first see his new child? The new crew was the worst with whom Stanley had ever sailed but the good news was that a third son, Nigel, was born in February 1947. The journey home, from San Francisco, began in August 1947 with a four-day train journey across America. He spent many hours in the observation coach but was pleased to reach the hotel, near Times Square in New York, to await the arrival of the *Mauritania* which was to take him back to the UK. During the war, the liner, used as a troopship, had carried 340,000 military personnel and travelled 540,000 miles. It returned to post-war duty on 27th April.

"New York was very hot. All the cinemas on Broadway had their lights on and walking under the glass canopies, the heat was intense. I spent a couple of days with friends at Newport, Long Island and it was a relief to escape from the crowded city. I boarded the *Mauritania* on Friday afternoon and we sailed just before midnight on 22nd August. I stood on the deck, admiring the New York skyline and its myriad lights. Night or day, New York is a fascinating sight. I was travelling first class but was not really prepared for the luxury." Stanley was most impressed by the food, which, less than two years after being starved in captivity, was natural. One of the ship's officers, who had been in the prison camp with Stanley, showed him around the vessel. "I did not fancy running between Southampton and New York and there seemed to be no time to relax. Never out of sight of land for more than four or five days and never visiting any other ports. I preferred the long leisurely days and nights at sea in the tropics, chugging along at 10 knots and finishing up in a port in the Far East that nobody had ever heard of." Fellow passengers included a few American generals and an unidentified film star whom Stanley had seen on the screen, looking beautiful, but, standing next to him at the purser's office she did not warrant a second glance.

On 28th August, a car met him at Southampton, to take him to London, en route to Devon and his enlarged family. "The weather was fine and I was about to meet my third son for the first time. Maidie met me at Paignton station. On reaching home, I expected to be ushered into Nigel's presence. I was told he was asleep but could see him at 10.00 pm when he woke for feeding. At the appointed time, he was picked out of his cot. He looked at me for a few seconds then he smiled, stretched out his hand and touched my cheek. In everybody's life there are some unforgettable moments. I have had many and this was one of them."

The happy father was home for nearly two months but then spent 11 months on a 16,000 turbo electric vessel, the *Theodoxus* during which time some 78,000 miles were covered. In September 1948, Stanley went on leave. After a long legal struggle with a very difficult tenant, the family had regained possession of the London home in Muswell Hill and were now living in the house that the couple had bought in 1932. Six weeks later, on 15th November 1948, Stanley took command of another American-built vessel, the *Trigonosemus*. About one year later, after leaving Kuwait, a message from London said that a Shell tanker had lost its propeller and was drifting in the Persian Gulf. "We were to pick her up and tow her into Clarence Strait so that she could anchor off Bandar Abbas in southern Iran. Sailors dream about salvage jobs, to pick up a helpless ship and to tow her into port. The amount of the salvage is decided by the value of the salvaged vessel and its cargo, the risks run by the rescue ship and time taken. The crew's imagination ran riot: some even thought about purchasing houses. I was not indifferent as the master always receives the largest share but I kept a lid on my imagination.

"We were to assist a ship from our own company and the risks were minimal. We met the distressed vessel, which was carrying a full cargo of Kuwaiti crude, at daybreak, the weather was fine, a flat calm sea, no wind and no mischievous currents to upset either ship. Our ship handled like a tug boat and we were able to get near without any risk of damage. We secured our tow rope and proceeded slowly and reached our destination after 22 hours. We had not even broken a rope yarn. I was very satisfied." Shell thanked Stanley and subsequently, the crew were awarded one month's wages and he received three. After being responsible for carrying 190,000 tons of cargo and steaming 128,000 miles, for 17 months, Stanley departed for leave. Between May and September 1950, the proud father was at home and was able to enjoy a family holiday in Bournemouth in July. The sons were now aged 14, 10 and three.

Next, Stanley relieved the fleet commodore on the 18,000 ton *Hyalina,* a handsome ship with good accommodation and several rooms for passengers. It had a speed of 17 knots, good in the 1950s, and was equipped with radar. Passing Dover, Stanley was surprised to see the outline of the harbour exactly reproduced on the screen. "It was a monumental improvement in coastal navigation. So often I had cautiously felt my way in thick fog, up the English channel, through the Dover Straits, and across the North Sea, listening to ships' sirens, and the fog signals from lighthouses and light vessels, trying to decide the bearing and distance."

For several years, Shell had allowed senior personnel to carry their wives on board for one voyage a year. Because of the problem of leaving three boys at home, the Algars had been unable to take advantage of this concession, but at last, arrangements were made. Ships without a passenger certificate were not allowed to carry passengers so any non-crew member was signed on ships' articles as a supernumerary, at a wage of one shilling per month. Presumably advised by Shell, the London *Evening Standard* covered the story that Maidie was to accompany her husband on a voyage. A cringe-inducing full page article opened with "if you call at their London home, the brothers will tell you that mummy has gone to sea with daddy to Curacao."

"Before my wife signed on, I explained the consequences of any dereliction of duty, including drunkenness, insolence to the captain, refusal to obey orders etc. She was completely unimpressed and was so glad of a rest, I think that she would have signed on without the financial incentive." Stanley threatened to reduce his wife's wages for insubordination but she was unmoved and the captain withdrew his remark lest it provoke the imposition of sanctions on him on his next leave. After seeing Dominca, with its rich vegetation, Curacao with its low volcanic hills and cactus, was less impressive but it was always interesting entering the harbour at Willemstad, the capital of the Netherlands Antilles. "A pontoon bridge is drawn clear of the narrow channel as the ship enters. The town is on each side but there is a fort and the governor's residence on the starboard side. At the end of the channel, the bay comes slowly into view revealing the wharves with the numerous tankers alongside and the vast and numerous storage tanks."

At 4.00 am, two days later, the *Hyalina* sailed for home. The weather was fine, the sea was calm and the cloudless sky enabled Stanley to point out stars that could not be detected in London. Part of the cargo was discharged near Southampton. "Fearing later retaliation, I signed my wife off as a crew member reluctantly giving her a 'very good' on her discharge. However, I did not give her the shilling and she never forgot this and accused me of pocketing it. I was naturally sorry to lose her especially as our next voyage was around the world. I had never done this before."

Stanley was intrigued at the thought of seeing the East again where he had spent his first eight years with Shell but had only returned once since 1938. "As we rounded the north tip of Sumatra and entered the Strait of Malacca, I recalled earlier days. The Straits were like a sheet of glass, an occasional Chinese junk with flapping sails, and its reflection mirrored in the sea, the heat haze, and the distant land faintly discernable and the inevitable regular procession of ships of the Straits steamship company and the passing of passenger ships bound for home. I had served on ships as small as 1,600 tons but now I was to arrive as captain of an 18,000 ton vessel. We anchored off Polo Bukom. After transacting ship's business, I went for a walk. The streets and even the shops were the same as I recalled from the 1920s but I was haunted by memories of so many of the men with whom I had sailed and who were now dead, victims of the war."

In less than two days, the *Hyalina* was in the Java Sea, between Borneo and Java, en route for New Zealand. From Java a string of islands stretches for nearly 2,000 miles almost on latitude of 8 degrees south. After Java came Bali, Lombok, Sumbawa and many smaller islands the last of which was Wetar. "It was an entrancing and romantic part of the world for me, where, in my younger days, the shipping consisted mostly of small Dutch KPM steamers which had a near monopoly of trade in the islands. For a few days, the conditions were idyllic. The Java Sea and then the Banda Sea were calm and the nights amazingly beautiful. After the blazing sun of the day had set, the night came quickly as there is no twilight in the tropics. We were steaming through a quiet placid sea. It was very dark and the only noise was the rustle of the water along the ship's side and the occasional splash as a fish broke the surface. It was incredibly peaceful.

"Slowly, to the east, a pale white glow appeared, announcing the presence of the moon. The glow became more pronounced until, suddenly, the tip of the moon appeared above the horizon. As it climbed slowly, it appeared reluctant to leave the horizon and for a few minutes, its shape was distorted as the lower edge clung to the sea. Then nature

254

asserted itself and the moon was free and rising and immediately a narrow silver path appeared on the black dark sea, leading direct from the moon to the ships. As the moon climbed higher the path became wider until it spread over the entire sea and we were gliding along on a completely silver sea. It was beautiful."

A few days later the vessel arrived at Thursday Island, off the north east tip of Australia, and a pilot came aboard to guide the tanker through the many islands and reefs of the Great Barrier Reef. In New Zealand, for the first time for 20 years, Stanley was interviewed by the local paper, the *Dominion* of Wellington. The piece said that he was 52 but looked 32 and was proud of his 583 foot long, 18,000 dwt vessel. The reporter commented favourably on "the individual accommodation for all the crew, a beautifully-appointed smoke room and a galley of tempting odours". The article noted that Stanley had been on 19 tankers, the smallest of which had been 1,400 tons. The interviewee "noted nonchalantly that the *Agnita* had been collared in the South Atlantic by the *Steinmark*, (sic), (the *Kormoran's* initial name was *Steiermark*) and that he had spent four years in a prisoner-of-war camp. He had had to swim for his life, on his first voyage, (wrong) when his vessel sank after a collision in Scapa Flow. In the First World War, he had been torpedoed once and mined twice. He said that he had been a very lucky man."

Just before Christmas, the *Hyalina* ventured out into an inhospitable North Sea to clean tanks and returned to the Tyne at 5.30 am on the 24th December. Stanley caught the 4.30 pm train from Newcastle, arriving home at 11.00 pm on Christmas Eve 1951. It was to be his first Christmas at home since 1939. One month later, Stanley's travels resumed. This time he was to load in Texas for Singapore and New Zealand and thence back to the Persian Gulf to load crude oil. "The entrance to the Persian Gulf is comparatively narrow. We approached it at about midnight and, as we rounded the southerly point, it seemed as if slowly, someone was opening an oven door and we were about to be incinerated. It was a pitch black night and, as we steamed along, the phosphorescence caused the bow wave to become a bright green flame, which sparkled along the ship's side until the wave astern of us was a broad green band of bubbling green water."

Gulf heat is a dry heat and perspiration dries on the skin immediately. Salt tablets were issued to replace the salt lost in the body but a fireman, who had been working in the boiler room, had not taken his pills. His eyes seemed to have sunk deep into their sockets and he looked awful. Two days later, having taken the salt tablets, he had recovered. The temperature was 137 degrees Fahrenheit in the sun and 110 in the shade.

The *Hyalina* docked at Falmouth in August 1952 and Stanley left what had been his happiest ship. In his 22 months on board, they had steamed 169,000 miles and carried many cargoes without mishap. Shell had acquired several large tankers, each of 28,000 tons and Stanley hoped that he might be given command of one but it was now summer and he was on holiday. On the 8th November 1952, Stanley, still on leave, led the Merchant Navy contingent at the Albert Hall memorial service and Raymond Baxter, commentating on BBC television, noted his long service and the fact that he had been a prisoner for four years in Germany.

At the end of his leave, in December, Stanley's wish to be appointed to what, then, was the equal largest oil tanker in the world came true. He was to relieve the commodore of the fleet on the super tanker *Verena* and was later appointed master of another 28,000 tonner, the *Caprinus*. The voyages, once again, were from the Persian Gulf to the continent or the UK. With effect from 1st October 1953, Stanley was promoted to senior master and his monthly pay rose to £135. This meant that he was one of the six most senior masters in one of the biggest fleets in the world. He had moved from number 130 on the third officer's rank list in 1922 and finished just two places short of being commodore.

Stanley, 55 in the following year, would have to retire. Pondering retirement, he was uncertain on whether that was what he wanted. In 1915, when visiting the shipping office in Sunderland, several young men waiting to begin their examination for the second officer's certificate, asked him why he was waiting. Hearing that he wanted to become an apprentice, they laughed. Now, nearly 40 years later, were they right? The early days had been hard and unhappy. Would he choose another life if he started all over again? His response was similar to that with which he had responded to his mother when she asked him a similar question in 1918. "I could not imagine myself in any job not connected with sea and ships."

CHAPTER 21

Retirement approaches

For many years, Stanley had looked forward to leaving the sea but as retirement approached, memories of the hard times were fading or being softened in retrospect whilst the more pleasant aspects of seagoing were beginning to predominate.

"I had spent many weary hours on watch, thinking longingly of "an all night in bed", and when in command I had thought of undisturbed nights, free of all responsibility. I remembered the bad weather, the ship rolling and pitching, and occasionally shuddering as a mountainous sea crashed aboard and pounded the ship, the wind howling through the rigging, the icy rain and the spray stinging my face. The vivid impressions are being smoothed by the memories of the satisfaction I always felt when we were clear of the storm, the lessening violence of the wind and sea, the break-up of the black sky, and the gradual emergence of the sun, the ports and the doors being opened, the drying decks, and the perceptible increase in the ship's speed.

"I recall the anxious hours on the bridge during fog in a narrow channel, for example, the mounting tension as a ship is heard and the relief as its signals become weaker in the blanket fog and finally the freedom from anxiety when we encountered clear weather and good visibility. I remember the heat in the Persian Gulf, the clammy uncomfortable monsoons, the long, bitter crossings of the North Atlantic and Pacific Ocean in the winter. Compared to life ashore, I now see life at sea as one of constantly changing colour and pattern.

"I shall miss the beautiful tropical days and nights, the calm sea and cloudless sky, the porpoises frolicking around the bows, the quick excited flashes of flying fish breaking the surface, the bow wave lit by phosphorescence into green flames, the sense of tranquillity and loneliness when the only sound to be heard was the subdued hum from the engine room and the soft bubbling of the water swishing along the ship's side. I shall miss the Sunday morning inspection and walking around a clean ship, the pre-lunch drink and the discussions of the work to be done in the following week. No more shall I experience the excitement of arriving in port, being on the bridge at dawn, the early morning cup of tea, the pilot boarding, sometimes bringing mail. Gone will be the sense of achievement and satisfaction in bringing a ship, its cargo and crew, safety home from half way around the world.

"I shall be moved by my farewell to the sea with its kaleidoscope of life, fine weather and foul, sunshine and blizzard, terrific heat and numbing cold, responsibility and joyfulness. No longer shall I have to bid goodbye to good shipmates at the end of a long voyage. I shall miss being the head of an efficient and harmonious team, but, most of all, I shall miss the comradeship of men. Soon I shall be living close to my family, sharing in their affection and friendship, as I have always wanted. I shall be able to relax, free of the responsibilities of a ships' captain."

After six months on the *Caprinus,* Stanley left it at Le Havre on 29th April 1954 before, what he knew, would be his last Shell voyage. He joined the *Velletia* at Eastham on 23rd July, relieving the commodore. The first voyage was from Kuwait and ultimately to Singapore, a journey of 11,500 miles over 32 days. Approaching and, later in, Singapore, Stanley saw all the old familiar landmarks but this time there was an added poignancy: it was to be his last visit to the East. He spent a few hours ashore in Singapore and, walking along the Colliers Quay and North Bridge Road, was overcome with melancholia. "I recalled my first visit to Singapore, as a young man of 22, eager, excited and enthusiastic about his job, the sea and the East. Did I pity or envy that young man? Both, I suspect."

After Singapore, the *Velletia* loaded in Kuwait for Thameshaven. "The moment that I had anticipated for years had come and my wife and three sons were there to meet me. When mooring at the wharf the third officer always attended the engine room telegraph and gave the movements, such as 'full steam ahead' etc as ordered by the captain or pilot. When the ship was securely moored, the final signal to the engine room was 'finished with engines'. I walked to the telegraph and rang the signal myself, not the usual one but several times. The engineer understood. It was not just finished with engines but it was finished with the captain too.

I left on 3rd December 1954 and as we drove away, I looked back, and for a few moments, thought of all the men I had sailed with in Shell, many of whom had been lost in the war. I remembered so many incidents and I had a sudden impulse, which I quickly quelled, to ask the driver to stop for a moment. I turned and watched and the last glimpse was of a yellow funnel with its red Shell emblem."

On 19th December, he wrote a warm and appreciative letter to his employers, citing what they had done for him and for his colleagues over 32 years. He left Shell, officially, on 28th February 1955. His average annual salary, over the previous five years, was £1,432 so his pension began at £545.11.2. Fortunately, it was index-linked. In his last full year, his old-age pension was £2,735 and his Shell pension had advanced to £9,880 giving him a pension-related income of £12,615.

Many years later, when in his eighties, Stanley pondered his life and times again, free of more immediate emotions and recollections. "Even in peacetime, there are many disasters that can suddenly overwhelm a ship, especially a tanker, including fire and explosions, shipwreck, collisions, stranding on a rocky coast and even violence on board. I have visited many countries around the world but opportunities to explore inland have been limited because tankers seldom stay long in port. I have visited many towns, temples, pagodas, castles and mosques and I have even seen many marvellous spectacles from a ship's bridge. My time on watch has allowed me to see many hundreds of sunrises and sunsets.

"In the tropics I have waited for the sun to come up. A calm sea, cloudless sky and a faint glow to the east. Slowly, the glow would become brighter as the sun neared the horizon. Then the tip of the sun would appear and the last vestige of night had gone. For a little time it seemed as if the sun was reluctant to reveal itself and even when almost clear, the lower tip of the sun would cling to the horizon until the shape of the sun was distorted into a pear shape. The there would be a green flash as the sun broke clear and it became a golden ball climbing into the sky, and the sea reflected the golden light. I would drink my morning tea and inhale the fragrance of bacon from the galley. The world seemed a very pleasant place.

"Even in bad weather, daybreak was interesting. The sea, dark, rough and sullen, and the fractured clouds fleeing across the sky. The sun would rise, like a weak watery object, showing intermittently through the broken clouds. Then the sun would eventually win and disperse the dull dark clouds.

Some winter nights when the wind is howling, I recall the really bad weather at sea. The hours on the bridge, the wind blowing the spray into my face, the ship rolling, pitching and being pounded by the mountainous seas. Watching the huge waves advancing on the ship and threatening to overwhelm us. The ship slowly lifting its bows high, to meet the sea, sometimes too late, and the wave would splash on board and go swooping along the deck to carry away anything too weak to withstand it. The ship would shudder and creak in protest and then prepare itself for the next onslaught. It was an exhilarating experience standing on the bridge, carefully nursing the ship to avoid damage. We were alone in our own small world with the wind howling and whipping the tops off the waves and sweeping them away to leeward in a fine spray which reduced visibility. We seemed so insignificant. A sudden lurch, or roll and we could quickly disappear, a few air bubbles drifting to the surface would soon cease and then all signs of us would be lost and the sea would continue to rage and fume."

"So many memories come flooding back, sometimes prompted by a few notes of music, a book, or a scene on television and again, I am entering Sydney harbour on a summer afternoon. The harbour slowly opening up, scores of small boats waving cheerfully as we pass, or I am going into Hong Kong or another eastern port where the whole harbour is crowded with large ocean-going vessels, smaller coasters, Chinese junks with eyes painted on their bows and their ragged brown sails, or the ubiquitous sampans."

"Above all, I remember the men. Conditions on some ships were so hard that they tended to produce men who were equal to their surroundings. In those early days, virtually all ships could be away for up to three years so we knew each well. In most ships we worked together smoothly and had a pride in 'our' ship. Life itself made us indifferent to the petty discomforts and sometimes the excessive hours we had to work. I met some strange and outstanding characters, particularly in my early days. The First World War accelerated the end of sailing ships but on my first ship, in 1915, we had several sailors who had spent many years in sailing ships and who bemoaned their passing. They claimed that, in their younger days, it was wooden ships and iron men now it is iron ships and wooden men The sea will never change for wooden or iron men."

Epilogue

At 55, Stanley decided against retiring completely. Within 48 hours of leaving Shell, he was offered the post of assistant marine superintendent with a foreign company at a salary of £1,200. Occasionally, he relieved masters and his last command was the *Alva Cape,* which he left on New Year's Day 1957. A shipping depression in 1958 meant that the company had to lay up some ships and Stanley rejected a request to return to sea. Thus ended his 42 year-long career at sea during which time, as master, he had travelled 900,413 miles without a serious incident. (In June 1966, the *Alva Cape* exploded in New York harbour after a collision. The captain of the *Alva Cape* was amongst the 33 fatalities.)

Stanley then accepted a boring job in the City of London before retiring finally in 1965, at the age of 66. When he left Shell in 1954, after 32 years service, his ambition was to be a pensioner for longer than he had been an employee. He succeeded: when he died in 1992, he had drawn a pension for 38 years.

His retirement, like his career, was influenced by a keen sense of justice, compassion, kindness and financial prudence. He did not allow the retirement years to be wasted. "The bad old days of retiring at nearly 70, sitting in an arm chair and slowly dying, are gone. There is so much to be interested in: times are too exciting just to ponder what you did many years ago." Stanley's interest in the outside world never waned. His long retirement was marked by new friendships, overseas holidays, new hobbies, including gardening and do it yourself, learning Italian, motoring, watching cricket at Lords, going out for meals and visits to the cinema and theatre. Stanley took great pleasure in the activities and careers of his three sons and he spent many hours composing trenchant and critical letters to erring politicians and others who had irritated him.

He remained relatively open-minded and became more liberal in his later years. In his old age, he was not slow to criticise garrulous politicians and misguided trade union leaders and showed a surprising depth of anger towards those whom he felt were unworthy of their "big jobs" or those who had upset him, such as his mother. Towards the end of his long life, inevitably, he became confused by some modern technology and complained about what he perceived as high prices.

Increasing old age eventually took its toll. After a long illness, Maidie died in October 1990, aged 79, and Stanley gradually lost his will to live. Earlier that year, he wrote, "I've been very lucky, living to nearly 90, having Maidie who has always done her best for me and three sons who have also given me cause for pride".

Returning home, after visiting Philip and Jenny, he used to wave goodbye, saying as he did so, "goodbye old chap." On one such occasion, it was to be the last time that the oldest son saw his father. On the 27th June, 1992, this brave, competent and considerate master mariner, generous and kind father and decent man succumbed to myocardial ischemia and coronary atheroma. After nearly 100 years, he had shown consistent integrity, decency and honesty in an ungrateful world that treated him badly, denying him family life both as a child and young father, yet he never seemed bitter and always remembered his friends and colleagues whose lives had been snatched away. His very strong and enduring love for Maidie, his wife, and family and a desire to do the best for them, not least through sustained self-sacrifice, were key characteristics. A passion for justice, his sense of humour and an engaging optimism carried him through circumstances that would have felled a lesser man. "I've been lucky," was one of his favourite comments. Some 12 billion lived at some time in the century: many millions might not have agreed with this modest man.

Also by Philip Algar

It's Just Not Village Cricket

Woodfield Magna Confronts the 21st Century

ISBN:978-1-907219-09-2

The picturesque rural village of Woodfield Magna, some 50 miles from London, has changed little over the centuries. Some of its residents, at peace in the churchyard for many years and almost as active as some of the locals, would still recognise much of the village.

Surrounded by helpful hills, Woodfield Magna seems detached from the outside world but its inhabitants, keen to enjoy some of the benefits of the 21st century, nevertheless remain opposed to changes that could destroy the character of the village. Incomers would not appreciate the leisurely pace of Woodfield life. Families, once established in this attractive village, tend to stay there for life, subsequently passing on their homes to younger members of the family.

How long can the village sustain its stance? How will it react to a concerted attempt from a London-based company, lacking substantial funds, but still able to change everything for ever, for its own commercial gain? How could it advance its plans whilst still hiding its real intentions from the wily local residents? The story is told through some of the leading locals and their complicated relationships and takes in aspects of village life, including the all-important local cricket team which, unknowingly, could have a key role in determining Woodfield's future. As the plot unfolds, it takes a mocking look at big business, public relations, the media and local government, all of which have a role in determining whether the village will survive in its current state.

If you enjoyed Goodbye Old Chap
you may also enjoy reading:

'No Retreat, A Story of Loyalty, Courage and Dunkirk'
by Chris Coley
ISBN: 978-1-907219-05-4

This is the story of Wallace Moxon who was killed
defending the beaches of Dunkirk from the advancing German
armies. His son, the author's father-in-law, had kept a
notebook in which Lance Corporal Moxon had recorded the
final orders he was to carry out in leading a squad of young
soldiers. During the defence of Dunkirk Lance Corporal
Wallace and his men were allocated a position and given
orders not to fall back under any circumstance. In other words
they were sentenced to death or capture; the most the
rearguard could hope to do was delay the progress of the
German troops. The story of Wallace and the men of his final
command is only one of literally thousands of tales of tragedy
that befell the soldiers of the British army during those days in
1940; and yet great solace could be taken from the very acts of
gallantry and bravery that made possible the whole endeavour
of saving the much needed fighting men and averting a total
disaster.

Visit Peakpublish.com for more information on our authors
and books,

peakpublish

New Titles From Peak Platform

Peakpublish - Non-fiction

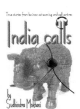

India Calls
by
Sudhindra Mokhasi
True Call Centre Stories

Playing for England
by
John Hemmingham
The England Supporters Band

Just Call Me Daisy
by
Lyndsey Bradley
Breast-feeding Mothers' Stories

Coal Dust to Stardust
by Jackie Toaduff
Billy Elliot Pales in
Comparison

The Best of France
by
Trevor Snow
8 Self-drive Tours

Jumping Fish - Fiction

Boji the Dolphin
by
Robert Alan-Havers
In Search of Independence

Not Quite Suicidal
by
Zoe Speakman
Life Can Only Get better

344 A story of the
Pretoria Pit Disaster
by
Andrea Jane Finney
Inspired by a Mother's Tale

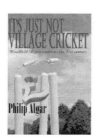

It's Just Not Village Cricket
by
Philip Algar

Selected Short Stories by
Bolwar Mahamad Kunhi
Translated work by award-winning
Indian Writer

Visit Peakplatform.com for more information